The
Professions
in
Ethical Context:
Vocations
to
Justice and Love

Francis A. Eigo, O.S.A.
Editor

The Villanova University Press

The Villanova University Press
Villanova, Pennsylvania 19085
Library of Congress Cataloging in Publication Data
Main entry under title:
The Professions in ethical context.

Includes index.
1. Professional ethics.
I. Eigo, Francis A.
BJ1725.P76   1986   174   86-7732
ISBN 0-87723-043-9

à

"mes trois neveux":

"Je ne cesse de rendre grâces

à Dieu à votre sujet

pour la grâce de Dieu

qui vous a été donnée

dans le Christ Jésus.

En lui, en effet, vous avez été comblés

de toutes les richesses . . .

C'est lui qui vous affermira

jusqu' au bout . . ."

(Première Épître aux Corinthiens 1:4–8).

Contents

Contributors

WILLIAM J. BYRON, S.J., President of the Catholic University of America, consultant, advisor, teacher, lecturer, editor of *The Causes of World Hunger*, has written extensively, including his book, *Toward Stewardship: An Interim Ethic of Poverty, Pollution and Power*, and has published widely, in books, magazines, journals, and newspapers.

SISTER MARGARET GORMAN, R.S.C.J., who is presently on the faculty of Boston College and has served as lecturer, consultant, editor, is the author of a number of articles, essays, and books, among which is her latest, *Psychology and Religion: A Book of Readings*.

CHRISTOPHER F. MOONEY, S.J., a member of the Pennsylvania bar and presently Academic Vice President of Fairfield University, has previously served as Chairman of Fordham University's Theology Department, President of Woodstock College, and Assistant Dean at the University of Pennsylvania Law School. The author of *Teilhard de Chardin and the Mystery of Christ* (which won the National Catholic Book Award), *The Making of Man, Man Without Tears, Religion and the American Dream, Inequality and the American Conscience,* and *Public Virtue: Law and the Social Character of Religion*, he holds doctorates in both theology and law, and in recent years has had as his major interest the interface between religious and legal values.

EDMUND D. PELLEGRINO, M.D., Director of the Kennedy Institute of Ethics and Professor of Medicine and Medical Humanities at Georgetown University, is the founding editor of the *Journal of Medicine and Philosophy* and the author of a variety of publications, including such books as *Humanism and the Physician* and coauthor of *A Philosophical Basis of Medical Practice*.

KENNETH L. VAUX, Professor and Chief of the Section of Ethics of the Department of Internal Medicine at the University of Illinois Medical Center, has edited a number of books, contributed to numerous books and journals, and authored such books as *Subduing the Cosmos, Biomedical Ethics, This Mortal Coil, Will to Live/Will to Die.*

WILLIAM J. WERPEHOWSKI, who teaches Christian Ethics at Villanova University, is a lecturer, consultant, editor, coeditor of a forthcoming book, *Christian Love and Moral Philosophy*, and the author of a number of scholarly articles as well as a book in preparation, *Social Justice, Social Selves: An Essay in Christian Political Ethics.*

Introduction

This eighteenth volume of the *Proceedings of the Villanova University Theology Institute* treats the professions as vocations to justice and love from an ethical perspective. After William J. Werpehowski's introductory essay, there are essays on the following as vocations to justice and love: Education (Margaret Gorman's), Law (Christopher F. Mooney's), Health Care (Edmund D. Pellegrino's), Business (William J. Byron's), Science and Technology (Kenneth L. Vaux's).

Because of its subject matter, this volume should be especially valuable for teachers and students at the college, university, and professional schools levels.

A word of gratitude to the following is especially fitting: the members of the Theology Institute Committee (Emily Binns, Bernard Lazor, O.S.A., Bernard Prusak, Patricia Fry) and the contributing essayists.

Francis A. Eigo, O.S.A.,
Editor

The Professions: Vocations to Justice and Love

William Werpehowski

> . . . we live by faith in our vocations, in that faith, in serving God, serves men, and in serving men, serves God. . . . A man therefore that serves Christ in serving of men, he doth his work sincerely as in God's presence, and as one that hath an heavenly work, and therefore comfortably as knowing God approves of his way and work.
>
> John Cotton

> Therefore, let there be no false opposition between professional and social activities on the one part, and religious life on the other. The Christian who neglects his temporal duties neglects his duties toward his neighbor and even God, and jeopardizes his eternal salvation. Christians should rather rejoice that they can follow the example of Christ, who worked as an artisan. In the exercise of all their earthly activities, they can thereby gather their humane, domestic, professional, social, and technological enterprises into one vital synthesis with religious values, under whose supreme direction all things are harmonized unto God's glory.
>
> *Gaudium et Spes*

I

The Puritan divine, John Cotton, writing and preaching some three hundred years before the meetings of the Second Vatican Council, adopts a position echoed in that Council's *Pastoral Constitution*.[1] It is that our work in the world, as it serves the neighbor, may be a form of genuine service to God. In addition (and, for the purposes of this essay, more importantly), a claim common to both texts appears to be that continuity of character, the personal integrity or wholeness or lived moral unity of the Christian, may be maintained even as that Christian serves in his or her occupation. One might add, in the same spirit, that performance in one's earthly station may honor both God and neighbor, may give to each what is due; or, one could say that the two great commandments, to love God and neighbor, may be aptly realized therein. Both Cotton's remarks about serving "comfortably" in the light of God's approval and the Constitution's commendation of a "synthesis" of earthly activities and religious values tell us that the Christian's work may be a vocation to justice and love.

And, what of those forms of work we call "the professions"? What are they, and does the same possibility exist for their Christian practitioners? Three characteristics are often cited as necessary features of a profession.[2] First, rather extensive training is required to practice a profession. Second, the training involves a significant intellectual component. Taken together, these characteristics suggest that professionals are distinguished by, and bound to one another in terms of, the common possession of esoteric and relatively specialized knowledge. But, the idea of this sort of bond, evoking the image of a circle of members turned toward one another, must be qualified by the third feature: professionals use their trained ability to provide an important service to society. Thus, the circle's members are Janus-faced, looking inward and outward, to one another inside and to those to be served outside. The picture I have drawn may enable a better understanding of other common, if not necessary, features of a profession. A process of certification or licensing attests to the public accountability which professionals, such as doctors and lawyers, must acknowledge; yet, the same process is compatible with a particular profession's self-protecting monopoly over the provision of services. Professional organizations exist to advance the economic interests of professionals; but, the economic pursuit is often qualified by efforts to better serve the public. "One does not expect to find carpenters' or automobile workers' unions striking for well-designed and constructed buildings or automobiles, yet public school teachers do strike for smaller classes and other benefits for students, and physicians and nurses for improved conditions for patients."[3] Finally, professionals are often autonomous in their work; the power of doctors and lawyers, for example, to exercise discretionary judgment is an implication of the expertise which they have and use for others. On the other hand, autonomy writ large makes for professional self-regulation, with accompanying removal from public and nonprofessional evaluation.

Beyond these uses, the picture may help us as we apply to the professions the proposals of John Cotton and Vatican II. Looking to one another and being with one another, professionals have the opportunity to be schooled in virtues that enable the realization of goods internal to professional practice. Healing well, teaching well, being a judicious legal advocate — these are goods attained through practices in which justice, courage, and honesty are necessary components of relationships among professionals and would-be professionals. "We have to learn to recognize what is due to whom; we have to be prepared to take whatever self-endangering risks are demanded along the way; and we have to listen carefully to what we are told about our own inadequacies and to reply with the same carefulness for the facts."[4] At the same time, these virtues serve ends which have to do with advancing the well-being of others. Looking and reaching outward, healers will cure and care for the sick, advocates will defend persons' rights, teachers will educate and edify. Surely, we may say, such service coincides with the Christian's commitment to the neighbor's rightful share of human goods. Just as surely, therefore, the professions may be vocations to justice and love. The character-constituting commitments of the Christian may be maintained and not destroyed in professional life.

What follows is an attempt to preserve and defend the conclusion just offered; but to do that, I will have to subvert, in some ways, the analysis which putatively warranted the conclusion. The analysis is, of course, descriptively simplistic in that it construes the professional's "service" as if it applied nonproblematically to some monolithic "public." Clearly, a professional's moral responsibilities to those outside the profession extend not only to "clients" directly served (the patient, the student, et cetera), but also to third parties affected by his or her professional activities. One can also speak of responsibilities to citizens generally, who are, for example, owed fair consideration with regard to the availability of professional services.[5] This problem of imprecision in the account indicates another: the exact meaning of "justice" and "love" is specified neither with respect to substantive content, nor in terms of the objects of moral regard. Whatever love and justice *abstractly* require, an account of their *concrete* requirements will differ, depending on who—a client, a third party, a fellow-citizen—is taken to be lovingly and/or justly regarded. But, the defects can be remedied by complicating, not (in part) overturning, my analysis above. A certain implied idea of the continuity or unity of Christian identity, an idea that would authorize placing some prepared grid of "love" and "justice" upon conduct, calls for such radical reconsideration. A close look at the various senses of "vocation," "love," and "justice," operative in a professional context, will suggest why.

II

"At least since the Reformation," writes Edward LeRoy Long, Jr., "Christian vocation has been understood to involve service of God in the productive and professional activities that sustain daily life, and Christian ethicists have been attentive to the fact that moral questions arise in the course of daily work."[6] But, the "moral questions" that arise can be viewed from different perspectives. There is, first of all, the ethics of one's task *qua* worker, i.e., the moral demands, in a professional context, of lawyer or doctor or engineer, *as such*. There is, secondly, the ethics of one's working task in its relation to broader public notions of citizenship and the common good. Finally, there is the ethics of one's work in its connection with the total set of circumstance and relationships constituting one's personal situation and shaping one's personal character. The phrase, "ethics of vocation," may apply to any or all of these perspectives. Let us consider each one in turn.

The first perspective attends primarily to the constraints that the activities of work themselves present to the moral agent participating in them. Thus, for Martin Luther, the Christian in his or her vocation must recognize its own "immanent law," and the service of God is significantly contained by standing within these limitations:

> If you are a manual laborer, you find that the Bible has been put into your workshop, into your hand, into your heart. It teaches and preaches how you should treat your neighbor. Just look at your tools — at your needle or thimble, your beer barrel, your goods, your scales or yardstick or measure — and you will read this statement inscribed on them. Everywhere you look, it stares at you. Nothing that you handle every day is so tiny that it does not continually tell you this, if you will only listen. Indeed, there is no shortage of preaching. You have as many preachers as you have transactions, goods, tools, and other equipment in your house and home. All this is continually crying out to you: "Friend, use me in your relations with your neighbor as you would want your neighbor to use his property in his relations with you."[7]

Luther's appeal to the "Golden Rule" is deceptively simple because, as a formal principle, the rule needs to be filled with the moral content that the point, limitations, and possibilities of the "tools of the trade" provide for the one who would serve the neighbor with them. The point or *telos* of those tools, in addition, may be understood in a way that is congruent, but not entirely congruent, with some current institutional framework establishing concrete possibilities and limitations. For example, it can be persuasively argued that a good lawyer, or a good teacher, or a good advertiser, is someone who does the best job possible *"with the material he or she has to work with."*[8] This means, with respect to the ends of a professional activity, that there is a range of moral considerations that apply to the activity in question; a lawyer must not make claims on behalf of a client that distort or pervert the law, nor can he or she try, as lawyer, to gain an advantage for a client by dishonest or unfair tactics.[9] The task is vigorously to defend a client's legal rights within the limits of the law for the purpose of just, impartial adjudication. Similarly, the good teacher may help students prepare for the Scholastic Aptitude Test, but not by providing them with stolen copies.[10] The task is to instruct students in a way which may help them attain goals that are more or less related to disciplining and nurturing a person's love of truth and value, on terms that are consistent with the practice of that very discipline. On the other hand, the means one rightly employs in one's activities may limit the kinds of "good" a good professional may be able to do:

> A good teacher is no worse a teacher for teaching stupid, lazy students; a

good advertiser is no worse an advertiser for promoting inferior products. Similarly, a good lawyer is no worse a lawyer for representing clients who are legally culpable or for defending clients who are morally but not legally guilty of performing any wrong. Like the good teacher and the good advertiser, the good lawyer must do the best he or she can for whatever client he or she has.[11]

A good physician, furthermore, may still be good even when his or her patients suffer and die. Of course, everything depends here on the way he or she attends as healer to patients in a competent and caring capacity, just as it depends for the lawyer as advocate on the way to attend to clients in a competent and fair-minded capacity, or for the teacher as, say, "Socratic midwife" to deal with students in a competent and "maieutic" capacity. The good one can do is determined by the point of what one is doing and the available means, institutionally allotted, at hand for doing it; but, the meaning of the "point" is not necessarily exhausted by the institutional arrangement.

Many of the problems of "professional ethics" derive from the framework sketched above. They concern the responsibilities of professionals to those they directly serve. Specification of the ends of their activity (healing, justice, the love of truth) will contribute to the establishment of a norm governing what counts as giving *what is due* a client (*suum cuique*). Justice in professional relationships means precisely that. Yet, serious disagreements may exist over what justice requires. Is the terminal cancer patient always (or ever) to be told the truth about his or her condition? In zealously defending legal rights in our American system of adversarial advocacy, does one believe that the "right" use of the law includes the use of rules of discovery, created to enable one side to find out crucial facts from the other, to delay trial or impose added expense on the other side?[12] Can the same law firm "rightfully" argue opposite points of law in different courts for different clients? A teleological framework does not by itself resolve the problems brought to the forum of practical wisdom.

Luther's doctrine of vocation, applied in relevant part here, may be an appropriate expression of the Christian notion of love of neighbor, and for at least two reasons. First, the requirements apply to *finite* human creatures who cannot effectively extend their love universally in the strict sense; the boundedness of one's vocation may aptly reflect the boundedness of one's effective service as a lover of neighbors.[13] Secondly, the requirements apply to *sinful* creatures who are tempted to celebrate their comparative achievements for the purpose of earning God's favor. This pretense is aptly countered by the insistence that obedient attention to God's ordering work with respect to our vocation leaves us more than enough to do; no time is left for the "pious works" we would choose for ourselves.[14] While the responsibilities of one's particular vocation appropriately express the requirements of neighbor-love for Luther, however, they do not exhaust the requirements; for, he calls as well for the "common order of Christian love" which stands above one's vocation and station, which includes "feeding the hungry, giving drink to the thirsty, forgiving enemies, praying for all men on earth, suffering all kinds of evil on earth, etc."[15]

It is also possible that the order of particular vocations may express Christian love in a way distinguishable from and yet internal to professional responsibilities, as the well-being of others is pursued in a manner that witnesses to the love of Christ, i.e., through the dispositions of faithfulness to others, irrespective of "merit," mercy, graciousness, and righteousness. I understand the last virtue to include the extension of one's sphere of responsibility beyond accepted norms of "justice," especially insofar as they jeopardize the vulnerable in particular application. So consider the following case for purposes of illustration:

> A youth, Spaulding, badly injured in an automobile wreck, sued for damages. The conscientious defense lawyer and his own doctor examine the youth; the doctor discovered a life-threatening aortic aneurysm, apparently caused by the accident, that Spaulding's doctors had not found. Spaulding was willing to settle the case for $6500, but the defense lawyer realized that if the youth learned of the aneurysm he would demand a much higher amount. The defense lawyer concealed the information and settled for $6500.[16]

The attorney could seek to justify his concealment in terms of the rules of the institutions of adversarial legal practice. The relevant norms are confidentiality and the related notion that a lawyer "should not use information in the course of the representation of a client to the disadvantage of the client."[17] The restrictions presumably encourage clients to give lawyers information necessary for effective advocacy in adversarial contexts, while insuring that a lawyer's adversarial zeal will not be compromised by possession of "compromising" information. If the adversary system of justice is warranted, as I will assume for the purposes of argument, this particular obligation required by it may be said to be warranted as well.

Yet, the value that would justify the adversary system, at least in connection with civil law,[18] is the truthful ascertainment of legal justice for the purpose of assigning benefits and burdens in its name. A norm of confidentiality applied in Spaulding's case, however, seems to contradict the value of justice which would justify the institutional system of adversarial advocacy; the system as justified, in turn, warrants the norm of confidentiality itself. Disclosure of information about the aneurysm would more truly contribute to legal justice, though perhaps at the cost of weakening bonds of loyalty between attorney and client and jeopardizing more generally, if minimally, the institutional stringency of adversarial advocacy itself. My claim is that disclosure in this case may be congruent with Christian righteousness and, hence, with Christian love or *agape*, because here an extended attention to the vulnerable in his need can both judge and correct an institutional norm for the purpose of realizing a more perfect *institu-tional* justice. While an appeal to the ideal of institutional justice might itself, in the abstract, warrant disclosure and overturn confidentiality, it might also be the case that the discernment of what institutional justice requires in the concrete situation is made possible by a moral stance of independent and unalterable regard for the neighbor's well-being, considered as but a child of God.[19] That love and justice coincide here affords no problem, for here righteous love may perfect a sort of justice which love itself should never fall below.

The Spaulding case can also introduce our second way of thinking about vocation, and this way both complements and complicates what I have already said concerning the intrainstitutional character of professional life. According to William Perkins (another seventeenth century Puritan), a vocation or calling is "a certain kind of life, ordained and imposed on man by God, for the common good."[20] Reference to the common good suggests that the object of one's service in one's vocation is not merely intrainstitutional. It *is* that, of course; Perkins uses the organic and functional imagery of the human body to make the point that service of the whole is always service as a member, in one's particular vocational sphere. Still, inasmuch as societies are, in a sense, "bodies," "and in these bodies there be several members which are men walking in several callings and offices, *the execution whereof, must tend to the happy and good estate of the rest;* yea of all men everywhere, as much as possible is. . . . And for the attainment hereunto, God hath ordained and disposed all callings, and in his providence designed the persons to beare them."[21] To follow the movement of God's providential work, therefore, the Christian professional may and must ask how it is that his or her vocational commitments attain to the common good of the society composed, not merely of clients, but of citizens (who may also be clients). The Spaulding case may force the attorney to ask: "how does the adversarial system of lawyer advocacy, to which I am committed, advance the common good? If features of the system do not support the value which warrants the system and which *citizens* seek, i.e., the justice to which they are entitled under the law, ought the *system* be modified?" With the reference to the common good, the question arises about the degree to which intrainstitutional norms really realize the good they promise, as viewed from the perspective of the polity generally, and of the good we would share together as members of it. Thus, "even the best conception of the good lawyer may not be morally good enough." i.e., "it may not be good enough for our society as an embodiment of values that will promote and preserve the moral quality of the relationships and lives of its citizens."[22]

As a focus on intraprofessional norms of vocation represents more nearly the tradition of Luther, attention to the way professional institutions may be transformed to better serve the common political and

social good willed by God represents more nearly the tradition of
Calvin.[23] The challenge in the latter case is for the Christian to take
God's continued sovereignty over the created but fallen world with real
seriousness; by God's gracious promise of redemption, the Christian
"lives by faith for the honor and service of God in a world the whole life
of which must be brought from sinful chaos into the ordered liberty of
the children of God."[24]

The shift from thinking about *professional ethics* (legal ethics,
medical ethics, business ethics) to thinking about the *ethics of a profession* is important because it cuts against the tendency to view professional ethics as determined and determinable solely by professionals
themselves. To stress the service function of professional institutions
for the common good implies that values outside of professional codes
of ethics may stand as criteria of adequacy for those codes. In the area
of medical ethics, for example, Robert Veatch argues that "an ethic
that professionals base on their own consensus of what their role entails
has no ethical force, at least with nonprofessionals. It is doubtful that
such a standard can be called an ethic at all. It is really more a set of
customs or mores governing behavior of members of a private
group."[25] What might these criteria be? Consider one proposal.
Michael Bayles lists a set of "liberal values" which a society like ours
claims to and ought to endorse—governance by law, freedom, protection from injury, equality of opportunity, privacy, and welfare (i.e.,
satisfaction of basic material needs)—and orders professional institutions to them:

> Norms for professional roles are to be justified by their promoting and
> preserving the values of a liberal society. The justification involves more
> than the primary value a profession promotes, although it plays an
> important part. . . . Different values will be affected depending on
> the context. For example, confidentiality promotes the value of privacy
> to clients, and making services available promotes equality of
> opportunity.[26]

As far as Christian ethics is concerned, if a theological warrant can be
found for something akin to these "liberal values," then professional
ethics may be freed from the prison house of a professionals' inner
ring, and a normative platform may be built for assessing the reform
of professional institutions, i.e., for assessing the ethics of a profession.
Hence, "justice" in this context is linked to what the profession owes
the *citizen* who may or may not also be a client, and the work of *agape*
can be understood to expand the range and depth of moral concern
for those affected by and needing the profession's service.

A related benefit of the shift is the way in which one's professional
vocation may be tied more closely to the idea of a "calling," in contrast
to the ideas of "job" and "career." In a recent and important study of
contemporary American individualism, Robert Bellah and colleagues
distinguish the first ("just making a living") and the second (where

one's progress through life is measured in terms of personal advancement in the workplace) from that

> practical ideal of activity and character that makes a person's work morally inseparable from his/her life. It subsumes the self into a community of disciplined practice and sound judgment whose activity has meaning and value in itself, not just in the output or profit that results from it. . . . The calling links a person to the larger community, a whole in which the calling of each is a contribution to the good of all.[27]

Against the prevalent tendency to view professional activity as merely instrumental to the private self's desires, focus on the "ethics of a profession" drives one to think how it is and may be that one's work is ordered to a public reality subject to moral evaluation in terms of the *common good*.

Reference to the common good of citizens may enable important substantive revisions in approaches to professional ethics. Consider two examples of such "re-visioning" or new ordering of moral perception from a standpoint beyond the narrower confines of an accepted professional-client relationship. Robert Veatch and others, convinced of the importance of the value of self-determination or autonomy in any moral reckoning about what citizens of a society like ours are owed, vigorously challenge the excessive paternalism of the dominant Hippocratic tradition in medical ethics. The idea that the physician always knows, unilaterally, what is in a patient's best interests is a product of the fallacy of generalization of expertise, in which it is assumed that medical knowledge about a patient's condition somehow qualifies one to presume moral knowledge about what therapy or régime is best for a person with a particular set of projects and values.[28] In another context, Thomas Shannon urges that the traditional idea of a profession be transformed to accommodate considerations of the good we share together as citizens; these considerations should have a real impact on the way professional scientists will protect the interests of their experimental subjects:

> Traditionally, professions have been viewed as specialized groups, quite often far removed from the public and its needs, and concerned primarily with their own interests and goals. Oftentimes, however, this can lead members of a profession into an adversary relation with society (i.e., society may not need or want what the profession has to offer) or into a paternalistic relation with society (the profession's knowing what is best for society). . . . [In contrast to this traditional view,] the profession is not . . . in a conflict situation (us against them). Rather, it is one institution among others seeking to contribute to the common good. It obviously has its own priorities and its own orientations, but what it has to offer is a contribution or service to society. Its primary focus is not exclusively its own preservation, but the preservation and well-being of the society of which it is a member and which it serves. Secondly, the professional is not simply a member of a profession. He or she is also a member

of various other civic or voluntary associations. As such a professional is, to use Michael Walzer's phrase, a "pluralist citizen," one who shares in ruling and being ruled precisely because of one's multiple membership in various associations.[29]

With this re-visioning, the scientist engaged in experimentation with human subjects will be better able to appreciate the variety of values that the experimentation may realize or defeat beyond merely "professional" interests, including the value of supporting the dignity of the subjects themselves.

As I have said, however, thinking about vocation in terms of its orientation to the common good—moving in thought from "vocational ethics" to the "ethics of a vocation"—introduces factors that complicate as well as enrich. First of all, at any point in time, a set of professional institutions may not be compatible with a professional ethics congruent with virtue in an extra-professional sense; or, moving more slowly, I should say that the virtues of a person who is a good citizen, all things considered, may not be fully compatible with the virtues of a person who is a good professional, intraprofessionally considered. The legal system, permitting and requiring the zealous advocacy of clients, even clients who would use the law (legally) to attain goals at odds with the common good, will tend to cut the advocates to its own size and shape. Susan Wolf puts the issue rather well, and deserves to be quoted at length:

> Although it is not part of the lawyer's intraprofessional moral responsibilities to refrain from defending such clients—indeed, intraprofessional responsibilities require that if a lawyer does take them as clients, he must zealously defend them—the lawyer who becomes a zealous advocate of such clients inevitably becomes morally tainted. Although a zealous defense of immoral clients who want to use the law to achieve immoral (but legal) goals requires no compromising of the professional's principles, it may force the lawyer to compromise his or her own personal moral integrity.
>
> It would be unrealistic . . . not to consider the effects on one's character that, while in no way required by the realization of the lawyer's professional ideal, are likely to result from the process of aspiring to achieve that ideal. The environment in which lawyers or would-be lawyers must place themselves and the training they must undergo may encourage them habitually to block out certain kinds of moral considerations or to develop certain patterns of reasoning that are likely to diminish their sensitivity to moral issues or their ability to recognize their full moral force.[30]

Of course, one may respond that the end of adversarial legal advocacy is justice; that the attainment of justice, broadly understood, must include the legal defense of moral rights (e.g., of those oppressed ones who lack even the basic necessities of a human life with dignity); that attorneys are, in most cases, perfectly free to refuse clients who would pursue immoral social goals through the law;[31] and that, in fact, attorneys' *intraprofessional* ideal should include serving clients who most deserve to win in the *moral* sense (as it is, of course, linked to the legal sense through the mediating category of justice).[32] The appropriate response is to concede each point but add a qualification. While the purpose of the adversary system is justice, and while that includes attention to moral rights, it is often the case that legal justice does not coincide with a reasonable understanding of what moral rights institutionally require; in these cases, a vigorous defense of legal claims for the purposes of adjudication may well introduce a conflict in moral dispositions. While it may be true that a good lawyer can and should refuse certain repugnant clients, especially in favor of clients who "deserve" to win, it can also be true that those whose moral rights are violated have a weaker legal claim concerning some contested question. What then?[33]

The person who wants to be a good lawyer (or a good doctor, or a good teacher) and a good citizen is given no guarantee that conflict will be absent in the sorts of moral (and morally relevant) skills and dispositions that each role would require. The institutional structures affecting and shaping an intraprofessional ideal may be criticized for the way they impede realization of the common good of citizens. While professionals should not be singled out to sort out and resolve the conflicts, certainly professionals possess some special interest and responsibility. But, the ability to engage in criticism and to discern conflict, we should recall, will be significantly affected by the consequences of adhering to the intraprofessional ideal liable to criticism.

The point can be established more solidly through reflection on an example where an intraprofessional ideal of loyalty to clients may conflict with *prima facie* duties to third parties and fellow-citizens. Consider Asher Bausch and his wife, Ashkenazic Jews, who

> went to the local genetics unit to be tested for the chances of having a child with Tay Sachs disease. This recessive genetic disorder is untreatable and produces blindness, motor paralysis, and other symptoms leading to death, usually before the age of three. The tests showed that Asher was a carrier but his wife was not. While he and his wife were not at risk of having a child with the defect, Asher's brothers had a 50 per cent chance of being carriers, and if they married an Ashkenazic Jew, the chances were 1 in 30 that she would be a carrier and so the odds were 1 in 60 that they would have an affected infant. When Dr. Cloe Dunlop explained these facts, Asher became upset. Dr. Dunlop asked Asher to send his brothers a letter the genetics unit had prepared suggesting that they be tested for the carrier status. Asher refused. He felt ashamed and could not bring himself to tell his brothers.

Would it be morally fitting for Dr. Dunlop to write the brothers and recommend that they have genetic screening?[34]

One could argue for disclosure in this case with the notion that a duty to the brothers overrides a duty of confidentiality owed to Mr. Bausch. Or, one might seek to establish a balance of competing moral considerations here, showing where the claims of confidentiality must end and responsibilities to third-parties emerge. It may be more illuminating, however, to entertain the thought that here we have a choice between different actions representative of different ideals of human life. On the one hand, there is the ideal of steadfast loyalty to those to whom one bears a special fiduciary relation; on the other, there is the ideal of seeking impartially to help and not harm others at risk by one's actions and omissions. We may have a choice here between two characters that may be imputed to Dr. Dunlop, characters expressing ways of life which

> explicitly or implicitly . . . may emerge as prohibited in virtue of the descriptions relevant to one way of life and as possibly required within another way of life. It is not only that the priorities to be aimed at are different in the two ways of life, both in respect of moral claims and dispositions, but also the questions that one asks about a course of conduct, before evaluating it, will tend to be different. [35]

If this last analysis is defensible, as I believe, the upshot is that certain role-responsibilities of professionals like Dr. Dunlop may conflict with other responsibilities in a way to generate a "moral cost," however the conflict is resolved. By "moral cost," I mean the loss of some cherished moral value which a moral agent has reason to regret.[36] In fact, either of the two projected options may be defended formally in terms of a professional's responsibility to advance the common good; in the one case, the values of loyalty and trustworthiness implicit in the intraprofessional ideal may more thoroughly shape the "questions asked" about conduct, while a more impartial perspective of beneficence and nonmaleficence may control in the second. With either of the options (disclosure or nondisclosure), further steps might be taken to address the costs exacted (e.g., Dr. Dunlop could advise that Mr. Bausch receive some counseling to overcome his shame so that he might be able to tell his brothers, or Dunlop could offer an explanation and statement of renewed commitment to Mr. Bausch *following* disclosure); but, that there are costs, and costs made possible by an intraprofessional ideal in conflict with other responsibilities, drives home the point that a dream of easy harmony among moral dispositions is only that.

That there are costs also drives home another point already mentioned. The professional's ability to perceive and identify moral conflict and moral cost is presupposed in the preceding account; yet, the consequences of adhering faithfully to the intraprofessional ideal may surely have an impact, and perhaps a significant impact, on that ability. There may well be a cost concerning the capacity for moral discernment to be acknowledged, given such adherence; loyalty to a patient or client may adversely affect the development of other moral dispositions to help and not harm persons who are outside the special relationship. If the conflict is to be perceived, however, some *sense* of conflict must be sustained on the part of the professional during and beyond the process of professional education:

> Professional education tends to take it as self-evident that it should aim to suppress qualms. There is indeed not much to be said for a system that simply makes the people who come out of it more uneasy, more unhappy, and less effective than they would otherwise be; moreover, since they are not in fact going to tolerate too intense a form of that condition, a system of education that tried to encourage it runs the risk, to that extent of being rejected. . . . It is quite certain to be rejected, and rightly so, if it merely punctuates an otherwise ruthlessly professional course with occasional encouragements to moral uneasiness, like a weekly address at military camp by a pacifist minister. What is needed is something very different, a general structure or tone that makes it clear that among the imperfections of the world in which the professional operates there is included the impossibility of entirely reconciling what the professional needs to do with what he or she would like only to have to do.[37]

Think again of the tasks of lawyers. A client wants to make a will disinheriting his children because they opposed the war in Vietnam. In drafting the will, the attorney goes along with a practice that arguably violates norms governing both good parenting and good citizenship (it violates the first, because parental love ought to have unconditional character; it violates the second because it treats punitively, and hence seeks to dominate, a political conversation that ought to be governed only by the rule of good reasons). Take the client who wishes to avoid tax expenditures through a loophole available only to the wealthy. The attorney who (legally) advances a client's interest through counsel on this matter supports a practice which arguably diminishes the prospects for free and more equal citizenship across all taxpayers. Reflect on the widespread assumption that a lawyer *qua* lawyer "will be encouraged to be competitive rather than cooperative; aggressive rather than accommodating; ruthless rather than compassionate; and pragmatic rather than principled."[38] Consider also that these traits correspond neatly with those emphasized and valued by the ethos of capitalism, and that, therefore, lawyers may well be lacking some appropriately critical stance toward that ethos when they confront it as citizens. Here once again, these professionals *qua* responsible citizens (and, as we shall see, responsible *persons*) ought to appreciate the moral costs of these actions; but, the appreciation attests to moral conflict while being also an effort to maintain a sort of moral integrity.

The *ethics of a profession*, as incorporated within a vision of one's "vocation," addresses more nearly what is owed to, and/or what it means to love, those neighbors who are not clients only but non-clients and citizens also. Thus, the sense or tone of "justice" and "love" in this regard is different from that found in connection with *professional ethics*. While the difference does not demand moral conflict in claims and dispositions, it is assuredly compatible with it.

"Vocation" may also apply more broadly. For Karl Barth, the term refers, not just to one's work, and not merely to one's work in relation to the common good of citizens, but to "the whole of the particularity, limitation and restriction in which every man meets the divine call and command, which wholly claims him in the totality of his previous existence, and to which above all wholeness and therefore total differentiation and specification are intrinsically proper as God intends and addresses this man and not another."[39] It is the "place of responsibility" where one stands before God, one's specific and situated determination with respect to one's stage of life, one's special historical circumstances, personal aptitude, and, finally, one's sphere of ordinary everyday activity.[40] From this situation, one may live freely, for God and for the neighbor. The "ethics of vocation" in this sense reaches a sort of limit, capturing the whole of what one is and has become as the basis of "where one stands" before God in readiness for future service in obedient love.

The breadth of this third sense of vocation invites us to think analogously of broad conceptions of "justice" and "love." "Justice" may refer generally to the patterns of human righteousness conforming to the gracious God's own; "love" may take on a related meaning: the independent and unalterable regard for the neighbor's well-being considered as but a human existent created by and destined for God. The standard for our valuing reflects the independence of God's own regard from criteria of worth grounded on merit or status or social productiveness. Alternatively, "justice" may refer to a limited moral regard which neighbor-love may surpass but should never fall below in the relations of human creaturely life.[41] Arguably, professional activity, understood as a vocation to justice and love, would conform to these standards, however they are worked out; the moral unity of the Christian life, moreover, would be realized in the application of these standards in the many contexts of one's life.

The abstractness of the analysis above betrays itself, however, when we extend our earlier thinking about the difference between professional ethics and the ethics of a profession. This last sense of "vocation" reminds us that our life before God is to be one in which we may always be able to recognize ourselves in continuity with the particular situatedness of our lives; but, however that continuity is to be understood, we must come to face the truth that that situatedness, too, is characterized by conflict in moral claims and dispositions. Just as a good lawyer may not be, *ipso facto,* a good citizen, given institutional arrangements, so the good lawyer, even if a good citizen, may not be so good a person. To speak of "love" and "justice" in general terms only begins to confront the challenge of making one's life of a piece, as well as the challenge *to* that challenge which life as we live it affords.

Columnists Ellen Goodman and Calvin Trillin write with great wisdom about the moral conflicts within our lives. Trillin's cranky and amusing exposés of the pretensions of political life are also telling appeals to reject the pretensions of citizen commitment in favor of the mundane personal adventures of food, friendship and family. One of Trillin's favorite antagonists is Harold the Committed, who insists: "It's a matter of paying lip service or making a political statement through every aspect of your life." Trillin responds that while he, too, opposes nuclear holocaust, he just does not get very political just before Halloween; there is just so much *else* to think about, such as what costume to wear to the Halloween parade, and what costume his daughters ought to wear. But, Harold pushes on:

> . . . Harold repeated a suggestion he seems to make every year: "Maybe your daughter, Abigail, could go as the dangers posed to our society by the military industrial complex."
>
> "We don't have anybody at home who can sew that well, Hal the C," I said. "Abigail's going as an M & M." Abigail has never been much impressed with Harold's costume suggestions, particularly since he persuaded his niece to go as a peace dove, and everyone thought she was supposed to be Donald Duck.[42]

I must risk the charge of overseriousness and say: the fun, even frivolity, of getting ready with one's family for the Halloween parade does indeed conflict with making political statements. The "moral cost" involved in conflicts *of this sort* is that a certain political unseriousness inevitably goes part and parcel with the personal and familial seriousness of having a good time together.

Ellen Goodman notes the shifting senses of identity and community in our nation, in which we "have replaced ethnic identity with professional identity, the way we replaced neighborhoods with the workplace." The change in identity she finds worrisome: "If our offices are our new neighborhoods, if our professional titles are our new ethnic tags, then how do we separate our selves from our jobs? Self-worth isn't just something to measure in the marketplace."[43] Beyond this, she ably discusses the tensions created by a particular ideal of the hardworking professional trying to get an "edge":

> The hard-driven, competitive people are seen naturally and emotionally as lousy spouses. Actuarily, they are seen as lousy insurance risks. But they are often the men and women we would like to have working for us. . . .
>
> Nobody wants to be married to a doctor who works weekends and makes house calls at two o'clock in the morning. But every patient would like to find one.
>
> No one admires a lawyer who spends vacations and weekends with a briefcase, except, of course, the client. . . .
>
> There is simply more of a conflict than we admit between the qualities we value in a person and those we value in a worker.[44]

There are resources in my analysis above that might qualify her analysis; perhaps, for example, seeing one's work as a "calling" and not just a "career" can mitigate the competitiveness. But, a great deal of truth remains in the quotation above, and it is truth exposed to us exactly when we relate professional life and its dispositions to other forms of life we value, such as family and friendship.[45]

We find, then, three senses of "vocation" and, correspondingly, different senses of "justice" and "love." Each of the senses, in either case, needs both of the others. An intraprofessional ideal inattentive to the common good is defective, just as a professional commitment to the reform of professional institutions is incomplete if not accommodated by a competent and considered adherence to intraprofessional ideals. We also, however, must see that good persons are not merely good professionals *or* good professionals who are also responsible citizens. Yet, the claim that each category may complement the other does not imply that moral conflict is absent *across* the categories as they indicate features of lives lived; on the contrary, as I have tried to show, moral conflict and some discontinuity in moral identity seem prevalent and even inevitable. We cannot completely and concretely encompass particular forms of neighbor-regard, like our work for clients, by more universal forms, like our work for citizens or children of God *simpliciter*. Moral costs are the remainder.

Theologically, the reality of moral costs reminds us that we are creatures and not the Creator, and that our lives and institutions are in many ways at odds with fittingly human (and therefore creaturely) ends. Our limited perspectives and affections limit our capacities to engage completely a more universal love. Our efforts to do so are necessary and appropriate, though, since the Christian is called by God to participate rightly in the form of God's own love. But, we risk sacrificing intimacy and loyalty and even kindness in the pursuit of a more universal justice or love, just as we risk dispositions to impartiality in the special and particular loyalties of our lives. Our individual and collective moral failures place us in circumstances in which the efforts to rectify those failures present costs as well. So, if Cotton's remarks about serving in one's vocation comfortably and Vatican II's mention of a dynamic synthesis of values mean that there is for us the promise of a neat balance or harmony of moral requirements and dispositions in the way we serve God and humanity; or, if they mean that moral identity is unambiguous, without conflict and moral loss; or, if they mean that some general notion of "love" and "justice" may be directly applied to the variety of our moral relationships, then there are good reasons for rejecting their position.

Rather than move in any of these directions, one may offer a far simpler interpretation. One may say 1) that professional life does include real possibilities for divine service and 2) that that service may be part of a personal narrative in which a measure of unity or moral identity is preserved with and through the moral conflicts and moral losses of a single life. We can understand the first point only after we explicate the second.

The category of narrative may work well to account for moral identity in this way, first, because it combines the features of unpredictability and teleology:

> We live out our lives . . . in the light of certain conceptions of a possible shared future, a future in which certain possibilities beckon us forward and others repel us; some seem already foreclosed and others perhaps inevitable. There is no present which is not informed by some image of some future and an image of the future which always presents itself in the form of a *telos* — or of a variety of ends or goals — toward which we are either moving or failing to move in the present. Unpredictability and teleology therefore coexist as part of our lives; like characters in a fictional narrative we do not know what will happen next, but nonetheless our lives have a certain form which projects itself toward our future. [46]

Secondly, a *narrative* unity is not one in which a life is subsumed under some principle or principles, even teleological principles; rather, it is one in which that life is seen as process and quest. While the beginning of a quest may require some determinate conception of the ends that make human life fully human, the process that is the quest of that end amounts to "an education . . . as to the character of what is sought." [47] The virtues of the moral life, according to this conception, are not dispositions which foreclose moral conflict, but which "sustain us in the relevant kind of quest for the good, by enabling us to overcome the harms, dangers, temptations and distractions which we encounter, and which will furnish us with increasing self-knowledge and increasing knowledge of the good." [48] Finally, a narrative conception of moral identity, together with the virtues included within that conception, can illuminate how "there may be better or worse ways for individuals to live through the tragic confrontation of good with good," i.e., how to deal with moral cost:[49]

> The tragic protagonist may behave heroically or unheroically, generously or ungenerously, gracefully or gracelessly, prudently or imprudently. To perform his or her task better rather than worse will be to do both what is better for him or her *qua* individual and/or *qua* parent or child or *qua* citizen or member of a profession, or perhaps *qua* some or all of these.[50]

That is, the order which a story or narrative offers can accommodate and make intelligible the actions of a *person* who must choose in a way that involves moral cost, given that person's multiple roles, relationships and commitments.[51]

The narrative that constitutes the unity of one's life cannot be abstracted from historical traditions; rather, it must be included within such traditions, for they provide contexts for the conversations about the very goods that constitute the traditions in question and, accordingly, the goods which may constitute a life. In addition, the virtues that may enable pursuit of the good through the narrative of one's life may also sustain the relevant traditions. Within Christian traditions, and in the face of moral conflict, therefore, the narratives of Christian professionals may display virtues which realize goods internal to professional practice (e.g., the good of healing, or education, or architectural design), which sustain them in their continual quest for a good life taken as a whole, and which also sustain the traditions which situate them historically. If the professions are "vocations to justice and love," they are so in this sense. In what follows, I shall discuss some virtues relevant to professional life and expressive of what Christians might call justice and love; thus, I will move directly to the issue of the shape that Christian service of God and humanity in professional life may take.

III

The Christian life may be well understood as a narrative, but a narrative of a particular kind. The Christian life is, first, a *pilgrimage;* it is a journey to home in God, and this is to say that it is a journey during which we are not fully "at home." Since the world in which we journey belongs to the gracious God, it may bear goods of creation that serve as consolation; right enjoyment of these goods, moreover, may educate the pilgrim in the sort of enjoyments he or she will find with God at journey's end. Since the world in which we journey also bears the mark of estrangement from God, consolation and education are experienced in the midst of suffering and moral evil. Secondly, the pilgrimage of the Christian is the pilgrimage of a *justified sinner.* Accordingly, the Christian always stands before the God whom he or she seeks as one both measured and forgiven by the grace of the just and merciful God; as such, the pilgrim trusts in the Lord's promise of forgiveness, and responds with a humble gratitude. Finally, this pilgrimage would be of a justified sinner *along a path of self-giving.* To traverse that path is to witness to and be empowered by the power of suffering and self-expending love that unmasks the forces of destruction and domination as finally futile and vain.[52] It is also to pursue the proximate goal of reconciliation for those neighbors estranged from themselves, from others, and from God. Thus, pilgrims may participate in the power of God, a power that reconciles through self-expending love, as it is definitively displayed and triumphant in the story of Jesus Christ.

The service of the professional who is also a pilgrim of the sort just described would bear, ideally, characteristic marks. The professional would serve the client in a way that would secure the client's trust concerning the tasks at hand. The client is served justly when the goods of healing, or of education, or of the rule of law, et cetera—goods which witness to the goodness of God's creation and God's will to preserve it—are provided by the professional through dispositions of honesty, candor, discretion, competence, diligence, and loyalty.[53] Other things being equal, the client must not be defrauded or deceived, and his or her privacy must be respected. The professional must know his or her craft well, pursue it perseverantly, and for the good of the client. The professional is being just to the client when these dispositions govern, in line, of course, with the particular professional service offered.

These dispositions in the sphere of justice may be preserved and perfected by dispositions in the sphere of love. Honesty, candor, and discretion can amount to a self-protective minimalism in professional life; the professional who does not cheat, lie, or divulge confidences may see his or her moral task completed thereby; or, such badges of rectitude may shield, almost by design, the deeper responsibilities associated with telling the truth, keeping confidences, and so forth. Merely to tell Mr. X the truth that he is likely to die in six months from lung cancer is to overlook the way the truth should be told, i.e., with compassion and constancy, patiently and perhaps indirectly. Merely to honor Mr. Bausch's request that his brothers not be told is to overlook the way Bausch himself may still need the services of the healer to help him understand his situation so to overcome his shame. In short, these virtues are liable to offer too little or even to break down without that form of love called *fidelity:* a steadfast bond of faithfulness to the well-being of the other in his or her wholeness (as, of course, that wholeness pertains to the particular service in question). Fidelity, moreover, is that concern for the client maintained even in the midst of despair, suffering, and loss. To use the truth or confidentiality to protect ourselves from these evils is to lose sight of the Christian idea that suffering, loss, and even death are not *ultimate* evils—indeed, they are evils to be overcome by way of the resurrection promise, evils which do not now foreclose the possibility that genuine value, and the value of reconciliation, may be realized in their midst.[54]

In the case of professional competence, diligence, and loyalty, the dangers include the pride in accomplishment that can be countered by *humility;* overprotectiveness regarding the client, countered by *patience* and *hope;* and vanity about one's service, countered by *gratitude* and *self-giving.* The attainment of competence in the esoteric skills of one's profession can lead one all too easily into the desire to "lord it over" clients and the general public. Consider doctors who reject patients' questions as ignorant, researchers who remain suspicious and contemptuous of a public concerned about the ethics of experimentation, teachers who refuse to accept criticism or intellectual challenges from students. *Humility* is the virtue founded in the sense that our achievements are ordered to service and not domination, since they are straw but for the divine promise of mercy and fellowship which may make use of them apart from our pretensions. Consider also the diligent and loyal professional who takes himself or herself so seriously that he or she comes to believe in his or her own indispensability for the well-being of the client; from this stance, doctors may lie to patients in order to protect them from the truth that "can't be handled," and teachers may refuse students the opportunity to take initiatives, however clumsily, in class because they will be "wasting their time" or "not covering the material." *Patience* is the virtue founded in recognition that we are but pilgrims, that we must learn to wait for the good when appropriate, and that the source of the good for which we wait hardly lies exclusively in our hands. *Hope* in a providence other than our own may enable the patience to let the truth be told and to let the initiatives be taken. Let me give another example. The intellectual freedom that an academy like Villanova University, a Catholic institution, ought to offer is not founded primarily on a "liberal" commitment to academic neutrality in the marketplace of ideas, but rather on the patient hope that enables a commitment to particular truths being recognized in various ways, at various times, through peaceful and not dominating means, i.e., through conversation and not exclusion, through the willingness to help and be helped, rather than the desire to control and confront. Finally, there is the danger that the professional may glory, not so much in one's craft, but in one's service to others. Such a stance would be held in the absence of the sense that what one is as a professional, and a person, one has in great part been given, and that the fitting response is gratefully to give in return. This cycle of gift responding to gift, moreover, makes for a pattern of *self-giving*, since one can "give up" the notion that what one controls and possesses for oneself, to the exclusion of others and their needs, constitutes one's identity; on the contrary, one's identity is established by what one has been given, and it is expressed by conforming to the pattern of giving that establishes it.[55]

These dispositions of love transforming, if you will, the "natural justice" of the professional-client relationship have correlates, I think, in the relationship between professionals and citizens or third parties generally.[56] Suppose, for the sake of argument, that we accept Bayles's proposal that professional norms and ideals ought to foster "liberal values," and suppose also that we follow him in listing three obligations of professionals toward third parties: truthfulness, nonmaleficence, and fairness.[57] It seems that these strictures may be compatible with strategies of self-protectiveness and, beyond that, slothful acquiescence in the status quo. *Courage in hope* to name the injustices of one's professional institutions, and *righteousness,* enabling one to discern the needs of vulnerable strangers, are two virtues relevant here. There are, of course, others, including those mentioned in the preceding paragraph. I will not analyze them here, but it suffices to say that the paradigm vision of the pilgrimage of a justified sinner along a path of self-giving may illuminate other pertinent moral skills in this context.

IV

The virtues that can make professional life a vocation to justice and love may not overcome the moral conflicts discussed in Part II of this essay. Costs are inevitable, given the finite and sinful creatures we are. But, the categories of narrative and pilgrimage enable us to see the way it is possible both to be at peace with the reality of moral loss in our lives and to be renewed in the quest for making our lives a single "living sacrifice" to God through service of the neighbor. There is no unity to our life apart from the unity of its narrative, a narrative which is, for the Christian pilgrim on the way, always unclear in its precise shape. The pilgrim lives by faith in a promise the fulfillment of which stands at the end of a journey, a fulfillment for which he or she hopes; but, still the pilgrim may catch only a glimpse of the end, and consequently, can never see his or her own life as a whole. The moral losses of a single life may and should be occasions for regret, but not for despair; for, the hope is just that this life will be seen as a whole by the gracious God who wills and continues to will to be a covenant-partner. We may be at peace at least in the respect that we would trust in a promise that refuses us the option of setting the terms by which we measure our own lives' moral unity or fulfillment. On the other hand, that there are moral losses in our lives may inspire the creativity and imagination and courage to mitigate them, just because the pilgrim is freed to show forth the power and sovereignty of God even with respect to them. If there is an incongruity between who we want to be and whom we want to work for us, and if that incongruity has a source in systemic powers of acquisitiveness, or domination, or indifference to the needs of others, then the path of self-giving pertains in a way that addresses the conflict as well as the false powers. One can say the same about the problem of "good lawyers" being "good citizens," or "good persons." Reconciliation in this connection, too, may be a possibility.[58]

Here, in conclusion, we find the proper sense of Cotton's talk about "comfortable service" and Vatican II's talk of a "synthesis" of values. Let us say that the service of the Christian professional may be comfortable because we live by faith in a gracious God; but, it is not a complacent service. A synthesis of values is possible to the professional, not because it may be free of moral loss, but because the way of the pilgrim may transform relationships and institutions through the power of loving self-giving.[59]

NOTES

[1] John Cotton, "Christian Calling," in Perry Miller, ed., *The American Puritans: Their Prose and Poetry* (Garden City, NY: Doubleday Anchor, 1956), pp. 176-77; *Gaudium et Spes*, in Walter M. Abbott and Joseph Gallagher, eds., *The Documents of Vatican II* (New York: American Press, 1966), p. 243.

[2] Michael D. Bayles, *Professional Ethics* (Belmont, CA: Wadsworth, 1981), pp. 7–8. Cf. Richard Wasserstrom, "Lawyers as Professionals: Some Moral Issues," in Tom L. Beauchamp and Norman E. Bowie, eds., *Ethical Theory and Business* (Englewood Cliffs, NJ: Prentice-Hall, 1979), pp. 325–37; and Stanley Hauerwas, *Truthfulness and Tragedy* (Notre Dame: University of Notre Dame Press, 1977), pp. 189–90.

[3] Bayles, *Professional Ethics*, p. 8.

[4] Alasdair MacIntyre, *After Virtue* (Notre Dame: University of Notre Dame Press, 1981), p. 178. On the notion of "practice," see pp. 175–77. Also cf. Stanley Hauerwas, *A Community of Character* (Notre Dame: University of Notre Dame Press, 1981), p. 126.

[5] Bayles, *Professional Ethics*, pp. 16–25, 92–106.

[6] Edward LeRoy Long, Jr., *A Survey of Recent Christian Ethics* (New York: Oxford University Press, 1982), p. 141.

[7] Martin Luther, quoted in Paul Althaus, *The Ethics of Martin Luther*, trans. Robert C. Schultz (Philadelphia: Fortress Press, 1972), p. 40, note 27.

[8] Susan Wolf, "Ethics, Legal Ethics, and the Ethics of Law," in David Luban, ed., *The Good Lawyer* (Totowa, NJ: Rowman and Allanheld, 1984), p. 47.

[9] *Ibid.*

[10] *Ibid.*

[11] *Ibid.*, p. 48.

[12] David Luban, "The Adversary System Excuse," in Luban, *op. cit.*, p. 88.

[13] Gilbert Meilaender, *Friendship* (Notre Dame: University of Notre Dame Press, 1981), pp. 86–103.

[14] Althaus, *The Ethics of Martin Luther*, p. 39.

[15] Martin Luther, *Ibid.*, page 40, note 28.

[16] Luban, "The Adversary System Excuse," p. 115.

[17] American Bar Association, *Model Code of Professional Responsibility and Code of Judicial Conduct* (Chicago: National Center for Professional Responsibility, 1982), p. 22.

[18] On the relevance of the contrast between civil law and criminal law, see Luban, "The Adversary System Excuse."

[19] This account of "equal regard" is ably defended by Gene Outka in *Agape: An Ethical Analysis* (New Haven: Yale University Press, 1972).

[20] "William Perkins on Callings," in Edmund S. Morgan, ed., *Puritan Political Ideas* (New York: Bobbs-Merrill, 1965), p. 36.

[21] *Ibid.*, p. 39, my emphasis. For a fine discussion of this text, see Meilaender, *Friendship*, pp. 89–91.

[22] Wolf, "Ethics, Legal Ethics, and the Ethics of Law," p. 54.

[23] For a provocative study of the contrast between Luther and Calvin, see Sheldon S. Wolin, *Politics and Vision* (Boston: Little, Brown and Co., 1960), pp. 141–94. The classic statement of the contrast is Max Weber, *The Protestant Ethic and the Spirit of Capitalism*, trans. Talcott Parsons (New York: Charles Scribner's Sons, 1958).

[24] E.G. Rupp, quoted in R.E.O. White, *Christian Ethics* (Atlanta: John Knox Press, 1981), p. 201.

[25] Robert M. Veatch, *A Theory of Medical Ethics* (New York: Basic Books, 1981), p. 107.

[26] Bayles, *Professional Ethics*, p. 19.

²⁷ Robert N. Bellah, *et al.*, *Habits of the Heart* (Berkeley: University of California Press, 1985), p. 66.
²⁸ Veatch, *A Theory of Medical Ethics*, p. 121. Cf. Alan Donagan, who argues that a similar position is an implication of norms immanent in medical practice itself: Alan Donagan, "Informed Consent in Therapy," in John Arras and Robert Hunt, eds., *Ethical Issues in Modern Medicine*, 2d ed. (Palo Alto: Mayfield, 1983), pp. 94–101.
²⁹ Thomas A. Shannon, "The Problems of Interests and Loyalties: Ethical Dilemmas in Obtaining Informed Consent," in Thomas A. Shannon, ed., *Bioethics*, rev. ed. (Ramsey, NJ: Paulist Press, 1981), p. 322. Cf. Michael Walzer, *Obligations* (Cambridge, MA: Harvard University Press, 1970), pp. 203–28.
³⁰ Wolf, "Ethics, Legal Ethics, and the Ethics of Law," pp. 51–52.
³¹ See Bayles, *Professional Ethics*, pp. 50–54.
³² Virginia Held, "The Division of Moral Labor and the Role of the Lawyer," in Luban, *op. cit.*, pp. 60–79.
³³ Held seems not to give this possibility sufficient attention. *Ibid.*, pp. 73–75.
³⁴ Bayles, *Professional Ethics*, p. 106.
³⁵ Stuart Hampshire, "Public and Private Morality," in Stuart Hampshire, ed., *Public and Private Morality* (Cambridge: Cambridge University Press, 1978), p. 48.
³⁶ This claim concerning "moral cost" does not imply, nor is it equivalent to, the proposal that genuine moral dilemmas exist. By "moral dilemma" I mean "a situation in which it actually is the case (rather than merely *seems* to be the case) that a moral transgression is unavoidable." Edmund N. Santurri, *Perplexity in the Moral Life* (Charlottesville: University of Virginia Press, forthcoming). Santurri's unrelenting theological and philosophical critique of the thesis that there are such situations is a valuable contribution to moral theory and theological ethics.
³⁷ Bernard Williams, "Professional Morality and its Dispositions," in Luban, *op. cit.*, p. 266.
³⁸ Wasserstrom, "Lawyers as Professionals: Some Moral Issues," p. 331.
³⁹ Karl Barth, *Church Dogmatics*, Vol. III/4 (Edinburgh: T. & T. Clark, 1961), pp. 599–600.
⁴⁰ *Ibid.*, pp. 607ff. I discuss Barth's notion of vocation at greater length in "Command and History in the Ethics of Karl Barth," *Journal of Religious Ethics* 9/2 (Fall 1981): 314–16.
⁴¹ Here I borrow from my forthcoming article, "Justice," in James Childress, ed., *The Dictionary of Christian Ethics*, 2d ed. (Philadelphia: Westminster Press, 1986).
⁴² Calvin Trillin, *With All Disrespect* (New York: Ticknor & Fields, 1985), pp. 78–79.
⁴³ Ellen Goodman, *Keeping in Touch* (New York: Summit Books, 1985), p. 21.
⁴⁴ *Ibid.*, pp. 46–47.
⁴⁵ Cf. Meilaender, *Friendship*, pp. 86–103, and the following statement by Martha Nussbaum: "Virtually any woman or man who both works and raises children is bound to face many conflicts between work and family; many times this person will have no choice but to neglect something that he or she values

doing, and would have done had the world arranged things differently. Many of these conflicts could indeed be removed by a juster and more rational public culture (by more equity in salaries, by better schemes of child care). But they will not all be removed this way. For the only way to guarantee that the demands of a child's love never encroach upon one's professional life is to deny the child's love—to arrange for it to be raised, and loved, by someone else. This is what many men have frequently done. And it seems important to stress that these conflicts are present as much for men as for women—though until now fewer men have acknowledged that (for example) in spending little time caring for their children they are missing something of intrinsic value. There is a cost in recognizing how many things are valuable: it is that one also sees how often the world makes it impossible to do everything that is good." "Women's Lot," *New York Review of Books* 33/1 (January 30, 1986): 11.

[46] MacIntrye, *After Virtue*, pp. 200-201.

[47] *Ibid.*, p. 204.

[48] *Ibid.*

[49] *Ibid.*, pp. 208.

[50] *Ibid.*, pp. 208-209. While I find this analysis illuminating, I question MacIntyre's passing remark that it implies that "no right choice" can be made by the tragic protagonist. The remark seems to reflect a belief about the reality of genuine moral dilemmas which I do not share. I also question MacIntyre's oversimple rejection of the unity of the virtues. *Ibid.*, pp. 167-68.

[51] Cf. Werpehowski, "Command and History in the Ethics of Karl Barth."

[52] Arthur C. McGill, *Suffering: A Test of Theological Method* (Philadelphia: Westminster Press, 1982), pp. 53-63, 83-98.

[53] Bayles, *Professional Ethics*, pp. 70-85.

[54] William F. May, *The Physician's Covenant* (Philadelphia: Westminster Press, 1983), *passim*.

[55] *Ibid.*, pp. 127-30; and McGill, *Suffering*, pp. 93-98.

[56] For a statement of "love transforming natural justice" to which I am indebted, see Paul Ramsey, *Nine Modern Moralists* (New York: New American Library, 1970), pp. 141-317.

[57] I discuss the limits and possibilities of theological endorsement of "liberal values" in "Political Liberalism and Christian Ethics," *The Thomist* 48/1 (January 1984): 81-115.

[58] It is also possible that regret over moral loss will be accompanied by the discovery that values in conflict sometimes "support and illuminate one another when all are respected—that citizenship can be instructed by the experience of knowing and intimately caring for one's children; that personal love can be richer and more interesting when both partners care about and seriously pursue some form of work; that children can be better educated if they see that adults who love and care for them also love and work for other valuable things." Nussbaum, "Women's Lot," 12.

[59] I want to thank Father Francis A. Eigo, O.S.A., Anne McGuire, Edmund N. Santurri, and Ronald F. Thiemann for their help and support during the time I was writing this essay. I dedicate the essay to Daniel Maguire, Christian ethicist, with whom I often disagree, and from whom I often learn.

Education: A Vocation to Justice and Love

Margaret Gorman

In this volume on the professions as vocations to Justice and Love, I would submit that education is concerned, perhaps more than any other profession, with a twofold goal. Not only must educators *exercise* justice and love in the *process* of educating, but they must include justice and love in the content of their teaching. While law, also, has both content and process concerned primarily with justice, the concern is very different.

Before discussing education as a vocation to justice and love, I need to raise some questions and/or make some clarifications. First, does the title assigned to the volume proclaim that it is of the *very essence of Education* to profess and to process justice and love? Second, has that been the view of educators in the *past?* Is it the concern of educators *today?* And third, are we merely stating that in the present and in the future, the goal of education *should* be to *teach* justice and love, and, in so doing, educators should *be* just and loving? Are we to talk about what is or what ought to be?

There are even more questions about what is meant by *justice*. As the word is understood by educators, especially in Catholic Schools and Universities today, *justice* includes some notion of *social justice*, of challenging the unjust structures of a political or economic system.

Such a notion of justice as *social justice* and of the education of persons who will critically question existing political and economic structures is a relatively new notion for educators, appearing implicitly with the first social encyclicals of Leo XIII in 1879 and really emerging explicitly in some of the documents of Vatican II in 1963, and more clearly and explicitly in the statements of the Bishops in 1971.

In order, therefore, to explore these questions more fully, I find it necessary to examine the goals and content of education as expressed and practiced in the past, even to the present, at least by way of a broad overview. I could have explored all the scriptural references to teaching as a calling to justice and love. But, I have chosen to explore the issue *descriptively* — rather that *prescriptively:* what has been done in education, not what should be done.

Power[1] has presented six goals that are today considered by educators, some of which have emerged rather recently and others have been present in most treatises on education beginning with Plato. The goal of education has been considered as (among others):

1. discipline of the mind,
2. character,
3. communication of knowledge and skills,
4. preparation for life,
5. growth,
6. personal fulfillment.

The long history of education reveals that the first three goals were paramount in either conflicting or complementary modes from the time of the Greeks to our own day. The last three are contemporary and American.

Of these, the goal of character or moral education (developing the cardinal virtues of prudence, justice, fortitude, and temperance) is most clearly related to the topic of education as a vocation to justice and love. But, as will be seen in the first part of this essay, the goal of character education was frequently replaced by an emphasis on career preparation or preparation for citizenship. Even preparation for citizenship often emphasized loyalty and service to the state as it was. Such preparation seldom emphasized justice and love, since that emphasis might imply a critique of the existing form of government.

With these caveats—that there are no unanimous agreements about the goal of education, that the practice of education throughout history has revealed this lack of unanimity, and that the concept of justice itself has taken on new meaning in the most recent documents of Roman Catholic Bishops and Popes (to include social justice), I will endeavor to explore the topic assigned to me in four very broad sections:

I. An overview of the philosophy or goals of education as formulated by the great educators in the past. Constraints of time and space limit this overview to very broad considerations and perhaps to arbitrary selection of the various educational theories. I have endeavored, however, to select what I consider to be representative theories of each era.

II. A presentation of the papal and episcopal papers which formulate the goal of education for justice, especially those documents of the second half of the twentieth century.

III. A demonstration of this developmental shift from an implicit goal of justice and love to the explicit goal as found in the statements of two educational religious orders or congregations with which I am most familiar—the Jesuits and the Religious of of the Sacred Heart.

The selection of these two religious orders in no way implies that other religious orders are not also committed to education for social justice. Time did not permit any thorough and comprehensive investigation of the many other groups (Catholic and non-Catholic) also dedicated to education for social justice.

IV. A presentation of the current themes in developmental and educational psychology which reinforce, by research and psychological theory, this growing concern to develop in students the ability to judge justly and act altruistically (the psychological term closest to what may be construed as *love* in an educational context).

V. Some conclusions and reflections on where education is and where it might go.

I. OVERVIEW OF THE CHANGING GOALS OF EDUCATION

GREEK

Plato, in an effort to expose the superficiality of the Sophists, formulated, through the words of Socrates, the first clear statement of the goals of education — the development of the virtuous person — prudent, just, courageous, and temperate. While knowledge may not necessarily be virtue, it is an essential foundation to ethical conduct.

It is interesting that, while Plato argued that men and women could and should receive the same education, he did not feel that all persons could become philosopher kings. Although his elitism may seem today to contradict a notion of justice based on equality, he and Socrates emphasized the goal of education as that of the development of character. The notion of love, of course, was not present as a goal, since the emphasis was on intellectual development.

Aristotle, too, because he emphasized that happiness is acting most humanly or acting virtuously, emphasized the development of virtue through knowledge.

ROMAN

Although Socrates, in *Protagoras*[2] and the *Gorgias*[3] particularly, had exposed the superficiality of the Sophists with their emphasis on speaking persuasively, the Romans, under the guidance of Cicero (106–43 B.C.) and Quintilian (A.D. 35–97), emphasized oratory and eloquence. Both implied that the essence of a good man is skill in speaking (although they did not claim the reverse). So, in Roman times the goal of education shifted away from education for *virtue* to education for *eloquence* as fostered by the study of rhetoric and literary works. These are the very sources which Plato had criticized so strongly as the opponents of truth.

EARLY CHRISTIANS

Because many of the early Christians believed that the second coming was imminent, they were far more concerned with educating for the kingdom than with educating according to the classical tradition.

Moreover, because Roman education consisted primarily in the classics, it was looked upon with suspicion, not necessarily as anti-Christian, but at least as un-Christian. In fact, until Constantine legalized Christianity in 313, Christians, although they were not forbidden, were discouraged from sending their children to Roman schools.

Yet, as time went on, to compete favorably in Roman society, one needed a good education, and that meant education in Roman schools. But, the issue was clear: Could the classics be taught without doing injury to faith? As early as the second century, Clement of Alexandria (150-220?) felt that classical literature could contribute to tolerance and could be compatible with Christian faith. He even maintained that classical learning could make a positive contribution to Christian character.[4]

During the next centuries, Jerome and Augustine[5] were to recognize the educational value of the classics, and at the same time they attempted to guard against any threat they might have been to Christian morals.

It is from Augustine, more than from any other early Christian educator, that we understand the role of love as the prime motivator in education. "My love is my weight; wherever I go, it is my love which brings me there."[6] Love as the internal motor of the soul, when rightly directed, leads to wisdom: "the intellectual understanding of eternal things." Learning must have purpose in view, the desire of the person to know something. For eternal things faith must precede knowledge:

> Do not seek to understand in order that you may believe, but believe in order that you may understand; for unless you believe, you will not understand.[7]

The teacher, then, cannot force his students to learn; he can only inspire them by reflecting God's love for man. The teacher meets his students "with a brother's, a father's and a mother's love."[8] And if teachers love God, the source of Truth (and, therefore, the source of all teaching and learning), they will also love the subjects and the students they teach. "Whatever is loved must inevitably communicate something of itself to the lover."[9] The clearest statement describing the vocation of teachers as one of love is given in his advice that teachers' love must be adapted to each student: "The same medicine is not to be given to all, although to all the same love is due — to some, love is gentle, to others, severe, an enemy to none, a mother to all."[10]

In showing that there are "external teachers" who will reveal material things and the "internal teacher" who shows the eternal truths, Augustine was true to his Christian Platonism. Thus, the human teacher should reflect the work of the Divine or internal teacher, since both are motivated by the same love: "Instruction is completed by love."[11]

Teachers should love not only God and their students; they should also love learning: "Be passionately in love with understanding."[12]

Howie[13] feels that Augustine made five principal contributions to education:

1. He declared that *wisdom* (the intellectual understanding of eternal things) rather than *science* (the rational understanding of temporal things) is the ultimate goal of education.

2. Because human beings can never fully penetrate the heart of existence, teachers should nourish a sense of wonder in their students.

3. While Augustine emphasizes love, he also stresses the basic importance of intellectual inquiry.

4. Perhaps of most relevance to the topic under discussion, Augustine showed that the personal relationship of teacher and student is the foundation of education.

5. Finally, Augustine warned against underestimating the importance of teaching and advocated the careful selection and preparation of teachers.

Thus, it is Augustine who clearly formulated the role of love in education — as a motivator to learn in the student, as a necessary quality in all teachers and, finally, as reflective of the Great Teacher, God.

AFTER AUGUSTINE

While Augustine advocated the study of the liberal arts in order to communicate better with the "pagans" in the culture, even in classical education a change in goals was occurring.

The goal of classical education as ornamental oratory was gradually changing. An educational program which prepared people to work in the marketplace in time became more attractive.

Meanwhile, Cassiodorus (480-575),[14] in *An Introduction to Divine and Human Readings*, went further than Augustine in his use of the classics. He explicitly named the liberal arts (grammar, rhetoric, logic, music and astronomy) and deliberately inserted them into Catholic educational practice as the foundation of all learning.[15]

With the fall of Rome in the fifth century, three centuries of scholastic neglect occurred, with a few pockets of brilliance.

By the ninth century, after severe losses during the Dark Ages, the schools were reopened. By the twelfth century, universities began to flourish.

A gradual shift in goals emerged. In the early Christian era, Christians were afraid of the classics and kept classical knowledge subservient to Christian wisdom. Moral rectitude was the primary goal, and reason was always subservient to faith, even though reason was respected. It may be deduced, then, that in these centuries justice and love, embodied in Christian wisdom and moral rectitude, were implicitly held as goals of education.

MIDDLE AGES AND RENAISSANCE

In the twelfth century, however, there was a return to the classics, and the compromises of Jerome and Augustine were forgotten. John of Salisbury (1120-1160) became the champion, not only of the classics, but also of their auxiliaries—grammar, logic, and rhetoric.[16] The reading of the classics thus became the sole curriculum.

However, to their credit, most medieval educators and theorists always recognized the limits of the classics. They saw that they were secular learning and primarily shaped the intellect. The church and the home were responsible for shaping moral and religious persons. The classics did not speak of the world made by God. Faith and the church were responsible for the formation of character.

While most histories of education do not discuss Thomas Aquinas, it would seem that, since Scholastic Philosophy dominated the curriculum and method of seminaries in the years preceding Vatican II, some reference in this historical overview should be made to his reflections on education.

These reflections are seen primarily in Question 11 of his *De Veritate*.[17] Thomas, who synthesized the insights of Plato and Aristotle, applied these insights to his view of education. The teacher, as instrumental cause, is to actualize the potency of the students for truth. There are both principles (which are innate) and facts, which come from the senses. As Collins in his introduction puts it:

> The intrinsic formal principle of education is precisely the learner's own intellectual progress, the activity whereby his mind (assisted by the teacher's instruction and personal example) traces out the connections among facts and between the principles of knowledge and the particular conclusions in the given field.[18]

In an almost uncanny anticipation of the American John Dewey's emphasis on learning as discovery (or perhaps Dewey had read Thomas), Thomas points out that there are two ways of reaching knowledge by natural reason:

> In one way, natural reason by itself reaches knowledge of unknown things, and this way is called *discovery;* in the other way, when someone else aids the learner's natural reason, and this is called *learning by instruction.*[19]

We will see later on that, as the psychologists examine moral development, some of them hold that there is an innate awareness of justice, actualized by the teacher in moral education. Just how related this is to Thomas' "notion of self-evident principles" (even though in his theory these are logical principles) is open to discussion:

> We would not attain the certainty of scientific knowledge from this unless there were within us the certainty of the principles to which the conclusions are reduced.[20]

In his consideration of the question, Is teaching an activity of the contemplative or the active life, he quotes Gregory who says that "the active life consists in giving bread to the hungry and in teaching the ignorant the word of wisdom." In his own reply he says that the "end toward which the active life is directed is the activity which is directed to the help of our neighbor" and concludes that education is more "properly a work of the active than of the contemplative life."[21]

I believe that this is the nearest we can get to a statement by Thomas that education is a vocation to justice and love. In this statement he maintains that, since the works of mercy are part of the active life, teaching is to be counted among the spiritual works of mercy.

By the time of the late fifteenth and early sixteenth centuries, however, such writers as Erasmus (1469-1530) and Philip were maintaining that the classics were not only bearers of secular wisdom, but they also helped to form character. They held that the discipline needed to master the classics was complementary to moral character.[22]

With the rupture of the Christian factions in 1517, however, classical education was used more to support religious orthodoxy and denominational allegiance than to form character.

Thus, by the sixteenth century, Christian educational theory did accept classical learning, but only rarely accepted it as helpful in the formation of character or faith.

EDUCATION IN THE MODERN WORLD

The preceding periods were marked by the belief that education could best be accomplished by studying the wisdom of the past, buried in the classics. Character, on the other hand, was best developed by a simple faith in religious orthodoxy.

The discoveries of the New World and the Protestant Reformation helped to weaken this unexamined trust in the words and works of the past. At first, there were criticisms about the use of Latin in the schools as persons began to explore the New World and to question the value of studying only the works of those who lived in the past. The physical world needed to be studied also.

It was John Amos Comenius (1592-1670), a Czechoslovakian or Moravian, who was one of the first to advocate what is since known as educational realism. He was one of the first to advocate education for everyone, rich and poor, boys and girls, in the vernacular, in a system of public schools. His great plea was for relevance and practicality in education:

> Nothing should be learned solely for its value at school, but for its use in life. . . . Whatever is taught should be taught as being of practical application in everyday life and of some definite use.[23]

In his schools, boys and girls both should begin their learning in the vernacular and, for the first time, in classes. As a realist, he insisted that learning start with the personal experience of the students and be related to life.

Without going into the philosophical contributions of John Locke (1632–1704), one may just indicate here his contributions to educational theory. With his rejection of the doctrine of innate ideas and self-evident propositions, so strongly held by the Platonists and Scholastics, Locke challenged the validity of authority and tradition. Reason, not authority or tradition, could ultimately judge what was true and useful. The inductive method was far superior to the deductive method. One did not need the classics; one needed only empirically verified knowledge to get at "the truth." His "tabula rasa" theory also indicated that every person began intellectual development in the same way. Thus, nurture was a more powerful force than nature in the process of education. Indirectly, he may have given rise to a supreme confidence in the power of education to improve the condition of human beings.[24]

Therefore, from the time of Comenius through the seventeenth century, more than ever before the goal of education was seen as a means to prepare persons to find suitable places in society. The goal of education was no longer character development, but had shifted, because of social and economic conditions, to preparation for life.

Jean-Jacques Rousseau (1712–1778) challenged the educational methods and goals of the past and, some would hold, had the greatest effect on education.[25] His basic theme was that it is not children who are evil but society: "God makes all things good; man meddles with them and they become evil."[26] Thus, instead of disciplining human beings and reforming a nature tarnished by original sin in order to enable them to live in society, Rousseau would strive to protect the child from the flaws of social life. However much we may wish to qualify that premise, it is true that Rousseau shifted the goal of education away from its too practical orientation of career or job preparation to the formation of the person. In this emphasis, however, he seemed to sacrifice public good and moved the pendulum away from the good of the society toward the development of the person. He also was one of the first to emphasize the developmental aspect of education. Perhaps one of the most important consequences of Rousseau's work is that more than ever it was recognized that education must seriously consider the nature of the child in whatever form it would take. However, his theories did not take effect immediately.

In reaction to Rousseau, a phase of educational theory was launched in which the competing goals of preparation for citizenship almost eclipsed the other goal of individual development, a situation due in part to the rise of nationalism. Germany and France, particularly, recognized the need for the State to undertake the work of education and thus develop citizens who would serve the State and take their places in society.

33

By this time, the Reformation, the French Revolution, and the closing of the Jesuit schools as a result of their suppression, had weakened the power and ability of the religious schools and shifted responsibility to the State.

Meanwhile, there were other thinkers supporting the ideas of Rousseau with his emphasis on the goal of education as the development of each person.

Although Immanuel Kant (1724-1804) has been called Rousseau's greatest disciple, especially in education, there are some significant differences between the thought of the two men. Recognizing the need for some discipline of the child's impulses, he stated that there need be no conflict between liberty and constraint. In fact, the goal of education would be to enable the child to find the inner law within himself. Restrictions thus can make for true liberty. Kant thus contributed to those educators who held that character formation is the primary goal of education.

With Johann Friedrich Herbart (1776-1841), education for character began to move toward education for citizenship and preparation for life which also meant education for the national interest and for patriotism. While Herbart is generally known in educational circles for the development of methods of instruction, he also reaffirmed the goal of education as the development of moral character, which by this time really included an understanding of one's duties to society and the way to fulfill them. Thus, the development of the person, the moral aim of education, and the good of the State become intertwined. The older goal of the reading of the classics and accumulation of knowledge of the ideas of the past was relegated to the background. As Power says:

> Education was intended to prepare persons for life, for life in a society whose foundations were already set in place, with a body of knowledge fully accredited in an empirical realism. Standing aside, uninvolved in the educational events of that time, and uninhibited by the threat of reprisal from nineteen century politics, we see personal interest, motive and genius sacrificed on the altar of nationalism. And educational philosophy, especially Herbart's, took part in this sacrifice.[27]

Perhaps we have come full circle back to Plato's goal of education to train good citizens on various levels to serve the State. In any case, this overview of Greek and European educational theory reveals the way the notion of moral character became closely intertwined with a notion of political morality as that which serves the State. In no instance was education directed toward a critical questioning of the State when it violated principles of justice, freedom, and equality.

OVERVIEW OF AMERICAN EDUCATION

The history of education in the United States, too, witnesses to this constant conflict between the goals of education: the development of the individual or the development of good, contributing citizens of the State.

In colonial times, there were few who reflected on educational theory. Most of the educators adhered, without reflection, to three goals: "religious orthodoxy, civility, and practical accomplishment."[28] Education was a private matter and was usually in the hands of the religious leaders.

Once we became a nation, the educational goals were even more practical. Both Franklin and Jefferson proposed their "reforms" in order to protect the democracy. While Franklin promoted the study of the English language and of the classics in English, Jefferson saw that universal manhood suffrage could work only with universal education on an elementary level. For, only an educated person can vote responsibly.

At the outset, there was a tradition that persons should be educated according to their means (thus contradicting Jefferson's view of universal education). Education was a private responsibility. However, gradually the conviction grew that "the purpose of schooling is to train citizens in civic duty,"[29] and not merely to train them within denominations. Both Jefferson and Franklin believed that educational progress in America would be directly in proportion to the lessening of the influence of religion on educational theory and practice.

The common-school movement was born when education was recognized as a responsibility of the public sector. However, it is generally conceded that the goal of public education at this time was not necessarily to develop educated persons who would be critical of the *status quo,* but rather to train people to conform to the existing social, economic, and civic order:

> . . . the purpose of education was to prepare persons for life, the social and economic life of the United States at that time. No room was made for social reconstruction.[30]

But, gradually this goal changed as American society began to be exposed to progressive ideas, especially to the idea that "all social institutions have a commitment to the improvement of mankind."[31] Thus, the perennial conflict was renewed, and again the question was raised: was the goal of education to *fit* the students into an *existing* society or to develop persons who might be able to *critique* that society?

While we can give here neither a presentation nor a critique of Pragmatism, John Dewey (1859-1952) must be seen in this overview as contributing to those who see education as enabling the students to grow to lead full and satisfying lives as citizens. Although progressivists turned to Dewey for philosophical justification, Dewey's philosophy is essentially different.[32]

Dewey has profoundly influenced those educators who see their task as facilitating the growth of the child intellectually and psychologically. The "banking" concept of education — that the child received the deposits of knowledge from the teacher and "spent" them as needed — was to be discarded. Instead, the very subject matter can and should stimulate the child to know and reflect. Instruction then becomes a

> continual reconstruction, moving from the child's present experience out into that represented by the organized bodies of truth that we call 'studies' and the studies, on the other hand, become integral parts of the child's conduct and character in organic relation to his present needs and aims.[33]

According to Dewey, teachers are

> neither hearers of lessons nor instructors delegated to teach students a body of dependable knowledge. They are guides and supervisors in a broad and open educational process.[34]

Thus, Dewey definitively rejected the old view of education as a learning of the classics.

RECENT CRITICISMS OF AMERICAN EDUCATION

Two recent documents examined both the goals and results of American Education in all spheres.[35] Neither report explicitly referred to justice and love. The report of the National Commission in 1983 is, I think, remarkable in the emptiness of its description of "Excellence in Education":

> We define "excellence" to mean several related things. At the level of the *individual learner,* it means performing on the boundary of individual ability in ways that test and push back personal limits, in school and the workplace. Excellence characterizes a *school or college* that sets high expectations and goals for all learners, then tries in every way possible to help students reach them. Excellence characterizes a *society* that has adopted these policies, for it will then be prepared through the education and skill of its people to respond to the challenges of a rapidly changing world. Our Nation's people and its schools and colleges must be committed to achieving excellence in all these senses.[36]

There was no clarification as to the nature of these high expectations and goals. If there was any reference to justice in the document, it was in terms of reconciling the goals of equality and high-quality schooling. The need to reconcile these goals was less for the promotion of justice and love and more for the improvement of society, particularly its economic condition:

> The twin goals of equality and high-quality schooling have profound and practical meaning for our economy and society and we cannot permit one to yield to the other either in principle or in practice.[37]

As this report describes the Learning Society, there is reference to "commitment to a set of values,"[38] but these are never specified. Education is important not only "because of what it contributes to one's career but also because of the value it adds to the general quality of one's life."[39]

A later report on Undergraduate Education (*Chronicle of Higher Education*[40]) criticizes such traditional criteria for judging excellence in higher education as endowments, resources, test scores of entering students, the intellectual attainments of faculty, et cetera. As the report indicates, these are "proxies for educational excellence." The committee establishes the following criteria which, at the end, do have some reference to justice and love. The report first lists as primary criteria:

1. *demonstrable improvements* in student knowledge, capacities, skills, and attitudes between entrance and graduation
2. which "occur within *established, clearly expressed and publicly announced and maintained standards of performance*"
3. and are achieved "*efficiently*, that is, that they are cost-effective in the use of student and institutional resources of time, effort, and money."[41]

Then, almost as an afterthought (although this, I must admit, is my perception) the report goes on to say:

Adequate measures of educational excellence must thus be couched in terms of *student outcomes* — principally such academic outcomes as knowledge, intellectual capacities and skills. Outcomes also may include other dimensions of student growth, such as self-confidence, persistence, leadership, *empathy, social responsibility, and understanding of cultural and intellectual differences.* (italics mine)[42]

Later on, in a perceptive statement on the role of the environment of an institution of higher learning, the report urges:

College presidents should strive to insure that the behavior of their institutions evidences the ideals of honesty, *justice,* freedom, equality, *generosity,* and respect for others — the necessary values of community . . . it is an exhortation directed to those leaders who are ultimately responsible for maintaining the values and standards for which colleges and universities have stood since their creation. If we expect students to develop those values that *are consonant with those of a democratic society, if we expect them to understand what ethical behavior means and how necessary it is to family, community, and national life,* then the leaders of academic institutions must insure that this tone dominates the campus environment. (italics mine)[43]

Thus, the view of contemporary American education might be said to be one of confusion and lack of clarity about goals and the various criteria of evaluation. Since the critique of the Carnegie Commission indicated that it spoke to all forms of education — public, private, and parochial, this report may well characterize all sectors of education.

CONCLUSION TO OVERVIEW

It must be noted in this overview that there were few references to statements on the goals of Christian education in the last one hundred years. This omission was deliberate in that we wish to consider in greater detail in the next section the various papal and Church statements on education for justice (which implicitly includes love) over the past one hundred years.

II. RECENT CHURCH STATEMENTS ON THE GOALS OF EDUCATION FOR JUSTICE

Although the labor encyclicals, *Rerum Novarum* and *Quadragesimo Anno*, were the first explicit modern statements recognizing justice as more than a matter of personal morality and although both Leo XIII and Pius XI explicitly referred to the teaching authority of the Church in them, I wish to consider them but briefly. Instead, I wish to consider in greater depth those Church documents explicitly referring to education and to education for justice.

Hollenbach[44] has given an excellent overview of modern Catholic teachings concerning justice. He indicated that *Rerum Novarum* initiated "a new phase in social and political self understanding of the Roman Catholic Church."[45] In the discussion of the two labor encyclicals mentioned above, one finds two themes that are relevant for this essay.

First, Hollenbach shows the way both popes, particularly Pius XI, indicated the close relationship between justice, especially social justice, and love:

> Justice alone, can, if faithfully observed, remove the causes of social conflict, but can never bring about union of minds and hearts.[46]

In fact, Pius speaks of "social love" as the soul of the new order of justice.[47]

Secondly, Hollenbach indicates the one limitation of these documents which was altered considerably by the documents of Vatican II and those following Vatican II. Because of the historical and political context in which they were living, both Leo XIII and Pius XI defended social inequality and a hierarchical form of society as characteristic of the natural state of things. Leo XIII stated:

> the inequality of rights and of power proceeds from the very author of nature.[48]

Hollenbach sums up the redefinition of the role of reason in Roman Catholic thinking which from now on included the contributions of the human sciences and challenged the notion of social inequality as "natural":

> No single method for analyzing the problems of social interaction can

produce a concretely normative set of conclusions about the demands of justice. Sociological and political analysis, contrary to the implicit assumptions of Leo XIII and Pius XI, cannot provide a model of society which will in some way fully embody the norm of justice in a definitive way. This rules out, at least in principle, claims such as those made by earlier popes that a social system based on private property or on a hierarchical distribution of authority and power is the only rational arrangement and therefore the only just arrangement. The same holds true for similar claims made for any concrete socialist system.[49]

Thus, the later documents recognize that no one form of government can be perfect. With these brief references to the earlier social encyclicals, I wish to examine in greater detail the papal and episcopal documents on education and on education for justice.

THE CHRISTIAN EDUCATION OF YOUTH (PIUS XI, 1929)

The first document to be considered is the encyclical of Pius XI, *The Christian Education of Youth*,[50] given on the last day of December 1929, just about a year and a half before his encyclical, *Quadragesimo Anno*. This was some years before the ecumenical movement, and its narrowness and triumphalism are somewhat surprising, given the enlightened discussion of social justice found in *Quadragesimo Anno*. The aim of education is, it stated, to prepare

> man for what he must be and for what he must do here below in order to attain the sublime end for which he was created . . . . . there can be no ideally perfect education which is not Christian education.[51]

While education belongs to the three societies—Family, State, and Church, it belongs preeminently to the Church "by reason of a double title in the supernatural order, conferred exclusively upon her by God Himself: absolutely superior therefore to any other title in the natural order."[52] Moreover, the Church has the "inalienable right as well as the indispensable duty . . . to watch over the entire education of her children in all institutions, public or private, not merely in regard to the religious instruction there given, but in regard to every other branch of learning and every regulation insofar as religion and morality are concerned."[53]

While declaring that both Family and Church have prior rights of education, Pius did indicate that it is

> the right, or so to speak, more correctly, it is the duty of the State to protect in its legislation, the prior rights, already described, of the family as regards the Christian education of its offspring, and consequently also to respect the supernatural rights of the Church in this same realm of Christian education.[54]

However, he felt that the so-called "neutral" or "lay" school where religion is excluded is "contrary to the fundamental principles of education" and is bound to become irreligious. He repeated the declarations of Leo XIII that frequenting of non-Catholic schools is forbidden for Catholic children and can be tolerated only "with permission of the ordinary."[55]

His list of the qualities of good teachers includes: "thorough preparation, intellectual and moral qualifications, pure and holy love for youth because they love Jesus Christ and His Church, having at heart the true good of family and country."[56]

The proper end of Christian education is "to cooperate with divine grace in forming the true and perfect Christian." This true Christian, product of Christian education, is

> the supernatural man who thinks, judges and acts constantly and consistently in accordance with right reason illumined by the supernatural light of the example and teaching of Christ . . . in other words, . . . the true and finished man of character. For it is not every kind of consistency and firmness of conduct based on subjective principles that make true character, but only constancy in following the eternal principles of *justice*. (italics mine)[57]

Thus, while almost claiming the sole ownership of Christian education, Pius does indicate that the goal of education is the formation of persons of just character. Educators are called to this and motivated by love.

VATICAN II ON EDUCATION

While this document on Education[58] is not one of the outstanding ones coming out of Vatican II, it did represent a significant advance over the directives of Pius XI. It is also representative of the spirit of Vatican II in that it no longer sees the Church as the sole guardian of Christian education and sees that Christians must involve themselves in working toward a better society. It is concerned only with a few basic principles and expects more specific statements to come later from the Bishops.

While still affirming, as Pius XI did, the primacy of the Church as teacher and the inalienable right of each person to education, it introduces some significant changes:

1. Education is also to prepare students to contribute to society — as well as to form the person with respect "to his ultimate goal . . . and to be willing to act energetically on behalf of the common good."[59]

2. Where sexual education in the schools was forbidden and allowed only to the parents by Pius XI, this document states: "As they advance in years they should be given positive and prudent sex education."[60]

3. Far from forbidding parents to enroll their children in non-Catholic schools, this document recognizes that there are many who are being trained in schools that are not Catholic and recognizes that the Church must be present as teacher in other forms.[61]

4. Where Pius XI almost fostered a separatism, this document

40 EDUCATION:

urges the Catholic graduate to become, as it were, "the saving leaven of the human family."[62]

5. Attention and even esteem are given to those Catholic schools which contain a large number of non-Catholic students, and emphasis is given to contemporary needs and knowledge.[63]

6. For the first time, reference is made to institutions of higher learning, both Catholic and non-Catholic or secular, and collaboration is urged. Theological departments and schools are urged to foster dialogue with our "separated brothers and with non-Christians, and solutions will be found for problems raised by the development of doctrine."[64]

Implicitly, rather than explicitly, this document expands the view of Christian Education and opens it, by its ecumenical approach and emphasis on working in society, to a broader view of education for justice and love. But, nowhere in this document nor in the document issued by Pius XI was there mention of the vocation of education as one of justice and love.

The other document of Vatican II which refers to education, *Gaudium et Spes,* does so in reference to education for peace. And since, in an earlier section, the document had indicated that peace is the work of justice, there is an indirect reference to education and justice. Again, the document also maintained that "the Church, founded on the Redeemer's love, contributes to the wider application of justice and charity among nations."[65]

JOHN XXIII

Even before Vatican II, John XXIII, in *Mater and Magistra*[66] (1961), had indicated that the Church's teaching on life must include social teaching and urged that these topics be included in Catholic schools on all levels and in seminaries as well as in all forms of communication. All Christians should not only know these social teachings, but they should experience and live them.

Then, in *Pacem in Terris*[67] (1963), John XXIII again referred to the lack of consistency between what persons believe and their actions. He felt this inconsistency was due to the lack of a solid Christian education, which should continue on the same level with scientific training. Religious education should not remain at an elementary level while scientific and technological training was given at an advanced level.

JUSTICE IN THE WORLD[68] (1971), Synod of Bishops

The outstanding recent statement of the need for education for justice is this one by the Bishops with its recognition that "action on behalf of justice and participation in the transformation of the world fully appear to us as a constitutive dimension of the preaching of the Gospel."[69]

Specifically also, the Bishops pointed out that education demands a renewal of heart: "It should inculcate a truly and entirely human way of life in *justice, love and simplicity.*"[70] (italics mine) They also pointed out that "education for social justice will critically examine the society in which persons live." Education should "make men ready to renounce those values when they cease to promote justice for all men."[71] In developing countries, conscientization is necessary so that persons are awakened to the injustice of the existing situation and the world can be transformed.

This document was to have a profound effect on the various religious orders engaged in education, as will be seen in the next section.

OTHER CHURCH DOCUMENTS

Paul VI was to reiterate constantly the message of justice and love throughout his pontificate, specifically in *Populorum Progressio*[72] (1967) and in addresses to various groups. Just before the statement of the Bishops in 1971, Paul, referring to the eightieth anniversary of *Rerum Novarum* in *Octagesima Adveniens,*[73] showed that the need for economic equality included the need for political participation as part of social justice. All Church documents had referred to the limitations on individual human rights because of the rights of others and the common good. In this encyclical, Paul VI explicitly referred to the need for education in this aspect of social justice:

> This indicates the importance of education for life in society, in which there are called to mind, not only information on each one's rights, but also their necessary correlative: the recognition of the duties of each one in regard to others.[74]

In 1972, in a message to the Diplomatic Corps, Paul indicated that the Church's contribution to the realization of justice took concrete form first in the education of its members. Such an education was not only on the cognitive and intellectual level, but aimed at action in daily life. As he said:

> This will be done by conquering, *through the power of love,* the limitations of one's own selfishness and that of others, by influencing, in order also to humanize them, legal structures in cases in which these structures may become an instrument of injustice.[75]

In 1974, the Pontifical Commission, in "Justitia et Pax," indicated that the Church's chief contribution to justice and the realization of human rights was through education: "The purpose of this education is to make Christians ever more conscious of the dignity of the human person, the brotherhood of man, the liberty and equality which all men share."[76] Later on, the document indicated that education for justice is the same as education for human rights. They are similar in that justice and respect for human rights are both implicit elements of the Gospel message. Nor should education for human rights be merely a theoretical exercise; human rights must be "put squarely in the actual context and dynamics of the society in which the person lives."[77]

Finally, John Paul II but briefly refers to education for justice in his encyclical letter, *Dives in Misericordia*[78] (1980). He, too, recognizes that justice in the teaching of the Church has now become social justice and must be applied to existing social conditions:

> It is not difficult to see that in the modern world the sense of justice has been awakening on a vast scale; and without doubt this emphasizes that which goes against justice in relationships between individuals, social groups and 'classes', between individual peoples and states, and finally between whole political systems, indeed between what are called 'worlds'.[79]

Thus, the official statements of the Church on education have, within the last century, emphasized education for justice. They have included, in the notion of justice, a recognition that it must be applied to social, political, and economic spheres. Education for justice means the development of persons not only able to live in a secular world, but also able to examine it critically and, if need be, to work towards its transformation.

III. EXAMPLES OF EDUCATION FOR JUSTICE FROM TWO TEACHING RELIGIOUS COMMUNITIES: THE JESUITS AND THE RELIGIOUS OF THE SACRED HEART

This section is an attempt to demonstrate more concretely two of the main themes of this essay:

1. that education as a vocation to justice and love has not been *explicitly* so stated in the various philosophies of education of the past, but only *implicitly* in the stated goal of education for character.

2. that the notion of justice has been considerably expanded within the last one hundred years to include social justice and a recognition that social structures must be critically examined and, if needed, transformed.

This will be demonstrated by a schematic examination of the various statements on education made by two educational religious orders: The Jesuits and the Religious of the Sacred Heart. The choice of them is made because of my familiarity with these two congregations. They are not atypical but rather typical, I believe, of the gradual explicit shift toward social justice as an educational goal of almost all Roman Catholic teaching orders.

THE JESUITS

It is beyond the scope of this essay to explore in depth the development of the philosophy of education of the Jesuits. Various writers, Fitzpatrick[80] (1933) and Donohue[81] (1963), have indicated the sources of the philosophy as the *Constitutions of the Society of Jesus,* the *Spiritual Exercises* and the *Ratio Studiorum.* The last, while usually considered *the* statement of Jesuit education, is really not a pedagogical treatise at all, nor does it discuss educational principles. It is, rather, a collection of rules.[82] It emerged out of the practical educational experience of the first Jesuit educators.

Fitzpatrick believes that the most significant contribution of Ignatius to education was in the *Spiritual Exercises.* The foundation statement is really a statement of the purpose of life. Since, fundamentally, education is to help students fulfill that purpose, it is an important educational statement:

> Man was created to praise, reverence and serve God our Lord, and by this means to save his soul; and the other things on the face of the earth were created for man's sake and in order to aid him in the prosecution of the end for which he was created. Whence it follows, that man ought to make use of them just so far as they help him to attain his end, and that he ought to withdraw himself from them just so far as they hinder him.[83]

The *Constitutions* of the Jesuits spoke more directly of education and love:

> The teachers should . . . inspire the students to the love and service of God our Lord and to a love of the virtues by which they please Him.[84]

According to Fitzpatrick,[85] the significant contribution of the Jesuits in the past is not in the content of education or in the curriculum. They usually adapted the curriculum to the different times and places. In the beginning, the Jesuit schools took over the humanistic and classical education of the Renaissance. The Jesuit contribution lay rather in the way the material was organized and used to develop each of their students.

While the Jesuits had always recognized that character education implies participation in the community, it was only after the social encyclicals that the emphasis shifted to the development of a sense of social responsibility for the various communities in which their students would be involved upon graduation. Even in 1949, the twenty-seventh General, John Baptist Janssens, exhorted the Jesuits:

> It is our aim above all in educating the young men we have accepted in the name of the Church to instill in their hearts the charity of Christ as it is applied to modern problems in the encyclicals and other papal documents . . . Let them learn to hunger and thirst after justice, the justice which sees to it that all men receive the due reward of their labors.[86]

But, the documents most relevant for this essay are those following Vatican II and, most notably, those following the publication of

"Justice in the World" in 1971: documents from the Thirty-First
General Congregation in 1966; *Men for Others,* the address of Pedro
Arrupe, Father General, to Jesuit Alumni in 1973 and, finally, the
documents from the Thirty-Second General Congregation, especially
that on *Our Mission Today: The Service of Faith and the Promotion of
Justice.*[87]

The Thirty-First Congregation in 1966 had elected Pedro Arrupe as
Father General. The Vatican Council had just closed, and throughout
the world there was growing skepticism concerning the wisdom and
justice of keeping large institutions which had large numbers of affluent students. This Congregation reaffirmed the value of and "high
regard for the apostolate of education as one of the primary ministries
of the Society." It repeated almost verbatim the directives of Father
Janssens in 1949 on education as a service of love.[88]

Even more important was the address of Father Arrupe to the Tenth
International Congress of Jesuit Alumni of Europe in Valencia, Spain,
on July 31, 1973, entitled *Men for Others.* This was two years after the
publication of the Bishops' *Justice in the World,* and the address
clearly reiterated their message. It was radical in that it not only called
for an understanding of justice as constitutive of the life of a Christian
in theory. It also called for action consistent with the acceptance of this
requirement.[89]

After having shown that education for justice has in recent years
been one of the chief concerns of the Church, Father Arrupe asks
frankly and answers honestly:

> Have we Jesuits educated you for justice? . . . You and I know what
> many of your Jesuit teachers will answer . . . in all sincerity and humil-
> ity: No, we have not. If the terms "justice" and "education for justice"
> carry all the depth of meaning which the Church gives them today, we
> have not educated you for justice.[90]

He also asks the alumni where the stress should be put in Jesuit
education:

1. Justice among men, or justice before God?
2. Love of God, or love of the neighbor?
3. Christian charity, or human justice?
4. Personal conversion, or social reform?
5. Liberation in this life, or salvation in the life to come?
6. Development through the inculcation of Christian values, or development through the application of scientific technologies and social
   ideologies?[91]

Just as the papal documents had shown the inextricable relation of
justice and love, so, too, does Arrupe say: "We are never sure that we
have love at all unless our love issues in works of justice."[92]

As he spoke to these alumni of continuing education, he said that it
must be a "call to conversion" and asked of them three things: to live

more simply, to draw no profit from clearly unjust sources, and, finally, to resolve to be agents of change in society, actively undertaking to reform unjust structures. He concluded by saying that the paramount objective of Jesuit education must now be to form men-for-others, resolved to do the three actions described above.

The Thirty-Second Congregation was even more explicit in declaring that work for justice is part of the identity of a Jesuit today: "The Jesuit is a man whose mission is to dedicate himself entirely to the service of faith and the promotion of justice."[93] The mission of the Society of Jesus today is "the service of faith of which the promotion of justice is an absolute requirement,"[94] and again: "We should pursue and intensify the work of formation in every sphere of education . . . we must help prepare both young people and adults to live and labor for others and with others to build a more just world."[95]

The address of Father Arrupe, more clearly than any of the directives of the two Congregations, indicated that this thrust toward social justice had not been part of Jesuit education in the past. His words and those of the two Congregations, however, indicated that henceforth Jesuit Education would be for justice and love.

The Jesuit High Schools in the United States are implementing this imperative for education for justice and love by requiring of all their students a certain number of hours serving the disadvantaged. Most of the high schools also require reflections on these experiences in the light of principles of social justice. The Jesuit Volunteer Program, both in the United States and internationally, is also aimed at educating the volunteers for their responsibility to reform the social injustices among the poor and in the Third World.

At Boston College, a new program has been set up to further the study of Faith, Peace and Justice. It is hoped that every department in the university will participate. For fifteen years, the Pulse program has emphasized practical experience in the study of justice. I am sure that there are many other programs on other Catholic campuses all endeavoring to implement the rather recent awareness that education is a vocation to Justice (meaning social justice) and Love.

THE RELIGIOUS OF THE SACRED HEART

The social encyclicals, the documents of Vatican II, the messages of the Latin American Bishops at Medellin in 1968, of the African Bishops in 1969 at Kampala, and of the Asian Bishops in Manila in 1970, all had profound influence on all international religious orders, especially as Arrupe indicated.[96] The religious orders of women were as affected as the religious orders of men.

One such educational order of women is the Society of the Sacred Heart, founded in France in 1800 for the education of young Christian women. Like the Jesuits, the aim of the society was to glorify God, in their case to glorify the Sacred Heart of Jesus, and education was to be the chief means for bringing about this goal. As various Plans of Studies of the Society explored the nature of education, a clearer statement of the purpose of education emerged: "Education, a work of progressive development, brings about that harmonious fulfillment of nature which favors the action of grace."[97] The goal was seen as the harmonious development of each child according to her capacities, with "a view to her future as a Christian in family and social life."[98]

> A total formation must take into account the compenetration and reciprocal reactions of the different powers, as well as — when dealing with the education of girls — the specific character of feminine psychology. It assures the harmonious development of nature which prepares for the action of grace.[99]

But, as early as the 1930s, the curriculum in the boarding schools included the social encyclicals of Leo XIII and Pius XI. The Decrees of the 22nd and 24th General Congregations, 1935, 1952, stated:

> In the last years of their education, the children must be initiated into the study of Catholic social doctrine and be effectively prepared for social action according to the directives of Holy Church . . . All Christian education therefore must be preoccupied with the social problems of our day; a fortiori must an education, centered on the love of the Heart of Jesus, open souls to a truly Catholic charity.[100]

This Plan of Studies then proceeded to list the documents to be examined, and it directs the teachers to

> (a) *Make them feel the need of this teaching:*
> — Show the agonizing character of the social question by giving a picture of the situation, quoting definite facts, giving statistics, facilitating correct information.
> — Enquiry on a particular situation: the work of young adolescents in a particular factory, the living conditions of workers in a specified workshop for luxury products, etc.
> — Contact with painful, complex, delicate situations for which, as at first sight, there seems to be no remedy. . . .
> (d) *Bring out the agreement of the Church's social doctrine with sound philosophy:*
> — Notions of the human person, of the common good, of justice and charity, of community.
> — Right conception of the family, education, work, property, of civil, national and international society, the mutual relations of these and their relations with the spiritual society.[101]

While stressing these concerns of social justice and, in a sense, anticipating the future directions of education, the Plan of Studies (1958) goes on to show that "all of this can prepare the children, theoretically and practically, for their future work in the home."[102]

Like Jesuit education, Sacred Heart education had the power to change with the times while retaining its fundamental goal of developing harmoniously all the capacities of each student. Thus, Vatican II and the social justice documents had a profound effect on the thrust of this education, as reflected also in the documents of the General Chapters of 1967, 1970, and 1976.[103]

Just as the Jesuits had now made education for justice and love explicit as a goal, so, too, were these documents to spell out explicitly the new awareness of education as a vocation to justice and love. This was done with considerable discussion, conflict, and re-examination of the original spirit of the Foundress.

Just as Father Arrupe had to admit that Jesuit education had not educated for justice, so the Religious of the Sacred Heart had to recognize in 1967 that certain obstacles prevented their witness to love:

> Identification with a particular social class, triumphalism, an air of self-satisfaction and a tendency to stress structures rather than persons.[104]

By the General Chapter of 1976 (after the Bishops Synod), the mission of the Society today had become clear. The third goal was stated in this way:

> For us, as an international apostolic community, the *educational dimension* of our mission is inseparable from the call to work for *justice*. In a world where people are often frustrated in their basic needs as in their deepest longings, we wish to work for justice, laboring together for development and liberation, with a preference for the poor and for those living on the margins of society.[105]

By 1982, in the version of the revised *Constitutions* submitted to the Congregation for Religious, this statement included work for peace:

> Whatever our work may be, it is animated by
> —a desire for the growth of the whole person;
> —a thirst for justice and peace in the world in response to the cry of the poor;
> —a longing to proclaim the Gospel.[106]

During the rather tumultuous years in the United States from 1968 to 1972, many of the Sacred Heart Schools closed, and lack of clarity about goals emerged because of the new directives from Vatican II. In 1973, plans for new collaboration were begun, and by 1975 the Network of Sacred Heart Schools was formed with nineteen schools. They are bound together by the same five goals—to educate to
—faith which is relevant in a secularized world
—a deep respect for intellectual values
—a social awareness which impels to action
—the building of community as a Christian value
—personal growth in an atmosphere of wise freedom.[107]
The third goal speaks most specifically to social justice and contains the following criteria:
1. The school awakens a critical sense which leads to reflection on

our society and its values.

   2. The curriculum includes study of the problems of the world community.

   3. The school provides the knowledge and skills needed for effective action on the problems of oppression and *injustice*. (italics mine)

   4. The school has programs which enable students to become actively involved in the wider community.[108]

Thus, while education for justice had been contained in the curriculum of Sacred Heart since 1935, at least in the United States, its social implications were *explicitly* recognized as a goal only forty years later.

This history of making explicit educational goals for social justice in Jesuit and Sacred Heart Education can most probably be found in the records of each Religious Order dedicated to education as one of its ministries. Some religious orders were founded especially to educate the poor. Clearly this was education for justice. But, the real emphasis on a justice which examines the social structures of a given society became part of educational goals, I believe, only in the nineteen sixties, after the messages of John XXIII, Vatican II, Paul VI and, most especially, the Bishops' Synod of 1971.

IV. BRIEF OVERVIEW OF DEVELOPMENTAL THEORIES OF JUSTICE AND ALTRUISM

Educators have been greatly influenced by the theories of Jean Piaget and the subsequent cognitive structural developmental psychologists. An understanding of the various stages of cognitive and emotional development given by psychologists helped to shift the view of the educator as one who *imparts knowledge* of moral principles to one who *facilitates* moral and emotional development.

From 1958 on, Lawrence Kohlberg's research and writings have profoundly influenced Catholic educators and developed considerable controversy. His model of the stages of moral judgment indicates that the development of the ability to make moral judgments eventually leads to decisions based on the principle of justice in the higher stages. A word of caution is necessary here. His value lies in his insights into the development of moral *judgment*. He does not present a coherent and total theory of the whole of the moral development of each person. Yet, he is profoundly concerned with the education of students to justice.

Perhaps even the titles of some of his chapters in *The Philosophy of Moral Development*[109] will indicate the way he has presented the aim of education as that of justice:

   Chapter 2: Education for Justice: A Modern Statement of the Socratic View

   Chapter 3: Development as the Aim of Education: The Dewey View

Epilogue: Education for Justice: The Vocation of Janusz Korczak. It is in the Epilogue that he discusses the life and death of Korczak as an educator with a vocation to justice and motivated by love. His description of Korczak is of one who viewed education as a vocation to justice and love.[110]

His greatest contributions to educational theory lie in his description of the way persons develop their judgments as to the reason an action is or is not moral (going from fear of punishment, to desire for reward, to group norms and authority standards and, finally, to justice and respect for the rights of all concerned). He shows the way to help develop persons who can make principled judgments based on justice. He does not, nor does he claim to, show the way to develop *just persons*. His is a theory of the development of the way to make moral judgments of *acts*, not a theory of the way to develop *moral persons*. As such, he contributes much to our awareness of the *cognitive* aspects of moral development. If developing moral *persons* is the goal of education, his contribution is but a part of a much larger picture.

He does refer to love in his description of Stage 7 which accepts "the finitude of the self's own life, while finding its meaning in a moral life, a life in which a sense of love for, and union with Life of God is expressed in a love for fellow human beings."[111]

And, in his most recent book,[112] where he presents the latest development of his theory, he does admit that he has not considered emotion, or *agape*, in his theory.[113] But, he considers care and responsibility as a subdivision of justice when applied to groups one knows well.[114]

Thus, while he views the role of the educator as one who facilitates students' capacity to make moral judgments based on justice, he does not recognize the role of love in the educator's task.

Other developmental psychologists have considered the need to develop a morality of love and care. Carol Gilligan, who first felt that this type of morality was unique to women, now recognizes this as another form of adult morality.[115]

Other psychologists are concerned about the development of empathy, altruism, prosocial behavior — all psychological terms for what could well be called a morality of love. One of the latest of these studies, *The Development and Maintenance of Prosocial Behavior: International Perspectives on Positive Morality*,[116] sums up much of the research on this aspect of moral development. Since many educators view education as a process of enabling the child to develop in all aspects, they will be greatly helped by the research in this area of the development of altruistic love.

The cognitive developmental psychologists have done more than just give the psychological bases for maintaining that the goal of education is justice and love.

They have also given us insights into the way moral judgments on justice issues can be developed by educators. The basic principle is that, when a person is on a certain cognitive stage and is confronted with an incident or situation that cannot be "solved" on the person's given stage, growth can and does occur. The person moves to construct a more adequate way of thinking about the justice issue. Thus, Patrick Gray, FBI director during Watergate, may well have been on Stage 4 of moral judgment since he was a retired Captain in the Navy. But, when his commander-in-chief tells him directly or indirectly to "Deep-six the evidence," the stage of obedience to law and authority was an insufficient basis on which to make his decision. It can be hypothesized that this incident may have precipitated Gray's movement toward Stage 5.

In a similar manner, when high school students are confronted with the poor and disadvantaged, they may well see that mere conformity to group norms (Stage 3) or the law will not help them to understand the conditions of some of the poor, made or kept poor by the legal system.

Thus, the service programs can be a potent force for stimulating movement toward more mature moral judgments on social issues. But, discussion of the issues is always necessary for the students to consolidate the growth in their thinking.

The same is true of growth in empathy, the forerunner of altruism, which may be considered to be the psychological term for that love referred to in "love your neighbor as yourself."

Hoffman[117] offers some speculations, based on his theoretical model of the development of empathy, as to the way to foster its development:

1. *Direct experience of emotions.* Children will be more likely to empathize with someone else's emotion if they have experienced the same emotion themselves. Since our society in the past has socialized males not to show emotion, it might well be that this practice might account for the lower empathetic responses sometimes found in males.

2. *Calling attention to the feelings of the victim.* Inductive techniques, that call attention to the victim's pain or encourage the child to imagine himself or herself in the victim's place, should help put the feelings of others into the child's consciousness and thus enhance the child's empathic potential.

3. *Role-taking opportunities* should help sharpen the child's cognitive sense of the other but it should be in positive social contexts rather than role-taking opportunities in competitive contexts. The latter might help develop manipulative rather than helping skills.

4. *Give much affection.* Giving children much affection would keep them open to the needs of others and empathic rather than absorbed in their own needs.

5. *Expose them to models who act altruistically* and express their sympathetic feelings. This should contribute to the child's acting empathically rather than criticizing the victim.

Hoffman concludes by pointing out "that empathy and helping may be fostered by relatively benign and nonpunitive socialization experiences."[118] Hoffman believes that empathy develops naturally and is present at an early age, and argues that "empathy may serve as a potential ally to parents and others with prosocial child-rearing goals for the child—something to be encouraged and nurtured rather than punished as egoistic motives must sometimes be."[119]

This brief reference to the work of pyschologists was presented because they, of all contemporary social scientists, are working with educators. And it is the cognitive psychologists, in their work on the development of justice and love (altruism), who can help to validate empirically the view of education as a vocation to (develop) justice and love.

V. SUMMARY AND CONCLUSIONS

We have attempted to demonstrate in our four part discussion of the topic, *Education: A Vocation to Justice and Love,* the following:

IN PART I

1. Over the course of history, the goals of education have shifted and been very diverse. The ancient Greeks, Plato and Aristotle, saw that the goal of education was to develop persons of virtue—primarily the virtues of prudence, justice, fortitude, and temperance. Although friendship was considered in their reflections, the goal of education was primarily intellectual. As far as I could determine, love of neighbor was not considered as an educational goal. This educational goal of developing moral persons eventually was thought to be accomplished by the study of the classics.

2. This content and goal continued with modifications even into the Christian era. Moral character development was considered more a task of the family and Church and less a task of the schools. Only Augustine, in his considerable reflections on the teacher and the student, refers to love as the motivator of learning. He clearly saw education as a vocation of love, for love, and by love.

3. Thomas Aquinas saw education as a work of the active life, a spiritual work of mercy—instructing the ignorant.

4. The Renaissance returned to the study of Greek and Roman classics as the means by which persons of character were educated.

5. With the advent of the Industrial Revolution, the split among Christians in the sixteenth century, and the rise of nationalism, new goals for education emerged, such as the goal of preparation for life here and now, and the training of citizens who would serve their nations.

6. Thus, reflections on education varied from a discussion of the *content* (classics) to the use of education for *political* means. Writers, such as Rousseau, focussed on the child and the natural development

of the child as the goal of education (a return to the Greek view of the person as the goal, but with a more developmental approach and without an emphasis on the virtues).

7. Even American education saw the need for education for political purposes, since a functioning democracy needed an educated electorate. Dewey, like Rousseau, emphasized the development of the child as the goal of education. The means of education were discovery and experience rather than books.

8. Today, there are no clear goals in American education. Two recent critiques referred to excellence without delineating excellence "for what?" There were but a passing reference to student outcomes and a mention of empathy and social responsibility, but no mention was made of justice.

IN PART II

1. The early social encyclicals on labor conditions emphasized the relationship of justice and love. However, both Leo XIII and Pius XI defended social inequality as inevitable. The notion of social justice as challenging existing social structures came only with the works of John XXIII.

2. The first modern encyclical on education was issued by Pius XI. The goal of Christian education was to form true, perfect, and just Christians. Teachers should be motivated by love, yet Catholic children were forbidden to go to non-Catholic schools without approval from the Bishop.

3. The Vatican II Document on Education expanded the narrow view of education given by Pius XI. Its ecumenical approach toward non-Catholic schools and non-Catholics in Catholic schools, as well as its recommendation to students to work within society for the common good, expanded the notion of Christian education toward one of justice and love.

4. John XXIII, in both *Mater et Magistra* and *Pacem in Terris*, was concerned about the social injustices in the world. He recognized that education should include the social dimension and religious education should be as advanced as technical and scientific education.

5. The most explicit work on education for justice was the statement of the Bishops' Synod, *Justice in the World*, in 1971. Justice was seen as "a constitutive dimension" of gospel teaching, as was action to transform the world. This spoke to all the elements of education for social justice — as part of the Good News of Jesus, which should emerge into action that would change unjust social structures.

6. Paul VI continued this message of the need for education in social justice which should result in action, in a critical attitude toward the secular world, and in working for its transformation.

IN PART III

1. The early forms of education exercised by the Jesuits were

adapted to the times.

2. The address of Father Arrupe in 1973 to the Alumni indicated that the Jesuits recognized that they had not educated for social justice in the past and that they must do so in the future. The Thirty-Second Congregation (1975) explicitly stated that the mission of the Society of Jesus is "the service of faith of which the promotion of justice is an absolute requirement," and education must prepare young people to build a more just world.

3. A similar movement toward education for social justice was seen in the more recent documents of the Religious of the Sacred Heart. Like the Jesuits, they had to admit to failure in an education for all based on justice and love. With the self-examination of their *Constitutions* directed by Vatican II, recent General Chapter Documents speak to the recognition of "education for justice" as a goal consistent with the original charism of the foundress.

4. In the United States, a Network of Schools drew up five goals, one of which specifically speaks to social justice.

5. The experience of the Jesuits and of the Religious of the Sacred Heart is probably typical of most educational orders.

6. Recent Church documents, the signs of the times, and the Holy Spirit have called us all to the true spirit of the Gospel teaching — that education is a vocation to justice and love.

IN PART IV

1. It is probably inevitable that as psychologists gained in influence and sophistication, they should become interested in the application of their research and theories to education. From the beginning of the second half of the twentieth century, Lawrence Kohlberg formulated his theory of education for justice, derived from his research and his notion of Socratic justice. He views the goal of education as facilitating the development of a sense of justice in all students.

2. Other developmental psychologists have studied the development of a morality of care, of empathy and altruism. They, too, have been outspoken in proposing that these qualities should be developed by educators.

3. So psychology, an empirically based social science, presents research material that would help educators in their goal of developing justice and love in themselves and in their students.

We are back to our original questions. Is the theme, "Education: A Vocation to Justice and Love," *descriptive* or *prescriptive?* It would seem from this rather broad review of the goals of education that the title of this essay is not *descriptive* of what happened in the past. That justice and love are *prescriptions* contained in the Gospel is clear. Recently, the Bishops affirmed justice as constitutive of Gospel Preaching.

It would seem, then, that the growing self consciousness of the

54 EDUCATION:

Church as it relates to contemporary social conditions has made *explicit* what was always *implicit* in the vocation of education. Not only, then, should education be a vocation to justice and love, but psychology has revealed to us the way these qualities develop, and papal documents have expanded the notion of justice far beyond that of Plato and Aristotle to include a profound critique of existing political, social and economic structures.

The challenge for educators has always been there. It is greater than ever before.

NOTES

[1] Edward J. Power, *Philosophy of Education: Studies in Philosophies, Schooling, and Educational Policies* (Englewood Cliffs: Prentice Hall, Inc., 1982), p. 250.

[2] Plato, *Protagoras*, trans. B. Jowett, in *The Dialogue of Plato*, 3rd ed. (London: Oxford University Press, 1892), 312a.

[3] Plato, *Gorgias*, trans. B. Jowett, in *The Dialogue of Plato*, 3rd ed. (London: Oxford University Press, 1892), 471de.

[4] Clement of Alexandria, "The Writings of Clement of Alexandria," in *The Ante Nicene Christian Library* (Edinburgh: T. & T. Clark, 1870), Vol. II, p. 100.

[5] George Howie, ed. and trans., *St. Augustine on Education* (Chicago: Henry Regnery Co., 1969).

[6] *Ibid.*, p. 11.

[7] *Ibid.*, p. 12.

[8] *Ibid.*, p. 13.

[9] *Ibid.*

[10] *Ibid.*

[11] *Ibid.*, p. 16.

[12] *Ibid.*, p. 18.

[13] *Ibid.*, pp. 27-28.

[14] Cassiodorus, *An Introduction to Divine and Human Readings*, trans. L.W. Jones (New York: Columbia University Press, 1946).

[15] Power, *Philosophy of Education*, p. 146.

[16] Daniel B. McGarry, *The Metalogicon of John of Salisbury* (Berkeley: University of California Press, 1955), Book III.

[17] Thomas Aquinas, *The Teacher: (Truth, Question Eleven)*, with a Foreword by James Collins, West Baden Translation (Chicago: Henry Regnery Co., 1953).

[18] *Ibid.*, p. x.

[19] *Ibid.*, p. 12.

[20] *Ibid.*, p. 16.

[21] *Ibid.*, pp. 36-38.

[22] Power, *Philosophy of Education*, p. 66.

[23] *Ibid.*

[24] *Ibid.*, p. 55.

[25] William Boyd and Edmund J. King, *The History of Education*, 10th ed. (New York: Barnes and Noble, 1973), p. 301.

²⁶ Jean-Jacques Rousseau, *Emile*, trans. Barbara Foxley (New York: E.P. Dutton, 1938), p. 5.

²⁷ Power, *Philosophy of Education*, p. 59.

²⁸ *Ibid.*, p. 60.

²⁹ *Ibid.*, p. 62.

³⁰ *Ibid.*, p. 64.

³¹ *Ibid.*, p. 62.

³² *Ibid.*, p. 140.

³³ Boyd, *History of Education*, p. 406.

³⁴ Power, *Philosophy of Education*, p. 140.

³⁵ The National Commission on Excellence in Education, *A Nation at Risk: The Imperative for Educational Reform* (Washington, D.C., 1983).

³⁶ *Ibid.*, p. 12.

³⁷ *Ibid.*, p. 14.

³⁸ *Ibid.*

³⁹ *Ibid.*

⁴⁰ *Chronicle of Higher Education*, 24 October 1984, pp. 37-45.

⁴¹ *Ibid.*, p. 37.

⁴² *Ibid.*

⁴³ *Ibid.*, p. 45.

⁴⁴ David Hollenbach, "Modern Catholic Teachings Concerning Justice," in *The Faith That Does Justice*, ed. John C. Haughey (New York: Paulist Press, 1977), pp. 207-34.

⁴⁵ *Ibid.*, p. 210.

⁴⁶ *Quadragesimo Anno*, in *The Church and the Reconstruction of the World*, ed. Terrence P. McLaughlin (Garden City, NY: Doubleday Image, 1957), No. 137, quoted in David Hollenbach, *op cit.*

⁴⁷ *Ibid.*, No. 88.

⁴⁸ Hollenbach, "Modern Catholic Teachings," p. 215.

⁴⁹ *Ibid.*, p. 217.

⁵⁰ Pius XI, *Christian Education of Youth*, in *Five Great Encyclicals* (New York: Paulist Press, 1939), pp. 37-68.

⁵¹ *Ibid.*, p. 39.

⁵² *Ibid.*, p. 40.

⁵³ *Ibid.*, p. 43.

⁵⁴ *Ibid.*, p. 48.

⁵⁵ *Ibid.*, p. 60.

⁵⁶ *Ibid.*, p. 63.

⁵⁷ *Ibid.*, p. 65.

⁵⁸ Walter M. Abbott, S.J., gen. ed., *The Documents of Vatican II* (New York: America Press, 1966), "Declaration on Christian Education," pp. 637-51.

⁵⁹ *Ibid.*, p. 639.

⁶⁰ *Ibid.*

⁶¹ *Ibid.*, p. 645.

⁶² *Ibid.*, p. 646.

⁶³ *Ibid.*, p. 647.

⁶⁴ *Ibid.*, p. 653.

⁶⁵ Walter M. Abbott, S.J., gen.ed., *The Documents of Vatican II* (New York: America Press, 1966), "The Church Today," p. 288, par. 96.

⁶⁶ David J. O'Brien and Thomas A. Shannon, ed., *Renewing the Earth: Catholic Documents on Peace, Justice and Liberation* (Garden City: Doubleday Image, 1977), *Christianity and Social Progress (Mater et Magistra)*, pp. 50-116.

⁶⁷ *Ibid.*, *Peace on Earth*, pp. 124-70.

⁶⁸ *Ibid.*, *Justice in the World*, pp. 390-408.

⁶⁹ *Ibid.*, p. 391.

⁷⁰ *Ibid.*, p. 402.

⁷¹ *Ibid.*

⁷² *Ibid.*, *On the Development of Peoples (Populorum Progressio)*, pp. 313-46.

⁷³ *Ibid.*, *A Call to Action: Letter on the Eightieth Anniversary of Rerum Novarum (Octagesima Adveniens)*, pp. 352-83.

⁷⁴ *Ibid.*, p. 365, No. 24.

⁷⁵ Vincent P. Mainelli, ed., *Social Justice: Official Catholic Teachings* (Wilmington, NC: McGrath Publishing Co., 1978), p. 312, No. 1141.

⁷⁶ *Ibid.*, "The Church and Human Rights: Pontifical Commission," "Justitia et Pax," p. 380, No. 1392.

⁷⁷ *Ibid.*, p. 383, No. 1407.

⁷⁸ Michael Welsh and Brian Davies, ed., *Proclaiming Justice and Peace: Documents from John XXIII—John Paul II* (Mystic, CT: Twenty-Third Publications), *Dives in Misericordia*, pp. 267-70.

⁷⁹ *Ibid.*, p. 269, No. 12.

⁸⁰ Edward A. Fitzpatrick, ed., *St. Ignatius and the Ratio Studiorum* (New York: McGraw-Hill Book Co., 1933).

⁸¹ John W. Donohue, S.J., *Jesuit Education: An Essay on the Foundation of Its Idea* (New York: Fordham University Press, 1963).

⁸² Fitzpatrick, *St. Ignatius and the Ratio*, pp. 23-24.

⁸³ *Ibid.*, p. 40, citing *Spiritual Exercises*.

⁸⁴ Donohue, *Jesuit Education*, p. 3, citing *Constitutions of the Society of Jesus*, IV, xvi, 4.

⁸⁵ Fitzpatrick, *St. Ignatius and the Ratio*, p. 15.

⁸⁶ Donohue, *Jesuit Education*, pp. 208-9.

⁸⁷ John W. Padberg, S.J., ed., *Documents of the Thirty-First and Thirty-Second General Congregations of the Society of Jesus: An English Translation of the Official Latin Texts of the General Congregations and of the Accompanying Papal Documents* (St. Louis: The Institute of Jesuit Source, 1977); Pedro Arrupe, S.J., *Men for Others: Education for Social Justice and Social Action Today* (Washington, D.C.: Jesuit Secondary Education Association, 1974).

⁸⁸ Padberg, *Documents*, pp. 230-32, par. 505-515.

⁸⁹ Arrupe, *Men for Others.*

⁹⁰ *Ibid.*, p. 2.

⁹¹ *Ibid.*, p. 6.

⁹² *Ibid.*, p. 7.

⁹³ Padberg, *Documents*, p. 408, par. 31.

⁹⁴ *Ibid.*, p. 411, par. 2.

⁹⁵ *Ibid.*, p. 432, par. 60.

⁹⁶ Arrupe, *Men for Others*, p. 5.

[97] *Spirit and Plan of Studies in The Society of The Sacred Heart of Jesus* (Farnborough: St. Michael's Abbey Press, 1958), p. 10, quoting *The Plan of Studies of 1922.*

[98] *Ibid.,* p. 14.

[99] *Ibid.,* p. 15.

[100] *Ibid.,* p. 45.

[101] *Ibid.,* pp. 46–47.

[102] *Ibid.,* p. 48.

[103] Society of The Sacred Heart, *Special Chapter: Orientations ad experimentum* (Purchase, NY: Manhattanville College, 1967); Society of The Sacred Heart, *Chapter 1970;* Society of The Sacred Heart, *Chapter 1976.*

[104] *Special Chapter, Orientations,* p. 21. Later on, other questions were asked: "In a world where hunger and ignorance can be overcome only by education we should ask ourselves if our pupils leave us with a real sense of social justice and the determination to work to change the world" (p. 63).

[105] *Chapter 1976,* p. 17.

[106] Society of The Sacred Heart of Jesus, *Constitutions* (Official Interim English Translation, 1982), p. 3, par. 14. See also par. 13 & 15.

[107] Sacred Heart Schools in The United States, *Goals and Criteria* (Newton, MA: Network of Schools, 1975), p. 1.

[108] *Ibid.,* p. 8.

[109] Lawrence Kohlberg, *The Philosophy of Moral Development: Moral Stages and the Idea of Justice* (San Francisco: Harper & Row, 1981).

[110] *Ibid.,* pp. 401–8.

[111] *Ibid.,* p. 401.

[112] Lawrence Kohlberg, *The Psychology of Moral Development: The Nature and Validity of Moral Stages* (San Francisco: Harper & Row, 1984).

[113] *Ibid.,* p. 227.

[114] *Ibid.,* p. 234.

[115] Carol Gilligan, *In a Different Voice: Psychological Theory and Women's Development* (Cambridge: Harvard University Press, 1982).

[116] Ervin Staub et al., *The Development and Maintenance of Prosocial Behavior: International Perspectives on Positive Morality* (New York: Plenum Publishers, 1984).

[117] Martin L. Hoffman, "Development of Prosocial Motivation: Empathy and Guilt," in N. Eisenberg, ed., *The Development of Prosocial Behavior* (New York: Academic Press, 1982).

[118] *Ibid.,* p. 306.

[119] *Ibid.*

Law: A Vocation to Justice and Love

Christopher F. Mooney, S.J.

The choice of law as a profession ought to pose some serious problems for anyone concerned with promoting justice and love in American society. The profession itself is at present a beleaguered institution. Conservatives criticize it for reaching too far into the economic and social spheres; liberals criticize it for being unavailable to those who cannot afford its cost; radicals criticize it for becoming an instrument of oppression and exploitation. There are many who think American society is law-drenched: we have altogether too much law and too many lawyers. Facts support this judgment. There are now more than six hundred thousand lawyers in the nation, one for every three hundred eighty-eight people; two thirds of all the lawyers in the world live here; and one third of these, almost two hundred thousand, have been in practice fewer than five years. The number of civil suits filed in federal courts has more than doubled since 1960 and increased by more than a third since 1970. The clog in state courts is even worse: in Cook County in Chicago, to choose one example, a negligence case can take as long as four years to get to trial. This rise in civil litigation comes at a time when courts are already inundated with criminal cases. Violent crime has increased by almost two hundred percent since 1960, and the total number of crimes by more than one hundred eighty percent.[1]

What is going on in American society and in the legal profession? How is a religious person to think about the practice of law today? There seems to be general agreement that the unique role of the lawyer as an independent advocate is being eroded by a rapidly growing segment of the American bar that views law as a business rather than as a profession. The large multi-state law firms are growing ever larger, and their complexity and bureaucracy inevitably chill their members' professional independence as well as isolate them from the humanity of their clients. A Harris poll several years ago, rating public confidence in sixteen institutions, found law firms at the bottom, along with Congress, organized labor, and advertising agencies. Hence, to speak of law as a vocation means that one has to ask not only, "What kind of lawyer does a person want to be?," but also, "What kind of person does a lawyer want to be?"

In the pages that follow I would like to begin with our Western concept of profession, as this was originally formulated, along with its companion concept of "calling." At this level of abstraction it would be quite easy for us to speak of the legal profession as a vocation to justice and love. Our difficulties begin as soon as we recognize to what extent this profession has been conditioned over the years by the traditionally litigious character of American society as well as by what American jurists have generally conceived to be the nature of American law. If we then go on to examine the present state of the legal profession and the type of education given to the typical American law student, we find even more problems. None of these can be either ignored or minimized if we want a realistic understanding of the way someone can function as a lawyer in America today and still be true to his or her religious faith commitment. For, such a person will have to deal not only with conflicts of justice between persons, but also with conflicts of the spirit that are far more threatening and painful.

I

We can speak of someone being "called" to a profession because of the way we have traditionally understood "profession" in the West. The term became secularized in the English language about the mid-seventeenth century, following its more restricted earlier usage to signify the taking of vows in a religious order. The concept itself, however, goes back to Graeco-Roman thought, especially as applied to the technical skills of lawyers and physicians. The Middle Ages added to the concept the requirement of university education in the arts and sciences, in order to support specialty skills with rational theory and a broad cultural background. Eventually, the concept developed a third feature, in addition to skills and learning; namely, those autonomous associations of professionals that defined their members' standards of performance and provided sanctions for any violation. Hence, certain characteristics have come to be associated with all professional activity: a high degree of generalized and systematic knowledge as well as technical competence in a specialized area; an orientation that is primarily to community service rather than to individual self interest; significant behavior control through internalized codes of ethics, formulated by voluntary organizations run by the professionals themselves.

Professions are distinguished from other occupations in that they justify their activities in terms other than self interest. Because the superior knowledge associated with them gives power and control in a community, it is important that such knowledge be used primarily in the community interest. Consequently, the reward system in profes-

CHRISTOPHER F. MOONEY, S.J.   61

sions consists not just in money, but in prestige, awards and community status. Professionals are also rewarded with a client's trust, and indeed ask for such trust, because they profess to know better than their
clients what ails them and their affairs. While they claim the right to
treat their clients by virtue of their specialized learning, they also
pledge not to exploit this situation for personal gain:

> These characteristics and collective claims of a profession are dependent
> upon a close solidarity, upon its members constituting in some measure a
> group apart with an ethos of its own. This in turn implies deep and
> lifelong commitment. A man who leaves a profession, once he is fully
> trained, licensed and initiated, is something of a renegade in the eyes of
> his fellows. . . . It takes a rite of passage to get him in; another to read
> him out. If he takes French leave, he seems to belittle the profession and
> his former colleagues.[2]

From what we have said so far, it is not difficult to see the reason the
concept of vocation has been linked so closely to that of profession: the
sense of commitment is central to both, even after the concept of vocation has been totally secularized. The legal profession has even been
compared to a secular national religion in America. "I often feel that I
am a black-robed priest," writes one judge.[3] The respect accorded to
law in our national life does in fact give to law some of the qualities of
a religion, and to the legal profession a resemblance to priesthood.
Legal ritual, like religious ritual, provides coherence and form within
a disorderly society. Lawyers are seen as secular clergy, praying before
the court, while judges are seen as secular bishops who wear flowing
robes and sit on raised platforms above all others in the courtroom:

> A trial with its controlled forms of address, cross-examination, and pro-
> cedural orderliness, offers a comforting framework to dispel feelings of
> helplessness. . . . The bar, like the Church, relies upon mysterious
> language and procedures to instill reverence. . . . The black robes of
> bishop and judge clothe mere mortals with the power of the Lord or the
> law. The courtroom is our cathedral, where contemporary passion plays
> are enacted. In both buildings silence, awe and deference—if not
> subservience—placate the authorities.[4]

But, the concept of vocation as applied to the legal profession has
other and more important connotations than that of civil religion. Just
as the major concern of medicine has always been for health, so that of
law has always been for justice. Law as a vocation is thus primarily to
be understood as a striving for justice. Indeed, law has often been
referred to as the art of doing justice. Trying to define justice as the
goal of law, however, is as difficult as trying to define "health" as the
goal of medicine. Like "beauty," these professional ideals elude rational analysis. It is much easier to recognize their opposites, injustice
and sickness. For the lawyer and physician this is also more important.
The problem for the legal profession, nevertheless, is the perennial
temptation to equate justice with the administration of justice, thereby

assuming that government in the person of the judge is the source of justice. Just legal procedures are obviously of paramount importance in a pluralistic society, but exclusive reliance upon them can result in thinking and speaking of justice in terms of coercion rather than truth.[5] This is the reason that in the 1972 Oliver Wendell Holmes, Jr., Lectures at Harvard, John Noonan of Berkeley could say that the "central problem . . . of the legal enterprise is the relation of love to power. We can often apply force to those we do not see, but we cannot, I think, love them. Only in the response of person to person can Augustine's sublime fusion be achieved, in which justice is defined as 'love serving only the one loved.'"[6]

The classical understanding of justice, originating in Natural Law theory, was that of giving to each person his or her due. Justice in this sense was thought to be the foundation of civil society. What Augustine asserted, however, was that civil society was in reality *not* based upon the principle of giving every person his or her due, but is rather based upon and held together by what persons love. In Book XIX of *The City of God* Augustine distinguishes between societies informed by the love of power and those informed by the power of love, and he then analyzes at length the way love functions as the bond of civil society. In this analysis, justice becomes the form of love which expresses the right ordering of human relations with reference to God's order and purpose. Love is thus the essence of justice and the key perspective for fashioning as well as criticizing law. Without love, there can be no order in society, since the public sphere would otherwise be continually disturbed by human willfulness, and persons would lack any real motive to render to others their due.

According to Augustine, then, justice to persons may be identified with love — an active service to another who is loved. This understanding of justice is so important because, as we shall see later in more detail, lawyers are conditioned by their training and practice to think in terms of rules and problems rather than persons. An exclusive concern for justice, understood professionally in its more procedural and administrative sense, is therefore clearly inadequate as a vocational ideal for the lawyer, educator or judge. Even understood in its larger sense as the principle that every person is entitled to his or her due, justice as a virtue must be complemented by the virtues of compassion and hope, so necessary in the interpersonal lives of lawyers and clients:

> The process is rightly understood only if rules and persons are seen as equally essential components, every rule depending on persons to frame, apply, and undergo it, every person using rules. Rules and persons in the analysis of law are complementary. By the same token, the paradigm of the impartial judge and the paradigm of the personally responsible judge are equally necessary.[7]

To contrast law and love, the one abstract, objective and impersonal, the other concrete, subjective and personal, is to misunderstand the nature of law, according to Harvard Professor Harold J. Berman. Law does not consist of general rules, but is rather a process, a living social institution for *applying* general rules. As such, it is concrete, subjective and personal. To think of it otherwise would be to treat justice as a purely intellectual problem:

> There is nothing abstract or impersonal about putting a man in jail because he committed a robbery, or enjoining the School Board of Little Rock, Arkansas, from excluding Negroes from the Central High School, or awarding a man who has been run down by an automobile money damages to pay his hospital bills. Law is not only rules and concepts; law is also, and primarily, a type of relationship among people. . . . The contrast between law and love exaggerates the role of rules in law and underestimates the role of decision and of relationship; further, it exaggerates the role of spontaneity in love, and underestimates the role of deliberation and restraint.[8]

To speak of law as a vocation to justice and love is thus to unite what tends to be separated in the professional life of the lawyer. Justice functions also on the interpersonal level, and love functions also on the social level. Thomas Shaffer sounds the leitmotiv of what we shall be discussing shortly, when he says that the legal culture of justice in America finds it very hard to say that a lawyer's life is really a ministry and that this ministry aims beyond justice to compassion and hope:

> Compassion is the heart of counseling and counseling is what lawyers do most of the time. Lawyers do not, most of the time, 'dispense' or 'administer' or serve justice: they serve people who know and who want to know how to live together. The professional culture's proclaimed concern with justice, because justice is often irrelevant to this enterprise, makes compassion more rather than less difficult.[9]

Just how difficult will be apparent shortly. For, what we have been doing thus far is speaking in theory. We must now examine very concretely the four major aspects of America's legal culture which condition a lawyer's vocation to justice and love and in large measure tend to inhibit its realization. I refer to the nature of American society, the nature of American law, the nature of American legal education, and the nature of the American legal profession. Only after such an examination can we talk realistically of the way an individual attorney, in the light of this conditioning, can still consider his or her life as a vocation to justice and love.

II

The legal profession in the United States developed gradually over two centuries in accordance with certain characteristics that were and continue to be endemic to American society. Alexis de Tocqueville observed as early as 1835 that "there is hardly a political question in the United States that does not sooner or later develop into a judicial one."[10] The source of this impetus was the pervasive influence of the British common law tradition, imported very early into the colonies to dominate the colonial legal system. As it originated, the common law of England (i.e., law formulated by judges as opposed to statutory law enacted by legislative bodies) was law developed by and for aristocrats. Legal historian Lawrence Friedman underlines this: "Leaf through the pages of Lord Coke's reports, compiled in the late 16th and early 17th century; here one will find a colorful set of litigants, all drawn from the very top of British society—lords and ladies, landed gentry, high-ranking clergymen, wealthy merchants. . . . The masses were hardly touched by this system and only indirectly under its rule."[11]

All this changed when the colonies gained independence. These "rights by Englishmen," elaborated over centuries in great detail by the English judiciary, now became democratized. The new nation was, in fact, founded on law and on a legal system that was centered on litigation. Historian Maxwell Bloomfield notes that in postrevolutionary times "a middle class public, cherishing the ideals of competition, utilitarianism, and self-advancement, found itself unwilling to forgo the advantages of an individualistic legal system in favor of some more equitable communitarian experiment."[12] The Bill of Rights referred to the rights of everyone. Democracy brought with it the idea that the people themselves could direct their own affairs and that they could use law to accomplish this. Americans took literally the language of their Constitution, their charters and statutes. "What good is a right that cannot be enforced and pleaded in court? If a right is observed there is no need to turn to judges; but if it is disregarded, to whom else ought one turn?"[13]

This dominant ethic of competitive individualism, that has been part of the American psyche from the beginning, inevitably fostered an adversary culture. The United States was, after all, founded by persons preoccupied with the assertion and maintenance of individual rights. Government, according to the Founders, was to be checked, with power balanced against power, so that personal liberty would remain intact. The great immigrations of the nineteenth and twentieth centuries brought millions of people to America who were distrustful of the government they knew in Europe and zealous to embrace and maintain their rights in the new world. Our classical liberal tradition is thus based on a fragmented model of society that emphasizes a negative responsibility to restrain power and to resist any clear center to the social system. No one will deny that this American emphasis upon personal freedom and competition has mobilized powerful energies in the nation, but it has also encouraged an open litigiousness based on rights claimed, adjudicated and enforced. Such litigiousness is not a legal, but a social phenomenon, It exists in other nations, of course, but in much more muted form, and in some Eastern cultures, like that of Japan for example, it is almost totally unknown.

This native adversary culture has been exacerbated during the past two generations by another American phenomenon: the radical separation of legal and religious values. Such separation has resulted from the triumph of the Enlightenment concept of law as something wholly instrumental and wholly invented, a pragmatic device for accomplishing specific political, economic and social objectives. We shall say more about this in the next section. For now, it is important to realize that this totally secular understanding of law, which goes back to the French and American revolutions and has for more than a century been espoused by most American jurists, has only recently penetrated the general social consciousness. Its parallel concept is that of religion as a wholly private affair, without any political or social dimension, and with no role to play in overcoming the forces of public disorder and strife. Harold Berman has emphasized that this secularizing of law and this spiritualizing of religion is something quite different from the separation of church and state mandated by the Constitution, which concerns the separation of religious from political and legal *institutions*. The contemporary phenomenon under scrutiny here is rather the almost total absence of any interaction between religious and legal *values*.[14]

I said a moment ago that our adversary culture was aggravated by this phenomenon. The reason is that without such interaction between values law tends to degenerate into legalism, and to rely exclusively on experiences of fairness and trust:

> It is precisely when law is trusted and therefore does not require coercion . . . that it is efficient. One who rules by law is not compelled to be present everywhere with his police force. . . . In the last analysis, what deters crime is the tradition of being law-abiding, and this in turn depends upon a deeply or passionately held conviction that law is not only an instrument of secular policy, but also part of the ultimate purpose and ultimate meaning of life.[15]

Banning from the realm of law the religious and moral discourse common to most Americans is thus hastening the decay of that civility between persons which finally enables the legal system to serve its fundamental goals of justice, mercy and community trust.

What we have in contemporary American society, then, is an instinctive national impulse to rely upon litigation to settle disputes, coupled with the relatively recent isolation of that impulse from those religious values which counsel prudence, civility, reflection, and trust. The consequent breakdown in community has fed the current explosion of lawsuits, which in turn has accelerated the breakdown of community. Several other sociological factors compound the problem. A change in our economic base is perhaps the most significant.

American society is gradually being transformed from an industrial into an information-based society, in which people interact far more than ever before with other people:

> The number of personal and business transactions has increased geometrically, encompassing a broad range of activities on paper and over wires, including phone calls, letters, messages, bills, checks, contracts and agreements. Because the medium we trade in is information—words, ideas, communications—we have become a more litigious society as some transactions undoubtedly go sour or are thrown into question.[16]

A rising population is another factor. The more people become concentrated in a single area, the greater number of collisions they tend to have with one another. There are also more young people and more old people in the United States today, and these usually have far more problems than the middle aged. A third factor is the ever increasing willingness in the nation to let courts settle matters that were once settled by legislatures, executives, parents, teachers or just pure chance. Judges are now asked to run prisons, hospitals and school systems, and their decisions may even in some cases replace those of physicians, labor unions and parents.

This last factor (the growing reliance upon courts), however, is not totally negative. On the one hand, the result has been an almost hopeless congestion in court dockets. The six Federal District Courts in New York, New Jersey and Connecticut, for example, between 1978 and 1983 had an increase of new cases that ranged between forty-four and one hundred forty percent, a range of increase that reflects the situation in most of the other ninety-four District Courts across the country.[17] On the other hand, such massive litigation, especially in federal courts, can be judged an index of societal health. The reason is that, following the *Brown* decision in 1954, the Supreme Court demonstrated an unprecedented sensitivity to the legal rights of disadvantaged citizens:

> As courts impeded discrimination based on race, gender or wealth, a generation of Americans looked to a vigorous, vigilant judiciary to enforce the Bill of Rights. The judiciary developed procedural safeguards in criminal law, protected the rights of the indigent, and expanded the right to counsel. New rules—superseding old notions of who could sue or be sued, and about what—reduced the immunity of public officials and enlarged litigation opportunities for victims of discrimination, harassment and official lawlessness.[18]

Besides this judicial activism in the 1950s and 1960s, Americans pursued the goal of equality in other ways. Public interest law firms developed along with a Federal Legal Services program. The underprivileged and disadvantaged could now file class-action lawsuits and use litigation to expose closed institutions, like prisons and hospitals, to public scrutiny and government regulation. Over the last generation the American impulse to litigate has thus been transformed, to some extent at least, into the vital ingredients of social justice. This is the reason we cannot evaluate our litigiousness outside the context of true injuries to people and their right to redress. Plaintiffs sue to heal these injuries and to vindicate these rights, and so the judiciary has inevitably become the ultimate authority that defines such legally redressable injury.

III

The litigious character of American society that we have just discussed is the first inhibiting factor in any person's pursuit of law as a vocation to justice and love. A second is the nature of American law itself. Practicing lawyers seldom think about the nature of law, and their penalty for avoiding such reflection is to be without any sense of the presuppositions underlying their profession and shaping their everyday lives as attorneys. But, merely because most lawyers are unconcerned with a legal world-view does not mean that they do not have one, or that it is not operative in their lives. As Douglas Sturm has said, jurisprudence is unavoidable for a lawyer: "One may not think about breathing but one breathes anyway. One may not deliberate about the economic system of a country, but one nonetheless fulfills some role in it. One's jurisprudence, however unsophisticated or subliminal, is nevertheless played out in one's conduct at law."[19] Is there a particular jurisprudence actually functioning in America today? There seems to be no question that what has come to be called legal realism is the living world-view of the average American lawyer. If presented with the issue, he or she would surely say that such realism is the most attractive theory of law for someone who wants to win a close case, or to counsel a businessman about to enter a complex commercial transaction. Legal realism has been defined as a perspective, a set of attitudes; namely, "recognition of law as means; recognition of change in society that may call for change in law; . . . recognition of the need for effort toward keeping perception of the facts uncolored by one's views on Ought; a distrust of the received set of rules and concepts as adequate indicators of what is happening in the courts."[20]

The origins of legal realism go back to the last century to one of the architects of American legal theory, Oliver Wendell Holmes, Jr. Positivist that he was, Holmes defined law as "prophesies of what the courts will do in fact, and nothing more pretentious."[21] Law thus represents what a society is like at any particular time; it reflects the values of a greater culture. In 1881 Holmes opened his study of *The Common Law* with this statement: "The life of the law has not been logic: it has been experience. The felt necessities of the time, the prevalent moral and political theories, intentions of public policy, avowed or unconscious, even the prejudices which judges share with their fellowmen, have had a good deal more to do than the syllogism in determining the rules by which men would be governed."[22] To know what law is, said Holmes, one must look upon it as a "bad man" does. The "bad man" has no respect for law as such and does not look upon it as telling him what is right or wrong. He obeys only if it is in his interest to obey. The threat of coercive sanction is what keeps him from disobedience. He thinks of law

> as simply part of the environment in which he does his business. He may break a contract, pay the assessed damages, and think little of it, so long as, on balance, his self-defined welfare has been served. . . . Law is a neutral object to be used where it might benefit, to be avoided where it might hurt, and to be put into the balance of calculations as one sets out one's policies for the future.[23]

Although Holmes was the first American to articulate in any complete way a positivist legal theory, the groundwork for such theory was laid by the rigid positivism of Thomas Hobbes. It was Hobbes who forced the decisive breach between theology and jurisprudence. The only human motive worth taking seriously, said Hobbes in *Leviathan,* is self preservation. Humans have only desires and appetites, and a good society can be created only by well articulated self interest. Hobbes considered human beings so irretrievably selfish and predatory that they had to be restrained by the absolute authority of the State. His understanding of lawlessness is the decisive element in his account of the source of law, for by lawlessness he means not only the absence of positive law, but the absence of any awareness among humans of what is right and wrong. In this conflict model of society, law becomes essentially a matter of force and coercion and not justice, an instrument to be used to secure order and to enhance one's struggle for power. Holmes was echoing Hobbes when he wrote that "the *ultima* ratio, not only *regum,* but of private persons, is force, and . . . at the bottom of all private relations, however tempered by sympathy and all the social feelings, is a justifiable self-preference." For Holmes, as for Hobbes, the function of law was simply to channel these private aggressions in an orderly fashion. Like Hobbes, he also believed that law had nothing at all to do with morality and could, if the majority of citizens so decided, promote what was immoral. "The first requirement of a sound body of law is, that it should correspond with the actual feelings and demands of the community, whether right or wrong."[24]

While contemporary legal realists would not judge humans as harshly as Hobbes, or even Holmes for that matter, most would, nevertheless, espouse a conflict model of society. Learned Hand's definition of justice, for example, was "the tolerable accommodation of the conflicting interests of society." Justice is thus seen as a compromise, giving the least offense to the most people, some rough equation between

order and fairness. Even a humanist like Karl Llewellyn can write that
in law we see

> the phenomenon of clashing interests of antagonistic persons or groups,
> with officials stepping in to favor some as against others. . . . Hence the
> eternal fight for the machinery of law, and of law-making, whereby the
> highly interested *A*s can hope partially to force their will upon equally
> but adversely interested *B*s and to put behind that control the passive
> approval and support of the great body of *C*s.[25]

For Llewellyn, as for legal realists and positivists generally, it is important to isolate the uniqueness of law, to underline its autonomy,
and to differentiate it from other forms of thought and action. Pushed
to extremes, this makes law purely instrumental and individualistic, a
pragmatic device for accomplishing certain political or economic objectives in society. Such extremes are, in fact, integral to the thought of
legal theorists like Hans Kelsen, who argues that "the concept of law
has no moral connotations whatsoever." To say that a certain social
order has the character of law, insists Kelsen, "does not imply the
moral judgment that this order is good or just. There are legal orders
which are, from a certain point of view, unjust. Law and justice are
two different concepts."[26] Few realists and positivists woud go as far as
Kelsen. Nor would they go as far as Holmes, who once wrote in a letter
to a friend: "I have said to my brethren [on the Supreme Court] many
times that I hate justice, which means that I know if a man begins to
talk about that, for one reason or another he is shirking thinking in
legal terms."[27] Most of today's jurists would say that, while an analysis
of the *is* of factual legal situations should not get entangled with any
ought to be, the professional decisions of individual lawyers are never
merely technical. At every level, these decisions are controlled by value
judgments of what ought or ought not to be. But, a realist like
Llewellyn would insist that with such value judgments "we desert entirely the solid sphere of objective observation, of possible agreement
among all trained observers, and enter the airy sphere of individual
ideals and subjectivity."[28]

For the positivists and the realists, then, the true essence of law is the
way disputes are settled by judges and administrators. The rules of law
are simply generalized statements of the behavior pattern of officials,
the source of which is to be found chiefly outside the law, in the
policies, prejudices, and preferences of these officials. "*What . . .
officials do about disputes is, to my mind, the law itself,*" says
Llewellyn.[29] This generally agreed-upon understanding of law in
America has inevitably fostered an adversary ethic which, when combined with the litigious character of American society discussed
earlier, produces the "fight" theory of justice. Out of this theory has
come our adversary system. It assumes that in the competitive strife of
a courtroom, the lawyers defending each litigant will energetically use

all the available evidence favorable to their client and unfavorable to their adversary. The trial court will thereby obtain all the relevant evidence and will consequently be able to apply to the actual facts the social policies embodied in the legal rules. In theory at least, such an adversary system supposedly gives to each person the means to defend his or her rights and interests. This, in turn, vindicates the American concept of the good society as one that secures the life, liberty, and property of its individual citizens and gives to each an equitable share of society's goods, roughly approximating our notions of distributive justice. For the legal realist the benefits to society are, therefore, clear:

> Litigation arises out of conflict. Conflict in turn arises in those fields of social activity where growth is taking place, where the relative strength of interest-groups is changing. Things are so arranged that where chang-ing social practice demands new law individual interest will see to it that suits will be brought which will furnish a substratum for the elaboration of the legal doctrine. There is happily a kind of automatic correlation between the interest of the individual litigant and the social need for new law.[30]

The justification of the adversary system is not difficult in the case of criminal prosecution. There, its purpose is both to protect the inno-cent person against the possibility of an unjust conviction as well as to preserve the integrity of society itself. It aims at keeping sound the pro-cedures by which society goes about condemning and punishing the criminal, and as such it has great symbolic value. In criminal law, therefore, the case for zealous advocacy is easy to make. American society especially, with its strong commitment to political freedom, has always valued any means that deters government from imprisoning those it distrusts and fears. The adversary system, by putting the heavy burden of proof on the State and at the same time guaranteeing to defendants access to loyal and independent advocates, prevents op-pression by the State. The real problems in the system begin to appear when it is taken out of the context of criminal prosecution and placed within a larger community context. Then, public interest tends to be conceived almost exclusively in terms of the rights and interests of in-dividual clients. While there may be obvious adversary behavior on the part of someone who breaks a contract, making enforced compliance by trial quite proper, most forms of human activity are not adversarial at all:

> The parent's role is not normally to oppose the child. The doctor's intent is to help, not to injure. But the growing desire for redress of injuries prompts us more and more to search for the wrongdoer. That search leads us with increasing frequency to view conduct and relationships as conflicting that not so long ago were unhesitatingly accepted as altruistic or benign.[31]

John Wigmore, who wrote the classic legal textbook on evidence, called the adversary system "the greatest legal engine ever invented for the discovery of truth."[32] But, the most common ground for criticizing the system today is precisely its incapacity to uncover the truth.[33] Mutual exaggeration of opposing claims, so widely accepted in practice, violates the whole theory of rational, scientific investigation. As a means of uncovering facts, the system can be extremely slow and inefficient, and its endless formalities and opportunities to delay make it terribly expensive. This means that generally the system will work for the naturally litigious and for the wealthy, but not for the poor. Public defenders and members of the public interest bar, who defend those unable to pay litigation costs, are usually overworked and ill equipped, and the services they give are bound to be spotty in application and distribution. If their battle is against more intelligent fighters who are better paid, more experienced or more vicious, they will usually lose. The Legal Services Corporation, moreover, estimates that it can service only a fraction of the poor people who need legal help. The interests of poorer and less sophisticated litigants would be much better served by removing their claims from the adversarial arena altogether. For, in that area they will find themselves more or less helpless and threatened, with their rights unprotected, their liberty threatened, and their property unsecured. Because it depends on force, the adversary system is thus inevitably biased toward the strong and seldom serves the aspirations of the general community. But, then, American culture as a whole, as we have seen, is not particularly communitarian, and its legal system will, in all likelihood, continue to follow suit with an emphasis on pragmatism, conflict, and coercion.

IV

The third factor inhibiting someone's pursuit of law as a vocation to justice and love is the nature of American legal education. The character and content of such education would seem to follow logically from both the nature of American law and the nature of American society. And so it does, as we shall see presently. But, American legal education also has a peculiar history of its own, conditioned by something quite distinct from either realism as a legal theory or the litigiousness of Americans generally. This "something" is the drive for classification and systemization, a phenomenon that began in 1871, when Christopher Langdell of Harvard, Dean of one of the very few law schools in the country at the time, formally announced his creation of the case method for the study of law.

The problem Langdell faced as a teacher was that in late nineteenth century America there already was too much law (i.e., too many courts in too many state and federal institutions) to serve as a basis for organized study at a university (as opposed to the more usual way of

then becoming a lawyer by apprenticing oneself to a practicing attorney). To deal with law as an organized body of knowledge, i.e., as a
university discipline, one had to find a way to make sense out of all
these cases. There had to be an identifiable body of information about
law that would serve as the proper subject matter for study, and there
also had to be a method of inquiry that would train a student to "think
like a lawyer." Langdell's solution was an ingenious combination of the
abstract and the concrete:

> Law, considered as a science, consists of certain principles or doctrines.
> To have such a mastery of these as to be able to apply them with con-
> stant facility and certainty to the ever-tangled skein of human affairs, is
> what constitutes the true lawyer; and hence to acquire that mastery
> should be the business of every earnest student of law. Each of these doc-
> trines has arrived at its present state by slow degrees; in other words it is
> a growth, extending in many cases through centuries. This growth is to
> be traced in the main through a series of cases; and much of the shortest
> and best, if not the only way of mastering doctrine effectually is by
> studying the cases in which it is embodied.[34]

Langdell's original idea, then, was that law is a science and that
legal truth is a species of scientific truth: once the one true rule of law
in a given area has been discovered, it will continue without change,
reducing the unruly diversity of cases to manageable unity. In his
brilliant study, *The Ages of American Law*, Grant Gilmore points out
that before Langdell legal texts contained the bare minimum of
theoretical discussion; what counted was what real people were doing
in the real world. What counted with Langdell, however, was precisely
the theory, the unitary set of rules that made sense of the cases which
illustrate the rules. Hence, not all cases were to be studied. The vast
majority of these, said Langdell, are worse than useless for any purpose
of systematic study. In other words, the rule of law does not in any
sense emerge from the study of real cases decided in the real world.
"The doctrine tests the cases, not the other way around."[35]

In 1881, in *The Common Law*, Oliver Wendell Holmes, Jr., gave
Langdell's pedagogical approach a certain intellectual respectability.
Holmes developed a philosophical hypothesis that all progress in law
and legal rules is toward an ideal state in which liability, both civil and
criminal, will be governed by objective standards, not by a person's
subjective state of mind or intent to cause harm. As a legal system
approached maturity, said Holmes, it will succeed in eliminating any
reference to what the defendant actually thought or willed. Individual
guilt or moral failure would both become irrelevant, and law would
deal with the "bad man" and the "good man" in exactly the same
way.[36] This was, in fact, the ideal behind Langdell's approach to the
law of contracts and the law of torts. Before Langdell, legal education
dealt with as many types of contracts as there were classes of people
who entered into them: contracts among farmers, workers, merchants,

brokers, auctioneers, seamen, corporations, shipowners, and between landlords and tenants, husbands and wives, parents and children — all these were studied by law students precisely as different, conditioned by circumstances, people, and content. Langdell, however, insisted that neither the status of the contracting parties nor the subject matter of their contract was to be taken into account in the "science of law." Law study should focus, not upon people, but only upon "faceless characters named A & B, whoever they might be and whatever it might be they were trying to accomplish." The study of "torts," i.e., personal injuries or non-contractual losses, was to be approached in the same way. "As with the new theory of contracts, the new theory of torts was designed to cover all possible situations in which any A might be ordered to pay damages to any B to compensate him for personal injury or property damage, with as little account as possible taken of who A and B were and the particular circumstances of their confrontation."[37]

Langdell and Holmes together set a tone and a style for legal education that has lasted more than a century. The American law school became over the years the principal instrument for restructuring our jurisprudence and reshaping our legal system. What future lawyers studied now were unitary theories to explain all conceivable single instances, and it was no longer necessary for them to take into account what was going on in the real world. For, law had become a "science," whose laboratory, as Langdell said, was the law library and whose experimental materials were the printed case books. Rules were separated from flesh and blood people, and law itself ceased to be considered a human activity affecting those acting and those acted upon and became, rather, a set of technical skills to be mastered and applied, first in the classroom and later in law office and courts. Rules became the subject matter of legal study, and the function of the "case" was simply to exemplify the rule. Judicial decisions also came in the form of rules, stated in such a way as to be applicable to all similar cases:

> Little or no attention is given to the persons in whose minds or in whose interaction the rules have lived — to the persons whose difficulties have occasioned the articulation of the rule, to the lawyers who have tried the case, to the judges who have decided it. . . . The prime teaching tools, the casebooks, have been composed to shed light on the life of the rule, not upon the part of the participants in the process.[38]

Langdell's dream of a system of legal rules that was self sufficient, absolutely certain, and impervious to change was never fully realized, of course, since American law can never be truly isolated from the economic, political, and social developments in American life. But, while the legal realists of modern times might hold up to scorn Langdell's overconceptualization of law, they had no intention whatso-

ever of abandoning the basic tenets either of Langdell's jurisprudence
(that law is a science and that such a thing existed as "the one true rule
of law") or of his pedagogy (that the primary task of legal education
was that of analysis, classification, and systematization). The realists
contented themselves with insisting that Langdell's so-called rules of
law were simply generalized statements of lawyers' behavior patterns,
the source of which was to be found chiefly outside the law, in the
policies, prejudices, and preferences of the lawyers themselves. For the
realists, "law is a science" was understood to mean "law is a social
science."[39]

Now, the point I am making by reviewing these developments in
American legal education is that they have had, and continue to have
today, a decisive effect on the way lawyers think about themselves and
their craft. "We believe," write the authors of a recent text for law
students, "that a subtle process of professionalization occurs during
law school without being addressed or even acknowledged. This learning by inadvertence means that the participants often fail to consider
fundamental questions about the identity they are assuming, and its
relation to their values."[40] This identity has, for more than a century,
been shaped by the ability to analyze, the capacity to be precise,
logical, and objective. Law students are trained not to make statements which cannot be defended by objective criteria, and so they
develop an ability to elaborate legal arguments unconnected with
personally-held beliefs. Such legal argument becomes, as a result, an
intellectually narrowing process, with the obvious risk that what is held
to be irrelevant to the main argument will gradually in one's thinking
become irrelevant altogether. Technical analysis that continually ex-
cludes human feeling and concern leads to a sense that these qualities
are somehow antithetical to a thoroughly rational inquiry. Justice,
however, is obviously something more than the analysis and application of rules, and its achievement requires more than just intellectual
skills. Indeed, when such skills alone are cultivated, feelings and emotions tend to become dulled, and the lawyer as a human person can
lose that sensitivity so essential in a one-to-one relationship with
clients. One lawyer has stated the problem in this way:

> Thinking, unabridged by the conscious application of other experience,
> endorses particular values—the values of order, certainty, and mastery.
> Such values are not always apposite to, or at least not consistently domi-
> nant in, the types of idiosyncratic problems many, if not most, lawyers
> confront. The unmitigated application of intellect tends to freeze out
> not only psychological but ethical dispositions as well. . . . The implica-
> tion for legal education is that, as a general observation, the qualities of
> personal sensitivity to others, a sense of justice, and concern for the
> general welfare need to be systematically nurtured, rather than
> developed, else they become overshadowed in the values attendant to
> concentrated intellectual inquiry.[41]

The risk of overintellectualization is, of course, a problem common to all professions. As early as 1925, Alfred North Whitehead warned of what he called the "professionalizing" of knowledge. "Each profession makes progress," he wrote,

> but it is progress in its own groove. Now to be mentally in a groove is to live in contemplating a given set of abstractions. The groove prevents straying across country, and the abstraction abstracts from something to which no further attention is paid. . . . Of course, no one is merely a mathematician or merely a lawyer. People have lives outside their professions or their businesses. But the point is the restraint of serious thought within a groove. The remainder of life is treated superficially with the imperfect categories of thought derived from one profession.[42]

The better the professional, then, the more he or she tends to be preoccupied with correct method and to separate this preoccupation from the interplay of diverse values. This explains the reason values have never been systematically analyzed in law schools: positivists and realists have always considered them unanalyzable, nothing more than inscrutable expressions of personal preference. Law professors may lavish analytic energy in tracing the continuity of values expressed in the opinions of the United States Supreme Court, but they generally shy away from any scrutiny of their own values or those of their students. Rarely are students ever encouraged to articulate value preferences at all, much less to supplement the cold logic of legal rules with a responsible and coherent value system of their own. Karl Llewellyn, whom we quoted earlier and who had enormous impact upon legal education, used to tell his first year law students at the University of Chicago that they were welcome to their morals, but that these morals had little to do with the culture of lawyers:

> The hardest job of the first year is to lop off your common sense, to knock your ethics into temporary anesthesia. Your view of social policy, your sense of justice—to knock these out of you along with woozy thinking, along with ideas all fuzzed along the edges. You are to acquire ability to think precisely, to analyze coldly, . . . to see, and see only, and manipulate, the machinery of the law. It is not easy thus to turn human beings into lawyers. . . . None the less, it is an almost impossible process to achieve the technique without sacrificing some humanity first.[43]

But, if in principle moral values are irrelevant to legal analysis and professional skill, might one not begin to suppose that living amorally is what it means to be a lawyer and that being a lawyer is what it means to be a person?

Only very recently has any of these problems in American legal education been addressed by the law schools themselves. In its 1984 annual meeting, the Association of American Law Schools for the first time had ethics in its theme. Law school deans and faculty worried especially about the narrowing of ethical perspective, recognizing it as a learned disability, an occupational hazard reinforced later on by the patterns of professional work. "The lack of concern of faculty members for the professional conduct of students," said Norman Redlich, Dean of New York University Law School, "is probably seen by students as a manifestation of similar standards which the faculty members set for themselves." Redlich called on faculty members to explain the importance of professional responsibility as a first step toward "an exploration of a broad range of ethical issues which the profession and the public have a right to expect of us." Speaker after speaker emphasized the heavy responsibility of faculty to encourage ethical standards by setting examples for their students. Terrance Sandalow, Dean of the University of Michigan Law School, argued that, because law school curricula generally lacked any moral foundation or guiding purpose, individual faculty members had to pay more attention to helping students "to realize their human potential and to act as moral beings." Otherwise, he said, legal education will continue to foster that "curious distinction that lawyers too frequently display — careful craftsmanship in the performance of professional responsibilities and a lack of concern for [craftsmanship] in dealing with political and social issues." Sandalow also called on law schools to place greater emphasis on developing students' "patience, perseverance and other qualities" that are "necessary to the success of any sustained moral undertaking."[44]

V

The character of American legal education just sketched is directly related to the fourth aspect of our legal culture, the functioning of the legal profession itself. This functioning has come under the sharpest criticism in recent years, perhaps none sharper than that of Derek Bok, President of Harvard University and former Dean of the Harvard Law School. In his annual report to Harvard's Board of Overseers, released in 1983, Bok asserted that the way students were being educated was in large measure responsible for the two major deficiencies of the American legal system, cost and access. He wrote:

> The hallmark of our curriculum continues to be its emphasis on training students to define the issues carefully and to marshal all the arguments and counterarguments on either side. Law schools celebrate this effort by constantly telling students that they are being taught 'to think like a lawyer.' But one can admire the virtues of careful analysis and still believe that the times cry out for more than these traditional skills. . . . The capacity to think like a lawyer has produced many triumphs, but it has also helped to produce a legal system that is among the most expensive and least efficient in the world.[45]

A "flawed system" is Bok's description of the profession as a whole. "There is far too much law for those who can afford it and far too little

tor those who cannot."[46] What I wish to emphasize here is that these
two deficiencies of the system, cost and access, also constitute together
a fourth inhibiting factor, originating in the legal profession itself, for
anyone pursuing that profession as a vocation to justice and love.

Bok acknowledges, of course, that the root problem with the profession goes much deeper than the two deficiencies he focuses upon.
Americans generally tend to forget that apprehensions about their
legal system correspond to their heavy dependence upon it, stemming
from the cultural values and the social structures we opt for as a
nation. The difficulties engendered by the litigation explosion of recent years thus cannot be blamed entirely upon lawyers. Lawyers
obviously benefit from the fees engendered by American litigiousness,
but one can hardly conclude from this that attorneys are the only cause
of the nation's propensity to sue. Turning more and more disputes over
to the judiciary, as we have done in recent years, clearly contributes to
social and economic problems, but the solution does not lie in simply
ridiculing the profession. This profession forces lawyers to confront the
most vicious as well as the most virtuous aspects of our national life and
to seek continually to bring order out of the chaos of human affairs.
People who quote the famous line from Shakespeare's Henry VI, "The
first thing we do, let's kill all the lawyers," usually forget that the
character who speaks that line, Jack Cade, is contemplating a dic-
tatorship. In a society where government by law is the norm and where
people want the security of law, lawyers are essential. The more laws a
nation has, however, the more laws will be broken, and the greater use
there will be for lawyers and courts. Yet law, as Jerold Auerbach has
said, is always more than rules and procedures, statutes and
precedents. For Americans, it is ultimately a national ideology, a set of
beliefs and a system of integrated values that provide elements of
predictability, stability and coherence.[47]

Nevertheless, Bok's question remains: why does the system work so
badly for poor people and so well for the affluent? Why does it continually fail its legitimacy test: unable to validate itself to the countless
disadvantaged, yet continuing to give special service to the privileged
few? "The blunt, inexcusable fact," says Bok, "is that this nation . . .
has developed a legal system that is the most expensive in the world,
yet cannot manage to protect the rights of most of its citizens." This
has happened, he continues, because a certain mindset conditions
almost all successful attorneys, all "leaders of the bar." This mindset
has two aspects. The first begins in law school, where the educational
experience gradually comes to be seen primarily as a conduit to
lucrative positions in the big law firms rather than as an opportunity to
ponder the larger questions of justice in society. These big firms not
only pay well, but they also provide the challenge of high-stake litigation and the glamor of social status. For Bok, this overwhelming
preference of top graduates for such positions represents "a massive

diversion of exceptional talent into pursuits that often add little to the
growth of the economy, the pursuit of culture or the enhancement of
the human spirit."[48] The result is a stratification of the bar into an
upper and lower tier. The upper tier is drawn from private liberal arts
colleges and élite national law schools and has traditionally consisted
of white upperclass males specializing in corporate tax law and anti-
trust work. In contrast, the lower tier consists mostly of solo practitioners from low status families and less prestigious law schools, who
(with some spectacular exceptions in the field of trial practice) tend to
rely on the grubbier aspects of practice, such as negligence, divorce
and criminal law.

A survey testing the idealism of the 1975 law graduates from the
University of California at Davis illustrates what Bok is talking about.
Considerable change was shown to have taken place between first and
third years. The proportion of those who expected to be working as
"poverty" or "public interest" lawyers one year after graduation
dwindled from fifty-seven percent in the first year to twenty-two percent in the third. Those motivated to practice law to "alleviate social
problems" fell from thirty-two percent to twenty percent.[49] "Corporate
work seldom intersects with the concerns for social justice that drew me
to law school," admitted a 1974 Harvard graduate at his tenth year
reunion.[50] Another Harvard student told a friend: "A lot of professors
tell me not to worry about politics and just go [to the large firms] for
the training; . . . but how do you help U.S. Steel hold up a pollution
abatement order during the day, then go home and read your mail
from the Sierra Club and tell yourself that you are a human being?"[51]
One recent Harvard class had sixty-nine percent entering corporate
work, while only one percent entered public service. In an address to
these graduates, Ralph Nader commented on the standards of success
held up to them as models by the legal profession:

> Where were we shown images of lawyers as organizers, determined advo-
> cates, rather than the disinterested hired hands of whoever could throw
> the price? . . . Was it really more absorbing to fuss over the details of
> some company's tax shelter than to face (as our education so seldom
> asked us to do) the gravest legal problems confronting society — corpor-
> ate and government corruption, the bilking of consumers, the dilemma
> of bringing adequate legal services to the poor?[52]

Lloyd N. Cutler, one of Washington's most prominent corporate
lawyers, writes the following of large firms like his own: "The rich who
pay our fees are less than 1 percent of our fellow citizens, but they get
at least 95% of our time. The disadvantaged we serve for nothing are
perhaps 20 to 25 percent of the population and get at most 5 percent
of our time. The remaining 75 percent cannot afford to consult us and
get virtually none of our time."[53] This problem is compounded by the
fact that there are now so many of these large firms and they are grow-

ing ever larger. Ten years ago, a dozen or so such firms had more than a hundred lawyers; today, close to a hundred have this many, and no fewer than sixty have more than two hundred. Legal departments of large corporations used to have one or two attorneys; today, staffs of fifty or more are not unusual. This slow shift in the profession's legal profile has been primarily responsible for the current efforts of the American Bar Association to revise its Code of Professional Conduct. The present Code, written in 1970, is geared mainly to the solo practitioner, whereas no more than a third of the nation's lawyers now practice by themselves or in small groups. While other factors may influence student choice of a large firm (such as the urgent need to repay loans assumed to finance their legal education), the major reason continues to be the mindset engendered by law schools and the legal culture, resulting in what a former president of the Federal Bar Council has called "a dreary metamorphosis of the legal profession to a business."[54] Professional success today, he laments, is measured by profits, and this extreme economic pressure is producing a bottom-line attitude that contributes to rising aggressiveness, incivility and cutthroat competition, and finally tends to undermine the professional independence of the average American lawyer.

Derek Bok sees a second aspect to this mindset of the professional attorney, one closely linked to the first; namely, a willingness to think of justice in purely procedural terms. Here is what he says:

> At bottom, ours is a society built on individualism, competition, and success. These values bring great personal freedom and mobilize powerful energies. At the same time, they arouse great temptations to shoulder aside one's competitors, to cut corners, to ignore the interests of others in the struggle to succeed. In such a world much responsibility rests upon those who umpire the contest. As society demands higher standards of fairness and decency, the rules of the game tend to multiply and the umpire's burden grows constantly heavier.
>
> Faced with these pressures judges and legislators have responded in a manner that reflects our distinctive legal tradition. One hallmark of that tradition is a steadfast faith in intricate procedures where evidence and arguments are presented through an adversary process to a neutral judge who renders a decision on the merits.[55]

The majority of lawyers and judges do, in fact, think of justice as primarily fair procedure and due process. As essential as these are for the rule of law in any society, however, exclusive focus on them inevitably induces overreliance upon as well as an overesteem for the adversary system. Bok notes "the familiar tilt of the law curriculum toward preparing students for legal combat." "Look at a typical catalogue," he says. "The bias is evident in the required first-year course in civil procedure, which is typically devoted entirely to the rules of federal courts with no suggestion for other methods of resolving disputes. Looking further, one can discover many courses in the intricacies of trial practice, appellate advocacy, litigation strategy, and the like—but few devoted to methods of mediation and negotiation."[56] Yet, the elaborate procedures of the adversary system are precisely the reason that legal services are so expensive and beyond the reach of most ordinary citizens. Those who work in that system look only at the individual case, not at the consequences of rules and decisions in their wider contexts. Laws and jurisdictions multiply into an uncoordinated quilt of rules which, taken together, have unexpected and often untoward social consequences. Because no one is responsible for the system as a whole, no one is able to control either its cost or its access.

The very complexity of these procedures induces in too many lawyers a tunnel-vision, a kind of legal gamesmanship: they raise every argument, no matter how settled the law; they argue points of law they do not themselves believe are right; they file appeals they have no intention of pursuing, simply in order to keep litigation alive; and they continue to dream of the "big case," lavishly financed and staffed, that can drag on in courts for years, until every motion and appeal are finally exhausted. Marvin Frankel, a former Federal District Court judge, believes that the fundamental reason lawyers are held in such low esteem is the role so many play as "hired guns." The public has "the vivid sense that we are not detached 'ministers of justice,' as people of the law might be in some utopia, but self-seeking shopkeepers whose wares are for sale."[57] The historic view was that a lawyer was an officer of the court and, therefore, an integral part of the scheme of justice. But, the conception today is that of a paid servant of the client, justified in using any technical lever supplied by the law to advance the latter's interest. For, in an adversary system the supposition is that, because the opposing interest is pulling an opposition set of levers, justice will somehow be done by the process itself in the resulting equilibrium. The aim of the individual advocate, however, is not justice, but only victory.[58] This "hired gun" mentality was expressed with admirable terseness a few years ago by the hiring partner of a major Wall Street firm, who remarked to a third year law recruit that the "greatest thrill" in litigation "is to win when you're *wrong*."[59]

The dilemma posed by the "hired gun" mentality is obvious: can an attorney be loyal to the traditional notions of lawyer-client privilege and of zealous advocacy and at the same time remain a good and moral person?[60] Little help has come from the organized bar to deal with this dilemma, because, strange as it may seem to the laity, there is simply no agreement in the profession as to what conduct is "ethical" or "unethical." Ethics are said to be derived from experience, which is the embodiment of a society's practical wisdom and shared notions about the moral justification of individual and collective conduct. Legal codes are crystallizations of these notions and should, ideally at least, encourage a person to view his or her conduct through a moral prism. The fallacy of such codes, however, is that they always reflect the limited experience of individual attorneys and of the profession generally. Given the wide diversity of this experience, as well as its limitation, one is not surprised that many lawyers really do not recognize moral dilemmas when confronted with them or have developed techniques to avoid or to rationalize them away.[61] One such technique we just mentioned: as an advocate in the adversary system, a lawyer has no responsibility for outcomes; as long as each client is zealously represented, the system itself will take care of justice. Richard Wasserstrom calls another technique "role-differentiated behavior" and describes it thus:

> For where the attorney-client relationship exists, it is often appropriate and many times even obligatory for the attorney to do things that, all other things being equal, an ordinary person need not and should not do. What is characteristic of this role of the lawyer is the lawyer's required indifference to a wide variety of ends and consequences that in other contexts would be of undeniable moral significance. . . . In this way the lawyer as professional comes to inhabit a simplified universe which is strikingly amoral—which regards as morally irrelevant any number of factors which non-professional citizens might take to be important, if not decisive, in their everyday lives.[62]

One feature of this simplified intellectual world is that it is often a very comfortable one to inhabit. Hence, the general lack of concern to seek remedies for the double mindset we have been discussing. Whether or not this system only sometimes satisfies the national longing for justice, whether or not it works badly or well, the organized bar seeks, nevertheless, to preserve it. Geoffrey Hazard of Yale Law School has compared current efforts to fine-tune the legal system to "running a bucket brigade when you're dealing with tidal waves of social change." Charles Halpern, Dean of the new CUNY Law School, makes the same point: "The real problem is that the people closest to the system and most responsible for the problems are the people for whom the system works beautifully."[63] The huge costs and delays of the system have been readily acknowledged but little addressed. Derek Bok observes:

> Though doctors are learning to assess the costs and benefits of medical procedures and new technologies, lawyers are not making a comparable effort to evaluate provisions for appeal, for legal representation, for adversary hearings, or for other legal safeguards to see whether they are worth in justice what they cost in money and delay. . . . Nor has anyone done much to explore the forces that encourage or inhibit litigation so that we can better predict the rise and fall of legal activity.[64]

The conclusion we must draw, then, is that, because of this double mindset conditioning the majority in the legal profession, the two great deficiencies of the profession itself, access and cost, will more than likely remain unaddressed and continue to constitute a serious inhibiting factor for someone's pursuit of law as a vocation to justice and love.

VI

Up to now my concern has been to highlight the four major problem areas endemic to the functioning of America's legal culture. For, these four areas also constitute the major obstacles that must eventually be faced and somehow grappled with by anyone who feels "called" as a lawyer to promote justice and love in society. How precisely these obstacles are to be overcome, however, is not all that clear. As I noted earlier, the legal profession expresses all too accurately those individualistic and material values cherished by most Americans. The freedom we prize so highly is very often conceived of as freedom to compete, acquire and possess, a *laissez-faire* mentality that relegates shared responsibilities and communitarian purposes to secondary importance. An ethic of justice and love, on the other hand, conceives of freedom in terms of concern for the neighbor as well as for oneself and tends to increase rather than decrease the scope of fellowship and community. When applied to American law, such an ethic challenges at one and the same time the pragmatism of our legal tradition, the impersonality of our legal education, and the preoccupation of the profession itself with technique, conflict, and profit. What grounds for hope can there be for a lawyer that some good for individuals and society will result from this ethical challenge?

For those who believe in God, of course, the ultimate ground for hope will be religious. For, they will be convinced that, through a continuing creative and salvific action, God is present somehow to all human experience, whether secular or sacred. From this point of view there is necessarily a religious dimension to all legal experience, whether or not individual attorneys have any awareness of this. That is to say, no human institution is an autonomous structure in which God has no interest, since every human institution influences the way people live in society, which, in turn, influences the way they think about God and their neighbor. Hence, it will generally be easier to live a good life and to find God in a just society than in an unjust one. The fact that secular institutions are never found to be all good, that most are indeed ambiguous, a mix of good and bad, is simply a reflection of the human condition. Religious institutions are not all good either, but share this same ambiguity of all things human.

Thus, the prior concern of the religious person is not what he or she should be doing in secular life, but what God might be doing. For, before any human being pursues justice and love, God pursues them. Before any human being promotes freedom and equality, God does. Though ultimately the purpose of God's providential design is the union of all persons with himself in the sphere of the sacred, his immediate purposes in the secular sphere must be secular, i.e., in conformity with the nature of a particular institution. These purposes God carries out through the meshing of divine providence with human prudence, through the instrumentality of men and women whose prudential judgments further any given providential design. Hence, persons in the legal profession who believe in God will also believe not only that their "call" comes from God, but that finally there is hope for the improvement of their profession because God is already concerned with their concerns, and that any initiatives on their part constitute a collaboration with the divine initiatives already present.

But, there are more immediate grounds for hope, and these come from the experience of vocation itself. Concretely, this experience is the sense of a threefold mission and of one's calling to carry it out. This mission is one of technical mastery, human concern, and social responsibility. The strength of one's hope will be proportionate to the depth of one's sensitivity and commitment. Let us summarize briefly the content and objectives of this threefold mission.

No lawyer can fulfill his or her vocation without first achieving a high degree of technical competence. I have emphasized at some length the risks involved in striving for such analytical rigor. But, unless one does strive for it, all talk about one's mission as an attorney to promote justice and love in society will be suspect. The problem is never with analytic skill as such, just as the problem is never with law as such. The risk is rather that the meaning of law will be reduced to technique, thereby restricting legal education to training in technique and understanding legal practice as the use of technique to manipulate human behavior. More specifically, the problem at all three levels is the separation of technique from values. This was the theme of the 1984 American Bar Association conference on legal education. "Law plus X equals justice. X is the value system," said Judge Dorothy W. Nelson of the Ninth U.S. Circuit Court of Appeals. She was supported by Robert MacCrate, partner in the New York firm of Sullivan and Cromwell and member of the American Bar Association Board of Governors: "Law schools must be more explicit in exploring the values underlying the law and its practice in order to assist those entering the practice and beyond to recognize and accept their responsibilities. We need a sense of what our values should be." Judge Robert E. Keeton of the U.S. District Court in Massachusetts and former associate dean of Harvard Law School was more explicit: "We are not talking about the value of skills training because of the skills learned. The deeper value is that it increases understanding of the legal system and the professional role. . . . You must experience the conflict of interest between two values." [65]

This perennial risk in law of separating technique from values should thus in no way obscure the importance of such technique to the professional as such. Karl Llewellyn once observed that technique

without values is wickedness, but values without technique is foolish-
ness. The aim is to become an accomplished technician without losing
sight of the values of justice and love which the vocation is all about.
This means that any lawyer has to spend a great deal of time in essentially boring endeavor and that vast amounts of trivial detail can be
mastered only with a lot of unrelieved drudgery. Grant Gilmore has
put it well: "If it is your dream to slay the corporate dragon in his lair
or to protect the environment against its predators, you will get
nowhere unless you have accepted the harsh necessity of making
yourself into at least as good a lawyer, on the nuts and bolts level, as
the lawyers for the dragons and the predators, who will be very good
indeed." [66] The quest of law for justice is often limited by technique
and sometimes even thwarted, but much more frequently the mastery
of technique makes possible the success of this quest, since such
mastery can engender suggestions of rightness that might otherwise not
have presented themselves. Gilmore's colleague at Yale, Charles Black,
once recalled a remark by a late professor of music at the University to
the effect that the aim of all training in singing is that the student at
last learn to sing naturally. "I profoundly believe," writes Black, "that
the final result of training in law is that one may come close to thinking
naturally about problems of justice. It is visibly true of law that a really
high technical proficiency liberates instead of binds, and this is one of
the surest diagnostic signs of art." [67]

Hence, before anyone can even begin to think about the way to deal
as a lawyer with issues of justice and love, that person must first want
to be a lawyer and to master the skills of the craft. This means that he
or she must want to be part of the legal establishment. The power to
influence society belongs to those who have gained recognized status
among peers; radicals and mavericks tend, in the long run, to carry
little weight in a profession. It is important to recognize, therefore,
before we examine the lawyer's second mission, that, in spite of the
obstacles acknowledged earlier, the legal profession is not devoid of interest in the way law affects human lives. The profession's history and
its ideals testify to law's humanistic base and to the underlying aspiration of lawyers to care for people. The problem with the profession is
not ideals and aspiration but practice. Legal education, as we saw, has
been almost exclusively concerned with principles and logical analysis
and generally avoids what appears to be the quagmire of moral inquiry. While ethical and social responsibilities are readily recognized
by the bar, lawyers tend to be inattentive to them in practice because
such inattention has been nurtured in law school. Law school and law
practice thus inevitably tend to distort the reality of the world of law by
interpreting the legal process as simply a set of rules. Whereas, in fact,
"the process consists in the interplay of the persons forming the rule
with the persons applying it and the persons submitting to it." [68] To be
"called" to the bar thus means to be called to a concern for persons in

society and, in particular, for the interpersonal relationships between lawyer and client.

The difficulty, of course, as Richard Wasserstrom has pointed out, is that lawyers in their professional role can, at the same time, be highly involved with a client's special interest and yet fail to view the client as a whole person, to be dealt with as an equal and treated with the respect and dignity deserved by an equal. One reason for this is the relationship of inequality that is intrinsic to all professionalism. By definition, the lawyer possesses an expertise not easily attainable outside the profession. Along with this expertise goes a special language by which lawyers communicate with other lawyers but not with clients. Since communication is one distinguishing characteristic of persons, this fact helps make the client less than a person in the lawyer's eyes. The client has the added disadvantage of not really being able to evaluate how well or badly the lawyer is performing. Not clients but fellow professionals evaluate lawyers, since, unlike clients, they have the power to criticize and regulate effectively. Finally, clients almost always have some serious life problem, and this tends to render them vulnerable and to induce dependence on lawyers for advice and well-being. This life problem, in turn, naturally leads the lawyer to see the client partially, to focus on that part of his or her person that can be altered, corrected, or otherwise assisted professionally. For all these reasons, the lawyer-client relationship conspires to depersonalize clients in lawyers' eyes and to foster responses to them that are manipulative and paternalistic. Such responses constitute that "role-differentiated behavior" referred to earlier, behavior which has great appeal for lawyers, who find it much easier to deal with clients as objects than as persons. Whether an individual client is actually dealt with as an object will, therefore, depend on whether a lawyer has so internalized this professional role that it has become the dominant role in life or whether he or she has been able to keep this role at a certain distance and in perspective in order to minimize its bad consequences without destroying the good that high professional competence can achieve.[69]

To fulfill a legal mission of human concern, then, a lawyer has to understand and practice legal skills, not just within the context of a legal problem, but also in the context of a human life. There has to be some focus upon the human condition as well as upon technical mastery. For, in touching a legal problem, this mastery also and inevitably touches a total life situation, a fact that can be ignored by the attorney only at the price of ignoring vocation and mission. Thomas Shaffer calls such concern an "ethics of care," an orientation governed by

> an aspiration to *care* for the client and to be cared for by him. It admits that the law-office conversation is moral and that those who speak to one another in law offices are interdependent and at risk. It aspires to moral

discourse as an exercise of love. . . . The risk of openness is a risk involving the person of the client, and acceptance of the principle (and of the
fact) that . . . it is not only an argument or interest being asserted but a
person and a relationship being lived.[70]

One consequence of this ethics of care is the need for a lawyer to
know something about the techniques for being open, for being sensitive to what, in fact, worries clients, not just what ought to worry
them. "He will learn to listen to what his client says, attend to what his
client feels, find out about the client's values. . . . Law students would
come to insist on education which trains them in the skills of sincerity,
congruence and acceptance."[71] Within such an ethical framework,
adversarial skills are not necessarily more valuable than those of
counsellor, concilliator, and compromiser. For, society needs lawyers
at home not only in conflict but also in arbitration, ombudsmanship,
mediation, and negotiation. "We tend to forget," said Chief Justice
Burger to the American Bar Association, "that we ought to be healers,
healers of conflicts. Doctors, in spite of astronomical medical costs,
still retain a high degree of public confidence because they are perceived as healers. Should lawyers not be healers? Healers, not warriors?
Healers, not procurers? Healers, not hired guns?"[72]

Perhaps a more important consequence of commitment to an ethics
of care is the likelihood that a lawyer's concept of justice will be effectively modified. I cited earlier Derek Bok's critique of the dangerous
mindset of most successful attorneys, one aspect of which is their willingness to think of justice in purely procedural terms, as being constituted exclusively by fair procedure and due process. Attentiveness to
the total life of the client as a human person, however, will inevitably
tend to push the concept of justice back from its public administration
to its private source in interpersonal relationships. This is much closer
to the biblical idea of the "just man"; it calls upon impulses to
cooperation and friendship, not on impulses to assert rights, demand
duties, or threaten force. In this sense the just relationship is synonymous with the loving relationship, the model being the love of God for
his people. Such a concept is also very close to the biblical concept of
"covenant," understood as a relationship of fidelity and mutual understanding. Such fidelity implies good faith, counsel, character, and
trust. Hence, the lawyer who truly listens to clients, who can empathize, who can pick up the unspoken feelings of participants in painful situations, is not only the person to whom people will confide and
share their deepest experiences, he or she is also a lawyer who fulfills in
a special way a vocation to justice and love.[73]

This ethics of individual care parallels closely an ethics of social
responsibility which characterizes the third mission of the legal profession; namely, care for the social order. Even though as a group they
are reluctant to admit it, lawyers have more to do with the direction

society takes than any other profession. We just discussed the power they have over clients that comes from superior training, knowledge, and skill, but their capacity to influence human life in business, government, and local communities is far greater, and their corresponding responsibility to use this power for good is both heavy and constitutive of the lawyer's vocation.[74] While the actual work of most lawyers is restricted to private practice, the legal profession itself functions as a crucial interactive structure in society. Whether it acts to obstruct, stabilize, or reform the social order, it acts always as an instrument of social change. "Organization," claims Harvard's Paul Freund, "is inextricably bound up with larger social patterns. Indeed, if there is a seamless web with regard to the legal profession it is just here, in its relationship to the economic, educational and political systems. . . . The distinctive role of the legal profession is to serve as the architect of structure and process."[75] The issue, of course, is what goals in society does the architect have? Every society is constituted by what Robert MacIver has called a "firmament of law," which represents to the world that particular order that constitutes the life-context of a people. This "cultural meaning of law," however, to use Douglas Sturm's phrase, is seldom discussed by lawyers, even by those who are judges, policy-makers, and legislators. Yet, the power they have to influence their culture is enormous, and, if an ethics of social responsibility does not govern their professional lives, then this power will inevitably tend to corrupt, as all power does.

In a recent study of American law, Lawrence M. Friedman of Stanford University develops the theme that law is both a product and a catalyst for social change. This capacity of law to mirror as well as to give form to society, he argues, explains the reason the humanistic study of law provides a unique vantage point for viewing the culture of which it is a part. Recent changes in our penal law, for example, especially the death penalty, reflect a general modern tendency to place much greater reliance on deadly force as a means of overcoming our frustration with crime, a tendency that seems also to be reflected in recent international policy. Yet, these harsher penalties, once solidified into statutory law, inevitably condition for years to come the humane character of American society as well as the way Americans in general view criminals as persons.[76] Hence, to be adequately practiced, law must be understood contextually, not in autonomous isolation as legal realists and positivists would claim. For, as we saw earlier, such a drive for the uniqueness of law serves only to support the dominant American ethic of competitive individualism and to absolve the legal profession from seeing itself as an inevitable part of more inclusive patterns of social interaction. Law simply cannot be isolated from all other means of articulating a social ethos.[77]

Openly recognizing in their public lives this contextual character of law is the first and perhaps most effective way for lawyers to realize their mission of social responsibility. Such recognition may well place them squarely against the mainstream of current legal thinking on the subject, but it will also enable them to evaluate the broader implications of the legal "system" and its norms. As practitioners, they will still occupy specific places in this system, but their sense of larger meanings will inevitably influence both the places they choose and the correctives to the system they elect to apply. If their work is in the adversary arena, for example, they will sense an obligation to society as well as to clients, and when there is a clear conflict between the two, this conflict will not necessarily be resolved by winning for the client. Cornell's Roger Cramton, then president of the Association of American Law Schools, said:

> There is a vast difference between the morally upright lawyer and the lawyer who conforms to the needs of the client and does anything to that end if it does not break the law. Total commitment to the client's cause pushes the lawyer toward amoral if not immoral acts. . . . Protecting the criminal defendant against the state is one thing, but maximizing the gain of a private corporation or individual is another. . . . A narrow focus that rests on the nuts and bolts of making a client win shows a lack of such civilizing qualities as trust and compassion. The result is not justice but social disaster.[78]

Cramton's call for more responsible patterns of advocacy highlights the continuing need for self criticism by the organized bar. This need is so urgent because every aspect of the legal profession is today under public scrutiny, from access, cost, and complexity to the overcrowding of courts and the oversupply of lawyers. People rightfully question whether the recent rapid growth in the number of lawyers has, in fact, been for the common good. The public has a right to know, for example, the reason rather obvious areas of law, such as divorce, probate, and personal injury, cannot be simplified and access to courts made easier and less expensive. Yet, change continues to be resisted, no-fault insurance being the only example of any significant development in these areas. There is also understandable concern about the extent that members of the profession serve the poor in our society. The alarming announcement in 1982 by the Census Bureau that fifteen per cent of all Americans were living below the poverty line, combined with the severe underfunding of the Legal Services Corporation and even threats of its abolition by the Reagan administration,[79] make an increase in responsibility for such voluntary service imperative. One example of such responsibility is a program organized in 1984 by the New York City Bar Association in which thirty of the largest firms and twenty corporate law departments pledged to devote thirty hours a year per lawyer to public service work, primarily to civil cases involving fraud, landlord-tenant matters, and the wrongful denial of government benefits. But, this program will involve only five thousand of the City's forty-five thousand lawyers and marks a much belated attempt to comply with the requirement of the Code of Professional Responsibility that all lawyers "participate or otherwise support provision of legal services to the disadvantaged." In 1980, this same Bar Association overwhelmingly rejected a two year study by one of its own special committees that proposed making thirty to fifty hours of public interest activity mandatory.

In underlining this need for a critical rethinking of the profession's functioning in society, I do not wish to imply that law has not greatly benefited the public sphere in recent years. The remarkable advances in civil rights law, poverty law, family law, environmental law, and consumer protection law testify to our country's capacity for innovation and vigorous response to pressing claims for social justice. But, all these laws are embodiments of values held by those who promoted, supported, and enacted them at a particular point in history. What has to be addressed now is our own point in history. If lawyers are to be true to their mission of social responsibility, they must be alert to the ever new demands being made on their profession and in constant search for values and tactics needed for response. What, for example, will be one's position as a lawyer on the key moral issue of our time: the value of human life? The Supreme Court's abortion and death penalty cases raise this issue in specifically legal terms. Upon what value sources will the lawyer draw to respond to this very public question of who is a member of the human community?[80]

Because lawyers guard our justice system in ever larger numbers, they must inevitably become more implicated in such issues and forced to shoulder ever greater responsibility for the public weal. And, here once again we encounter the relation of justice to love. For love, understood as *agape*, that force in human life which unites persons in the public as well as in the private spheres, is capable of energizing the lawyer's professional work so that it has meaning and direction for the larger human community. This same legal activity, on the other hand, is essential for love to have some structure in society. For, without the various branches of law that bring order to such areas as property, personal injuries, contracts, family obligations, criminal acts, and public administration, love would be forced to operate in social chaos. Of itself, law is constitutive neither of justice nor of love, but both of these forces need law and lawyers to become operative in a nation's life.[81] The laws of society often work against love, of course, and sometimes even against justice, but this only highlights all the more the need for lawyers dedicated to both virtues as well as to making them visible in the institutions of society as a whole.

I began by asking what grounds there were for hoping that some good for individuals and society will come from meeting the four challenges from our national character, our legal tradition, our law schools, and the organized bar. I want to end with a word of caution in regard to the grounds for hope that I have drawn from the lawyer's threefold mission: these grounds must be relied upon primarily for courage, not success. In using law to shape one's world, one is using no blunt instrument but one of extraordinary delicacy and precision. Such use is, therefore, an art, not at all the science that Langdell envisioned. For, the legal system as such is imperfect, "flawed," to use Derek Bok's word, and the results of its operation are very often unpredictable. This means that at any given moment law presents a set of possibilities, more or less likely to occur, the likelihood of occurrence being conditioned by human intuition, decision, and purpose. According to Charles Black, the central problem of this art of law is that of finding and using the openings provided by these possibilities. Black is worth quoting at length:

> The art of law is founded upon and practised within a set of tensions between aims not simultaneously realizable in full. On the one hand the aim of attaining justice . . . and on the other hand the aim of using the authority of law in a legitimate manner, employing but not straining the techniques sanctioned as legitimate within our legal culture. Living and working within this tension is not made the more easy by the fact that no reasoning about justice or even about practicability, and no reasoning about legal legitimacy, can ever be altogether demonstrated, like a demonstration in mathematics or even in physical science. What can be asked of the artist in law is . . . that he continually explore, with disciplined imagination, the means to justice within the legal system, and that at the same time he be continually responsive to the demand for reasoned justification within that system. The continued search for creative resolution of this tension is one of the main things the art of law is about.[82]

To encounter this tension creatively in one's life as a lawyer, however, will usually result neither in success nor in failure but more often in ambiguity. Black cites a remark by Sir Joshua Reynolds to the effect that the look of reality in painting results from showing a clear line when the line is clear and not showing a clear line when the line is not clear, and then notes that one of the central problems constantly recurring in the art of law is the problem of clarity and certainty. "I sought for certainty," writes Benjamin Cardozo of his first years as a judge. "I was oppressed and disheartened when I found that the quest for it was futile. . . . As the years have gone by, and as I have reflected more and more upon the nature of the judicial process, I have become reconciled to the uncertainty, because I have grown to see it as inevitable."[83] Lawyers "called" to a threefold mission must, therefore, become reconciled to uncertainty and to unclear lines. Nor should they be disheartened by the ambiguity they find in the art of doing justice, because this art in some sense is also a way of loving, and nothing is more ambiguous than human love. Hence, besides hope and courage, such lawyers need to make an act of faith as well. For, to practice law as a vocation is to fly blind, to approximate justice, and to wait with patience for the gift of love. Because disillusion is the great risk, the ambiguity of law itself must somehow become an object of faith and hope and a source of courage. Grant Gilmore sensed this when he wrote: "Law, like a radioactive substance, renews itself through a process of continual decay. The disease which threatens to destroy the *corpus juris* sets in motion the antibodies which enable it to survive."[84]

NOTES

[1] See Warren E. Burger, "The State of Justice," *American Bar Association Journal* (April 1984): 62-66; see also the lengthy article by Stuart Taylor, Jr., on page one fo *The New York Times* for 1 June 1983, dealing with the judicial system.

[2] Everett C. Hughes, "Professions," *Daedalus* 92 (1963): 657. See also Bernard Barber, "Some Problems in the Sociology of the Professions," *Ibid.*, 669-88; Duncan MacRae, Jr., "Professions and Social Sciences as Sources of Public Values," *Soundings* 60 (1977): 3-21.

[3] Louis G. Forer, "Some Problems in the Administration of Justice in a Secularized Society," *Mercer Law Review* 31 (1980): 449.

[4] Jerold S. Auerbach, "A Plague of Lawyers," *Harper's*, October 1976, p. 38.

[5] See the discussion of these issues by Thomas L. Shaffer, *On Being a Christian and a Lawyer* (Provo: Brigham Young University Press, 1981), pp. 160-64; Jerold S. Auerbach, *Justice Without Law?* (New York: Oxford University Press, 1983), pp. 138-47.

[6] John T. Noonan, Jr., *Persons and Masks of the Law* (New York: Farrar, Straus and Giroux, 1976), XII. The quotation is from *De moribus ecclesiae catholicae et de moribus Manichaeorum* in J. P. Migne, ed., *Patrologia latina*, vol. 32, 1322.

[7] Noonan, *op. cit.*, 18.

[8] Harold J. Berman, "The Influence of Christianity Upon the Development of Law," *Oklahoma Law Review* 12 (1959): 88.

[9] Shaffer, *op. cit.*, 162.

[10] Alexis de Tocqueville, *Democracy in America*, ed. J. P. Mayer and Max Lerner (New York: Harper & Row, 1966), p. 248.

[11] Lawrence M. Friedman, *A History of American Law* (New York: Simon and Schuster, 1975), pp. 20-21.

[12] Maxwell Bloomfield, *American Lawyers in a Changing Society*, 1776-1876 (Cambridge: Harvard University Press, 1976), p. 54.

[13] Jethro K. Lieberman, *The Litigious Society* (New York: Basic Books, 1983), p. 15.

[14] Harold J. Berman, "The Interaction of Law and Religion, *Mercer Law Review* 31 (1980): 412.

[15] *Ibid.*, 409.

[16] John Naisbitt, "Megatrends for Lawyers and Clients," *American Bar Association Journal* (June 1984): 45-46.

[17] As reported in *The New York Times*, 9 July 1984.

[18] Auerbach, *op. cit.*, 121.

[19] Douglas Sturm, "American Legal Realism and the Covenantal Myth: World Views in the Practice of Law," *Mercer Law Review* 31 (1980): 488. Sturm's article is a masterly analysis of our legal profession's reigning jurisprudence.

[20] Karl N. Llewellyn, *Jurisprudence: Realism in Theory and Practice* (Chicago: University of Chicago Press, 1962), pp. 68-69. Cited by Sturm, *art. cit.*, 489-90. For an overview of the movement, see Lon Fuller, "American Legal Philosophy at Mid-Century," *Journal of Legal Education* 6 (1954): 457-85.

[21] Oliver Wendell Holmes, Jr., "The Path of the Law," *Harvard Law Review* 10 (1897): 461.

[22] Oliver Wendell Holmes, Jr., *The Common Law* (Cambridge: Harvard University Press Edition, 1963), p. 5.

[23] Sturm, *art. cit.*, 495.

[24] Holmes, *The Common Law*, pp. 38, 36.

[25] Llewellyn, *op. cit.*, 36. Quoted by Sturm, *art. cit.*, 496.

[26] Hans Kelsen, *The General Theory of Law* (New York: Russell & Russell, 1945), p. 5.

[27] Quoted in Harold J. Berman, "Philosophical Aspects of American Law," in *Talks on American Law*, ed. Harold J. Berman (New York: Vintage Books, 1961), p. 229.

[28] Llewellyn, *op. cit.*, 86. Quoted by Sturm, *art. cit.*, 497.

[29] Karl N. Llewellyn, *The Bramble Bush* (Dobbs Ferry: Oceana Publications, 1960), p. 12. Italics in original.

[30] Karl N. Llewellyn, paraphrased by Lon Fuller, "American Legal Realism," *University of Pennsylvania Law Review* 82 (1934): 439.

[31] Lieberman, *op. cit.*, 169.

[32] John H. Wigmore, *Evidence in Trials of Common Law*, vol. 3 (Boston: Little, Brown and Company, 1923), p. 1367. Quoted by Lieberman, *op. cit.*, 168.

[33] See, for example, Anne Strick, *Injustice For All* (New York: G.P. Putnam's Sons, 1977); Marvin E. Frankel, *Partisan Justice* (New York: Hill and Wang, 1980); Jerold S. Auerbach, *Unequal Justice, Lawyers and Social Change in Modern America* (New York: Oxford University Press, 1976).

[34] From the preface of Langdell's 1871, *Cases on the Law of Contracts*, quoted by Robert S. Redmont, "Legal Education: The Beat of a Different Drummer," *New York University Law Review* 53 (1978): 677.

[35] Grant Gilmore, *The Ages of American Law* (New Haven: Yale University Press, 1977), p. 47. See also the early chapters of the historical study by Robert Stevens, *Law School: Legal Education in America from the 1850s to the 1980s* (Chapel Hill: University of North Carolina Press, 1984).

[36] *Ibid.*, p. 54. Gilmore's critique of this hypothesis is severe, and his judgment of Holmes as a person no less so. Far from being the tolerant aristocrat and defender of liberties as the myth would have it, the "real Holmes was savage, harsh and cruel, a bitter and lifelong pessimist who saw in the course of human life nothing but a continuing struggle in which the rich and powerful impose their will on the poor and weak." *Ibid.*, p. 49.

[37] *Ibid.*, pp. 46-47.

[38] Noonan, *op. cit.*, 6.

[39] Gilmore, *op. cit.*, 87.

⁴⁰ Elizabeth Dvorkin, Jack Himmelstein and Howard Lesnick, *Becoming a Lawyer* (St. Paul: West Publishing Company, 1981), p. 1.

⁴¹ Redmont, *art. cit.*, 685.

⁴² Alfred North Whitehead, *Science and the Modern World* (Cambridge: Harvard University Press, 1925), pp. 275-76.

⁴³ Llewellyn, *The Bramble Bush*, p. 101. A new movement in American legal education, known as "critical legal theory," takes as its starting point that the analytic reasoning learned in law schools cannot of itself provide either a method or a process for answering particular legal questions or for leading reasonable people to particular results in particular cases. Rather, what accomplishes this are the very political, social, moral, and religious value judgments from which most lawyers and judges claim to be independent. This does not mean that rule, principle, and policy analysis becomes unimportant, or that all outcomes in a given case are equally likely, but simply that any particular outcome is determined chiefly by its social context. That is to say, in a specific context one legal rationale among many will seem to be more reasonable or more "right" than the others because the values of that particular context support that result. Very important consequences would obviously follow from "critical legal theory" for legal education, the courts, and for the legal profession generally. But, while the number of its adherents is growing, the extent of its influence as well as its broader objectives for the restructuring of society are still not clear. Apparently, very important differences of opinion exist among those who consider themselves critical theorists. See the collection of essays by the leading theorists edited by David Kairys, *The Politics of Law* (New York: Pantheon, 1982), especially the essay by Harvard professor Duncan Kennedy, "Legal Education as Training for Hierarchy," pp. 40-61.

⁴⁴ See *The Chronicle of Higher Education*, 18 January 1984, for a full report on this unusual meeting.

⁴⁵ Derek C. Bok, "A Flawed System," *Harvard Magazine*, May/June 1983, p. 45.

⁴⁶ *Ibid.*, pp. 39-40.

⁴⁷ Auerbach, *Justice Without Law?*, 142.

⁴⁸ Bok, *art. cit.*, p. 41.

⁴⁹ Quoted by Errol G. Rohr, "An Interaction: Theology and Legal Education," *Capital University Law Review* 8 (1979): 436.

⁵⁰ Quoted in *The New York Times*, 30 April 1984.

⁵¹ Scott Turrow, *One L* (New York: Putnam, 1977), p. 100.

⁵² *Ibid.*, p. 147, note 15.

⁵³ Quoted in *The New York Times*, 1 June 1983.

⁵⁴ Peter Megargee Brown, "Misguided Lawyers," *The New York Times*, 6 December 1983. See also Tamar Lewin, "The New National Law Firms," *The New York Times*, 4 October 1984.

⁵⁵ Bok, *art. cit.*, p. 42.

⁵⁶ *Ibid.*, p. 45.

⁵⁷ Marvin E. Frankel, "An Immodest Proposal," *The New York Times Magazine*, December 4, 1977, p. 96.

⁵⁸ See the development of this argument by Monroe Freedman, *Lawyers' Ethics in an Adversary System* (Indianapolis: Bobbs-Merrill, 1975).

⁵⁹ Quoted by Philip M. Stern, "Lawyers and Ethics," *The New York Times*, 4 August 1980.

⁶⁰ This dilemma is discussed at length by Charles Fried, "The Lawyer as Friend: The Moral Foundations of the Lawyer-Client Relation," *Yale Law Journal* 85 (1976): 1060 ff.

⁶¹ See James F. Bresnahan, "Ethics and the Study and Practice of Law," *Journal of Legal Education* 28 (1976): 189 ff.

⁶² Richard Wasserstrom, "Lawyers as Professionals: Some Moral Issues," *Human Rights* 5 (1975): 5, 8.

⁶³ Quoted in *The New York Times*, 1 June 1983.

⁶⁴ Bok, *art. cit.*, pp. 44-45.

⁶⁵ Quoted in Susan K. Boyd, "A Look at Legal Education in the 21st Century," *Syllabus* 15 (1984): 1, 4, 8.

⁶⁶ Grant Gilmore, "What is a Law School?" *Connecticut Law Review* 15 (1982): 3.

⁶⁷ Charles L. Black, *Law As An Art* (Knoxville: University of Tennessee Press, 1978), p. 14.

⁶⁸ Noonan, *op. cit.*, 17.

⁶⁹ Wasserstrom, *art. cit.*, 15-23.

⁷⁰ Shaffer, *op. cit.*, 22, 29.

⁷¹ *Ibid.*, 30.

⁷² Burger, *art. cit.*, 66.

⁷³ On this approach, see Shaffer, *op. cit.*, 87-92, 135-39.

⁷⁴ Multiple examples of such power are given in a study, cited earlier, by Jerold Auerbach, *Unequal Justice*, and in Mark Green, *The Other Government, The Unseen Power of Washington Lawyers* (New York: Grossman Publishers, 1975).

⁷⁵ Paul A. Freund, "The Legal Profession," *Daedalus* 92 (1963): 690-92.

⁷⁶ Lawrence M. Friedman, *American Law* (New York: W. W. Norton & Company, 1984).

⁷⁷ See Douglas Sturm, "Modernity and the Meaning of Law," *Worldview*, September 1979, pp. 48-51.

⁷⁸ Quoted in Boyd, *art. cit.*, 4. I do not wish to become involved here in the very important but seemingly endless current discussion of the lawyer-client relationship within the narrow context of the Code of Professional Responsibility and the Model Rules of Professional Conduct. To do so would force us to deal in great detail with highly specialized subject matter. Whether these rules are to be understood as ethical or legal norms is one unresolved issue. Another is the interpretation of "zealous advocacy," and the relation of the "hired gun" interpretation of such advocacy to the interpretation suggested by the Cramton quotation. For examples of different points of view in this intra-professional debate and the dilemmas posed by certain lawyer-client situations, see Norman Redlich, *Professional Responsibility* (Boston: Little, Brown and Company, 1983); Geoffrey C. Hazard, Jr., *Ethics in the Practice of Law* (New Haven: Yale University Press, 1978); Monroe Freedman, *op. cit.*

⁷⁹ The Legal Services Corporation has become a focus of controversy for several reasons. Critics perceive the program as a political instrument of activist lawyers that is inefficient both in helping the poor and in the cost it places on the legal system. Defenders insist that there is every reason to make a large and fallible government accountable in its own courts for violating the legal rights of the poor. A dispassionate assessment of these and other underlying issues is given by Roger C. Cramton, "Why Legal Services for the Poor?," *American Bar Association Journal*, May 1982, pp. 550-56.

[80] See, on this value question, the comments of Edward M. Gaffney, Jr., "Biblical Religion and Constitutional Adjudication in a Secularized Society," *Mercer Law Review* 31 (1980): 422-48.

[81] For this insight I am indebted to Harold J. Berman, "The Influence of Christianity. . . ," pp. 88-89.

[82] Black, *op. cit.*, 13.

[83] Benjamin N. Cardozo, *The Nature of the Judicial Process* (New Haven: Yale University Press, 1971), p. 166.

[84] Quoted by Frederick M. Rowe, "For Grant Gilmore: A Student's Lament," *Yale Law Report* 29 (1982): 11.

Health Care: A Vocation to Justice and Love

Edmund D. Pellegrino, M.D.

> ". . . perfect charity is perfect justice."
> Saint Augustine, De Natura et Gratia, LXX, 64.

I. INTRODUCTION

A. *The Questions*

Love and justice are two virtues without which peaceable and civilized societies cannot exist. For non Christian societies, they are dictates of reason; for Christian societies, they are dictates of reason illuminated by faith. The spiritual challenge to all Christians is to live these virtues as they have been transvalued by the Gospel message.

Nowhere is the test of love and justice more urgently met than in the care of those at the margins of society — the very young, the aged, the poor, the oppressed, and the depressed. We may declare faith in the Christian message, but, unless love and justice eventuate in charitable justice, an authentic Christian life is not possible. As Augustine puts it, "for without charity, faith can be, but profit nothing."[1]

In this essay, I wish to examine the ways in which Christian perspectives on love and justice should shape our attitudes and behavior to the sick — ways in which scriptural, ecclesial, and episcopal teachings supplement and complement individual and societal obligations deducible by reason alone. What differences do Christian conceptions of love and justice make in the ethics of the health professions? What transforms a health profession into a Christian vocation to the health care ministry?

The scope of such an enquiry is unmanageable in any definitive way in a short essay. It is essential, therefore, to practice at least some economy in my pretensions and delimit my subject. For one thing, I shall not derive or cite the extensive biblical or scriptural sources for Christian conceptions of love and justice.[2] Nor shall I review the content of episcopal and ecclesial documents, particularly those since the Second Vatican Council which are so rich in fresh insight and particularly appropriate to the practice of love and justice in the modern world.[3] Finally, I will also skirt the exquisitely important question of the distinctiveness of Christian ethics. The differences, some sharp and some subtle, among the Church's most distinguished theologians on this point are sufficient to inhibit all but the most temerous commentator.[4]

I will delimit my task in still another way, and that is to concentrate on what is currently the most urgent confrontation with the principles of love and justice for Christians and non Christians — the challenge of economics and the marketplace to the altruistic spirit that both faith and reason dictate in the care of the sick.

B. *The Problem*

Christian churches and Christian communities have never been so directly challenged as they are today by fiscal expediency to compromise the Christian call to love and justice. For the last two decades, and especially in the last five years, the tendency has been to translate a legitimate concern for the rising costs of health care into a justification to commercialize and monetarize the care of the sick. The thesis is advanced that subjecting health care to market forces — competition, advertising, consumer choice — will control costs and demand and assure quality as well.

An outcome of the market mentality is to reduce health care to a commodity transaction, making it a service to be purchased like any other. Distribution, access, and availability of health care are left to the rules and ethics of the marketplace. The ancient medical ethical principles of beneficence and justice are thus to be reinterpreted in terms of economic utility.

On this view, medical ethics tends to be equated with the minimalist ethics of law and business transactions. The effacement of self interest and the altruism traditionally expected of health professionals are eroded as profit making and entrepreneurship are legitimated. The tension between altruism and self interest is not new to the medical profession. What is new is the encouragement of professional self interest as a respectable motive with social utility.

Catholic Christian health professionals — physicians, nurses, dentists, and administrators — cannot help being touched in fundamental ways by these forces. They are already embracing the metaphors of a commodity transaction — an industry instead of a ministry, entrepreneurship instead of vocation, and adequacy instead of equity. In the interests of fiscal survival many are accommodating to, or compromising with, the monetary mores of contemporary health care. The crucial questions are: how far may they go without losing their Catholic and Christian identity? How consistent is the industrial and commodity model of health care with the Christian concepts of love and justice?

Are the only alternatives survival at the expense of moral compromise or moral authenticity at the expense of extinction? Can
Catholic and other Christians responsibly avoid the dilemma by
retreating from the health care ministry as some have already done
and others are contemplating? Much depends on the essentiality of
care of the sick to the Church's evangelical mission. Is health care, or is
it not, a necessary call to all Christians to witness the difference the
good news of the Gospel makes in human affairs?

C. *The Method*

The content of these questions is, in part, philosophical and, in
part, theological. The answers are central to any formulation of contemporary medical and bioethics. It is fortunate, for this effort, that
these fields are enjoying an unprecedented flowering just at this time.
The thrust of this flowering is philosophical, and this is proper for the
morally pluralist, democratic society in which we live. The Christian,
too, must begin his examination philosophically — by the use of
reason, unaided by revelation.

But, for the Christian, philosophical bioethics is not enough. For
one thing, the dominant spirit of contemporary ethics is analytic
rather than normative.[5] It eschews ultimate normative principles, except, perhaps, utility or freedom. It is, as a consequence, difficult, if
not impossible, to validate morality, itself, or to select among competing ethical theories and ethical norms. Christian theological ethics,
however, does provide ordering principles derived from revelation,
and it links ethics with the sources of meaning of human existence. It is
a necessary supplement to philosophical ethics if a complete medical
morality is to be found.[6]

For these reasons, we must ascertain the ethical content of health
and medical care philosophically first — and this calls for an enquiry
into the two central principles of philosophical medical ethics —
beneficence and justice — together with the obligations that flow from
them. Then, it is necessary to inquire into the transformations of the
meanings of benevolence and justice, their shaping by the fact of
revelation. Finally, one can then examine the central question by using
the Christian concept of charity-based justice as a principle of discernment in confronting some of the concrete issues in medical care ethics
today. With these as principles of discernment, the moral commitment
of Christians to love and justice is translated in concrete acts, decisions,
and choices in personal and social ethics. A profession becomes a vocation to the health ministry when its actions are in conformity with
Christian ideals of love and justice.

I shall argue on both philosophical and theological grounds that the
concept of love and justice is inconsistent with the ethics of the marketplace, that all society is diminished when health care becomes a commodity and altruism is submerged by self interest. In addition, I shall

100   HEALTH CARE:

argue that Christian understandings of love and justice go beyond the
naturalistic interpretations and provide principles of discernment that
shape the responsibilities of health care ministry for individual professionals, the institutional care of the sick, the formulation of health
policy, and the relationships of the institutional Church and the people of God to health and health care.

   I have chosen not to emphasize potential differences between the
Catholic Christian interpretation of the health ministry and the *Christian* health ministry. I am mindful of the differences that may exist
between these conceptions — the longer and stronger tradition of rational argument and natural law in the Catholic ethics, the greater
emphasis on works than on faith, and the weight given the authorita-
tive teaching of the Official Magisterium and of tradition. I hope to
emphasize perceptions that might be common to the whole Christian
Community. I trust that my argument may not lose its force for those
who differ on these fundamental points.

   The argument I shall advance applies to all health professions, not
just medicine. For simplicity's sake, however, I shall use the term
"medicine" broadly to stand for all the healing professions — nurses,
dentists, allied health workers, as well as physicians. This is not to
argue that physician medicine subsumes the others or that they do not
have independent standing; however, by concentrating on the physician's role, I can make my enquiry more specific.

   The essay is divided into two sections. The first is argued philosophically under three subheadings; the second is argued theologically
under three subheadings.

II. BENEVOLENCE AND JUSTICE IN HEALTH CARE ETHICS: PHILOSOPHICAL PERSPECTIVES

A. *The Empirical Basis of Health Care Ethics: The Nature of Illness
   and Healing*

> "Then, isn't it the case that the doctor, insofar as he is a doctor, con-
> siders or commands not the doctor's advantage but that of the sick
> man?"
>
>   Plato, *Republic*, Book I, 342, D.

   We begin with what is deducible from reason about beneficence and
justice so that we can more clearly discern what is added by the Christian counterparts of these two principles. Virtue and beneficence are,
after all, ancient virtues, cogently and extensively expounded in pre-
Christian times and exemplified in the loftier aspirations of ancient
and classical medical codes. They are not discoveries limited to Christianity, but have been, and are, open to all who possess human reason.
Indeed, the actual practice of beneficence and justice by pre-Chris-
tians, or non-Christians, has, far too often, exceeded in sincerity and

genuineness that manifested by some Christians. Still, when interpreted authentically, Christian conceptions of justice or beneficence in medical care are different in inspiration and content from even their higher manifestations in non-Christian sources.

Since our inquiry into love and justice is focussed on their expression in health care, we must look at the central phenomena of illness and healing which give health care its moral qualities. The first question is whether or not illness is a special kind of human experience. If we are to argue against the increasingly prominent view that health care should be treated like any other commodity or service, then it is necessary to show wherein being ill differs from other human experiences — at least in degree, if not in kind. This requires some operational definitions of health, illness and healing — three concepts under vigorous discussion among philosophers of medicine.[7] These concepts can be fully defined only if we have a coherent theory of medicine. Such a theory is not yet fully developed. Thomasma and I have attempted an introduction to such a theory elsewhere. Some features of that effort are called up in the discussion that follows.[8]

Let us start with the empirical and phenomenological aspects of illness. In this view, "illness" is the subjective perception of a person that he (or she) has experienced a change from the customary state he regards as health. "Health" in this context refers to a patient's own interpretation of that state of functioning that permits him to do the things he wishes to do with a minimum of pain, disability, or restriction.[9] The person's perception of a change in existential states from health to illness is crucial, whether the change is acute or perceived over a period of time. The state a person regards as "health" need not be one free of disease or demonstrable disability. One may feel "well" and function even in the presence of manifest or covert pathological processes. Contrariwise, one may feel ill in the absence of a demonstrable structural or functional abnormality.

"Health," as I am using it here, refers, therefore, not to some ideal state of freedom from all social, physical, or emotional dysfunction. Rather, it is a state of balance, an equilibrium established between inborn or acquired diseases or limitations and the use of our bodies for transbodily purposes — to advance personal interests, plans, or aspirations. Each of us strikes such a balance which for us defines our personal definition of "health." The idea of health as balance is more analogous to the classical notions of *eukrasia, isonomia,* or *sophrosyne* than it is to some quantitative calibration of objective health determinants and measurements.[10]

Taking this subjective view of health and illness does not militate against assessing more objective criteria and remedying or preventing deviations from statistically defined criteria of normality. Nor does it preclude cultivating higher or better states of balance by positive health promotion. Rather, my concern here is for a person's experiential perception of whether or not he is in need of healing — of a restoration to some previous state of affairs to which he had adapted and adjusted his life. At that precise point, when the person who feels ill decides that he needs professional help, he becomes a "patient" — one who seeks to be healed by another person who "professes" to heal.

The patient, as the etymology of the word so clearly announces, "bears" a burden — a pain, a symptom, or a disability.[11] These burdens he recognizes as threatening to his personal conception of health. Their presence shatters his sense of wholeness. He can no longer cope without assistance. Now, as a "patient," the ill person presents himself to a health professional for advice, for relief of anxiety, for assistance in being healed, becoming whole again, to return, at least, to his prior state, if not a superior one.

Illness signals a change in existential states in the most crucial ways since illness assaults the whole person. Even a trivial or easily remediable illness, or injury, carries with it some compromise in the operations of one's humanity. The ill person lacks knowledge about what is wrong, whether it is serious, whether it can be cured, the way it will be cured, at what expense in time, money, pain, discomfort, loss of dignity and privacy. The ill person is also dependent on another for this information. He also lacks the skill and knowledge by himself to answer these questions and to effect the needed cure.

The ill person, moreover, has lost the free use of his body for his own transbodily purposes. Indeed, the body has in a sense revolted. It has taken the center of the stage. It demands attention. It demands to be served, rather than to serve. The body stands against the self; it becomes alien. The ontological unity that constitutes the well-functioning human person is compromised or even ruptured. Illness thus threatens our image of self — the identity we have fashioned as a result of the balances we have struck between our endowments, great or small, and our aspirations. The image and the meaning we have given to our lives must often be reconstructed if healing is to occur. How will the illness change us? What new demands will it place upon us? Will it mean that, at last, we must confront the fragility of personal existence and the reality of personal death?

These phenomenological characteristics of the experience of illness converge to make the patient a changed person. He has become a dependent, vulnerable, and exploitable human being. The sick person remains, ontologically, a human being, of course, but the freedom with which he can express his humanity is limited. Illness is, in effect, a wounding of the humanity of the one who is ill. The sick person has lost some of those precious freedoms we associate with being human.

Healing requires nothing less than repairing these wounds. It calls for a restoration to the former or a better state. If this is not possible, "healing" strives for whatever balance is still possible. Even the patient who is incurably ill can be healed to some extent. He can be helped to grasp control to the extent possible of his own living, to direct his own life, even in the face of obvious decline. He can be helped to regain some hope that his own death can be confronted in a human and personalized way. With assistance, the sick and dying person can refashion a new self image, one that confronts dying or incurability in his or her own way.

These selected phenomenological observations give only a superficial statement of the changes in existential states that constitute illness, health, and healing. They should suffice, however, to indicate that being ill and in need of healing is a special state of human existence and that the particularities of the experience are unique for each human person. Since the story, the narrative of each life, is unique, the "continuation" of that story in the face of illness is also unique.

Illness thus is different in degree and even, to some extent, in kind from being in need of some material commodity or service. Illness strikes much closer to what it is to be human. Hunger, poverty, injustice are states of deprivation, too. They share some of the phenomenological characteristics of illness. Yet, they are in a real sense external assaults — visited upon us by circumstances or other persons. They do not represent internal and intrinsic attacks on a person's capacity for survival — or for enjoying a satisfying life, if the external threats could be eliminated or diminished. Injustice or poverty limits possibilities, but they do not eliminate them as illness can.

Health, or well being, is an intrinsic human value. It is both a biological good — the well functioning of the whole organism — and a social good essential to the well functioning of society.[12] It is a different thing to be in need of healing from what it is to be in need of some commodity — a refrigerator, a new car, or even a new job. Illness, if not a unique state of deprivation, is one which, in degree at least, seriously undermines our capacity to live a fully human life and in ways that strike close to what it is to be a human being.

B. *The Act of Profession: The Promise of Healing*

In this special state of deprivation, the ill person seeks out the healer. The healer, in turn, offers himself or herself — that is to say, "professes" that he/she can and will heal. It is in the nexus of this personal transaction between one seeking help and one offering help that the ethical obligations of the healer are grounded. To promise to heal elicits expectations in the patient: that the physician will have the necessary competence and that he will put that competence at the service of the patient. The very nature of illness, what it does to persons, and the nature of the promise to heal, together create a necessity for trust. The physician must be the patient's advocate to warrant that trust. He has the obligation to practice a certain self effacement, suppressing his own self interests in favor of those of the patient. The physician must not use the vulnerability and exploitability inherent in the sick state to advance his own power, prestige, or profit. He must be compassionate because he cannot determine the good for this patient without feeling something of this patient's experience of illness, the patient's perception of his own good in this clinical situation, at this time in his life.

These expectations are heightened by the existential inequality of physician and patient. This is not an ontological inequality, for the patient remains fully a human person — entitled to the full measure of respect due all persons. But, illness imposes an existential inequality since the patient is less free, less knowledgeable, less powerful than he was when he was well. His humanity is less free to express itself. His control of his own destiny is compromised, and he is forced to trust in the character and virtue of the physician.

In a sense, the physician is also less free. He is bound, by the promise to heal, to this patient in a bond of trust. This bond limits the full expression of his own self interest. His promise to heal limits his freedom to pursue what might otherwise be legitimate goals — his own profit, prestige, or power. The physician's bond is forged by the promise to help, a bond of a type inconceivable in a business or commodity relationship.

In that circumstance of inequality, the physician is expected to make a decision for, and with, the patient and take an action which is technically correct and morally good. The two need not be, and increasingly are not, synonymous. Medical good does not exhaust the meanings of patient's good. We can think of an expanding number of situations today in which the assessment of the physician and the patient differ about whether or not a recommended treatment is worthwhile — blood for the Jehovah's witness, abortion for the Catholic, discontinuance of life support measures for the orthodox Jew, any kind of non spiritual healing for certain fundamentalist religious sects. Doing good for the patient is a complex act which calls for a balancing of techno-medical good (what benefits medical knowledge may bring) and the other dimensions of patient good — his preferences, his good as a human being to make autonomous decisions, or his spiritual or ultimate good.[13]

It is the confluence of these special existential aspects of illness, of professing to heal, and of healing, itself, that grounds medical ethics and gives it a special character within the broader context of human ethical behavior. Even on purely philosophical grounds, and without recourse to theological argument, the healing relationship transcends the buyer-seller relationship. Accordingly, the ethical obligations of patient and physician are of an order different from the obligations of buyer-seller.

It is those naturalistically deducible differences and specificities that ground medical morality and have in all major cultures enjoined higher degrees of commitment upon physicians than that expected in other members of society. We find those obligations spelled out in most of the ancient and modern modes of medical ethics in the Judaeo-Christian West, as in China and India.[14] These codifications vary in content and may, at some points, contradict one another. Yet, they all call for primary deference to the patient's well being, for competence, for avoiding injury to the patient, and respecting the vulnerability of the sick person.

Some will object that, despite these lofty aims, the medical profession has, in its individual members, so often and so egregiously lapsed that the idea of self effacement is a myth and a sham. There is no doubt that transgressions of the medical codes have, sadly, been all too frequent. But, that does not vitiate their intrinsic validity or the impressive fact that as many physicians have, in fact, honored these codes as have violated them — a record not equalled in any other endeavor, except the religious ministry.

It is important for the major emphasis of this essay — the meaning of Christian love and justice in the health ministry — that Christians appreciate the high level of aspiration, if not perfect adherence, that pre-Christian, pagan, and non-Christian medical ethics have attained. Benevolence and, less explicitly, justice are two virtues that civilized societies expect of their physicians for reasons that arise out of the nature of what it is physicians profess to do for those that are ill.

The challenge for Christians is to define what makes a Christian ministry of health care distinctive. What does it add to the loftier expressions of secular or non-Christian humanisms?[15] To examine that question further, we need first to look, still from the philosophical point of view, at the meanings of beneficence and justice inherent in the pre-Christian and non-Christian codes and in today's philosophical medical ethics.

C. *The Root Principles of Philosophical Medical Ethics*

I have outlined the philosophical grounding of medical ethics from which the major principles of traditional medical ethics can properly be deduced. Those principles are reducible to two: beneficence — doing the good of the patient, and justice — giving to each one his due. The other principles usually employed are, I believe, subservient to these two. Thus, autonomy — the obligation to enhance and to permit the patient's right of self determination and choice, is, to my mind, a component of beneficence, since doing the patient's good includes respecting his good — as he defines it, and his good as a rational being capable of exercising reason and making his own choices. Promise keeping, confidentiality, and truth telling can also be subsumed under a broadened conception of justice and/or beneficence.

Before we examine the ways in which the Christian conceptions of love and justice reshape the naturalistic conceptions of beneficence and justice, we must examine in more depth the explicit meanings of these two cardinal principles in contemporary philosophic ethics.

1. The Principle of Beneficence

Benevolence and beneficence — intending and doing the patient's good, i.e., acting in his or her best interests, is a complex notion.[16] The "good" of the patient subsumes at least four separate notions. The *first* is medical good — what the scientific and technological knowledge of medicine can effect to cure, contain, ameliorate, or prevent illness or disease. It consists in the judicious application of current medical knowledge and techniques. Its benefits are measured in terms of some quantitative effect on the unfolding of the natural history of the disease. Medical good in a given clinical situation is determined by "medical indications" — a statement of those clinical characteristics that make the application of given therapeutic modality worthwhile in certain classes of patients. "Worthwhileness" implies some possibility of good that materially outweighs the dangers and discomforts of a particular treatment.

In some models of beneficience, the whole good of the patient is equated with medical good and is the doctor's only proper concern. This is the doctrine of strong paternalism which holds that the physician only can know what is good for the patient, that the patient can never comprehend fully the risks and benefits, and that medical good is the only good the patient should seek from the physician.[17] Medical ethics in this view is measured by the canons of medical competence solely.

The *second* sense of patient good is the good as expressed in his preferences, his expressions of what he considers in his own best interests. This form of a patient good will vary markedly from patient to patient. It summates many values: the kind of life the patient would like to live, the risks he wishes to take and for what benefits. Each of us has a life plan and a set of values arranged in some order of preference, some set of things we wish to achieve and things to avoid. These values are based in culture, ethnicity, age, sex, occupation, family, and dozens of other facets of our individual lives.

When illness occurs and alternative treatments or outcomes are presented, each of us may weigh the possibilities differently. Each of us, therefore, has a somewhat different concept of our own best interests. No one else can presume to define those interests for us or the quality of life we may wish to lead. In clinical decisions, therefore, the medical good recommended by the physician must be placed within a matrix of personal preferences and shaped accordingly or even rejected.

When the physician encourages and permits the patient to make his own decisions, without deception or manipulation, he respects the principle of autonomy. This principle is fast becoming the prime principle of medical ethics in our democratic, pluralistic, and free society.[18] Autonomy is the *third* sense of the patient's good. It is a generic good proper to all humans as humans, as beings worthy of respect. It is grounded in the human capability for reason, choice, and judgment and in the capacity to express those choices in speech. Autonomy exercised in making moral choices becomes moral agency —the autonomous choice of a person among moral values and his accountability for the choices made. This is a good so intrinsic to being human that to violate it is to violate the very humanity of the patient, even if he chooses to refuse effective treatment and risk death as a result.

Much has been written about the patient's moral right to autonomy in contemporary medical ethics. It is placed by some authors in direct opposition to beneficence.[19] Those authors generally equate beneficence only with medical good. Taken this way, beneficence may indeed come into conflict with autonomy. But, if beneficence is looked at more broadly, it includes preservation of patient autonomy, because the patient's good is not limited to his medical good. Autonomy and beneficence in this view cannot be in conflict.

The *fourth* sense in which patient good may be understood is as ultimate good. This is the "good of last resort" in the sense that, when everything else is considered, this good predominates over all. This good is often expressed in spiritual terms and related to the final destiny of man. For the preservation of good of the soul or its spiritual advancement, humans may sacrifice all the preceding senses of good. They may even yield up their autonomy, as the religious do in the vow of obedience, sacrifice their lives or goods for others, or deny or endanger themselves to help others.

Even those who reject spiritual beliefs will have a good of "last resort," a good for which they may sacrifice all other goods. It may be a humanistic love of mankind, of country, the "greatest good" for all, the advance of science, the pursuit of utility, pleasure, nirvana, et cetera. Whatever it may be, ultimate good is the final ordering principle which will not be sacrificed in a crisis and will ultimately ground and justify moral choice.

I have arranged these four senses of patient good in an order of increasing hierarchical value. When they are in conflict, as they can well be, medical good is the least and ultimate good the highest good of the human person. Looked at this way, beneficence, even on strictly philosophical grounds, is a prime obligation of the physician. Beneficence means that he must respect each component of his patient's good. Because of the phenomenological features of the physician-patient relationship (emphasized in section I), the physician has a role-specific ethical obligation of trust and fidelity to act beneficently. This obligation goes beyond non-maleficence, which is simply not to do harm and, therefore, the most minimal construal of beneficence.

2. The Principle of Justice

The second great principle of philosophical medical ethics is justice—which, like beneficence, is grounded in what it is to be human. Aristotle puts it well: "Justice is essentially human, i.e., it suggests the mutual relations of men as men."[20] Justice is usually defined in some variation of the ancient dictum, suum cuique. This notion of rendering to each according to his due is intrinsic to the multitudinous definitions of justice advanced from Book I of Plato's Republic to the contemporary influential theories of Rawls and Nozick.[21] Each definition contains something of the suum cuique notion, but different shades of interpretation can yield radically different products when expressed in concrete human behavior. These differences become most apparent later when we examine justice in the allocation and rationing of resources.

Classically, justice has three dimensions, each of which is important in philosophical medical ethics—commutative, distributive, and social. Since each is modulated in a Christocentric ethic, each deserves some discussion first in philosophic terms.[22]

Commutative justice concerns the private relationships of persons. It is rooted in the essential equality and dignity of the persons making agreements or contracts with each other. It demands fidelity to promises, agreements, lack of coercion. In such agreements one may not take advantage of the other since the contracting parties are both equally human.

In medical relationships, commutative justice requires fidelity to the trust necessitated by the nature of medical acts. It requires the keeping of promises made by physicians to patients. It preserves the covenantal nature of the physician-patient relationship. On the empirical bases set forth in section I, justice requires that the physician be faithful to the obligations implicit in his promise to help the patient. It includes truth-telling as well, since patients cannot make free and personal choices without knowledge of the nature of the illness and its prognosis. Justice follows from the necessity of beneficence in medical relationships. It takes on a special character, however, because physician and patient are not really equal existentially, though both are still human.

The second sense of justice is distributive—it covers the responsibilities we owe each other as members of a society, or community, the claim each person has to some share in public goods even if his direct participation in the production of those goods may be remote. This claim arises from our mutual interdependence as social animals, each of whom can be fulfilled only in a communal life. In contemporary society, those common goods would include, for example, security, social services, a clean, safe environment, protection of natural resources, health care, housing, nutrition, et cetera. These are goods whose distribution is required if each member of a human community is to be a participant in that community. These are goods none of us could own or enjoy in isolation from our fellows. None of these can properly be considered "propriety" even in a capitalist society.

Health care is among those goods governed by the principle of distributive justice, since, without health, it is difficult or impossible to participate in society. In this sense, health is a precondition of a fully human life.[23] Likewise, it is difficult to conceive of a "healthy" society in which a significant number of its citizens are not healthy. How distributive justice is to be made operative in our society is today the subject of the most vigorous debate. Some of the most crucial questions in that debate are unanswered: What is the strength of the individual's claim? Is health a legal right, an obligation of society, or a luxury allowable only if sufficient affluence permits? By what criterion of justice shall health care be distributed? Should it be equity, merit, age, achievement, need, social worth, productivity, or ability to pay? What level of distribution is justified? Shall it be access and availability to all health services, none at all, or to some specified "fair" minimum?

John Rawls' impressive effort to elaborate a philosophical theory of justice emphasizes maximum liberty compatible with the freedom of all and the distribution of social inequities in such a way as to be to everyone's benefit.[24] "Injustice, then, is simply inequities that are not to the benefit of all."[25] In Rawls' view, we do not deserve our fate in the natural lottery. The ideal social contract is one in which we are all equal unless inequality favors the least advantaged or increases liberty. Rawls justifies his position on the basis of the "original position," the assumption that his is the contract we would choose if we did not know where in the natural lottery we would fall. Health care in this view would be distributed so as to advantage the least advantaged. It would favor egalitarianism and the establishment of social minimums for distribution and allocation of resources.

Nozick, on the other hand, interprets justice as preserving each one's entitlements—the advantages or disadvantages we receive in the natural lottery: our genetic, social, economic, political endowments.[26] Society, in this view, is not compelled in justice to remedy the quixotic distribution of goods that results from the natural lottery. If some are less healthy, less favored economically, or more powerful politically, this may or may not be unfair, but it is not unjust.[27] Nozick's view, applied to health care, favors liberty, as does Rawls'. But, in the distribution of inequities, goods, and resources, Nozick's favors non-egalitarianism. Nozick does not preclude a society voluntarily redressing the imbalances of the natural lottery. But, he would deny to the individual a moral claim in distributive justice to amelioration of the disparate entitlements resulting from his unfortunate position in the natural lottery. This concept of justice emphasizes individual differences and a pluralist conception of the principle that constitutes distributive justice.

The third sense of justice is social—the shared obligation of the members of a society to fashion and operate institutions and arrangements that will fulfill the obligations defined under distributive justice. This is justice in its socio-political expression. It calls for the creation of agencies, institutions, systems, and structures that will take account of the mutuality and interdependence which ground distributive justice. Social justice is a necessary condition of distributive justice without which the claims of individuals for participation in society's goods cannot be realized. In this view, it is a mutual obligation of all citizens to foster the formation of social organizations responsive to the claims of distributive and commutative justice.

As applied to health care, social justice is an even more vexed state than distributive justice. What is the most appropriate form of government and what degree of government regulation would best foster a just distribution of health care? What limits can be placed on individual freedom and entrepreneurship in the interests of optimizing social justice? What are the relative merits of a free market economy as opposed to centralized or planned mechanisms for health care distribution? How consistent are for-profit hospitals, the corporate practice of medicine, the licensing of physicians, the accreditation of medical schools, with a just distribution of health care? Obviously, some of the most crucial socio-political and economic questions of health care today turn on the interpretation we make of social justice.

Obviously, we cannot, in this essay, attempt to answer these questions in any definitive way. What I have sought to establish is only the range of possibilities inherent in the concept of justice as it applies specifically to health care. The theories of Rawls and Nozick offer opposing and even, on some points, contradictory ways to interpret justice. What is pertinent to our discussion is the way a Christian perspective on justice would influence our choices among these and other construals of justice derived philosophically. For this, we must turn now to the theological perspectives on love and justice.

This is by no means an exhaustive delineation of the senses in which justice may be taken. Compensatory and retributive justice, for example, have not been mentioned. They are important in health care and will be touched upon in the last section of this essay.

III. THE THEOLOGICAL PERSPECTIVE

"The enlarging of the heart is the delight we take in justice."
Saint Augustine, *In. Ps. CXVIII*, X, 6.

The Catholic Christian must attend to sources of moral guidance over and above philosophical analysis — to theological sources explicated in scripture, tradition, and the teaching authority of the Church. First, it is necessary to examine Christian teaching on love and justice and their inter-relationships and, then, the way these Christian conceptions act as principles of discernment in health care and transform the obligations of philosophical ethics. When those obligations are seen as a "call" to a specific ministry, they become a genuine vocation — a call that cannot lightly be ignored.

A. *Catholic Christian Teaching on Love and Justice*

Love and justice are central to the whole of Christian theology. On this point, Catholic Christian teachings are long, strong, and complex — far exceeding in richness any attempt to summarize them here. For the purposes of this essay, all I can do is to adumbrate the Catholic Christian perspective — particularly as it has been enriched in modern times by a series of important Papal Encyclicals on social justice, by the documents of Vatican II, the post-conciliar commentaries, and the pastoral letters of the World's Bishops.[28]

Christian notions of charity, *caritas* or *agape*, derive their unique meaning from the life, teaching, and example of Jesus Christ. The central message of the Gospels is the announcement of the good news of a God of Love. He sent His only Son who gave the ultimate demonstration of love when he suffered so that redemption might be made available to all mankind. Love of God and love of neighbor were Christ's daily exhortations to those who would follow him. Love is the touchstone to salvation, the only transforming power that can eradicate injustice from the world. Love is enjoined on all men and women because all are children of the same Father who loves us all.

Christian charity, as epitomized in the Gospel, went beyond the pagan notion of benevolence and beneficence, which could reach noble proportions on occasion.[29] Charity calls for love for all — enemy as well as friend, for the unjust as well as the just. Christian charity, as St. Paul so eloquently expounded upon it, called for a higher degree of self effacement, for the doing of good out of motives of love of God.[30] Its highest expressions call for sacrifice even to the loss of one's own life. Without other-directed love, the natural virtues could become suspect of some taint of self interest. To the extent they are so tainted, they become less congruent with the perfection of human love which is charity.

The patristic tradition reinforced this gospel teaching by requiring charity because of the mutuality of obligation we owe each other because Christ is in every person.[31] It is Christ we love in our fellows and in ourselves. The more perfect Christian charity is, the more it leads away from love of self and material goods and toward the dedication of self and material goods to the good of others. Christian love requires the kind of love that is free of utilitarian justification.

The differences between contemporary interpretations of beneficence and charity can be more concretely defined in health care ethics if we examine the spectrum of expressions possible for the principle of beneficence, philosophically construed. Thus, beneficence ranges from merely avoiding evil and/or harm to another to doing good as long as it does not require inconvenience to the doer, to doing good at some cost to the doer, to doing good even at a great cost, and finally, in the most heroic form, to sacrificing all one's goods or one's life for the other. Christian charity, or agapeistic beneficence, calls for wishing and doing good precisely under those circumstances where it might be most difficult to justify doing so on rational grounds alone. Charity is, in some senses, "unreasonable" in that it violates philosophical standards of moderation. It becomes reasonable only if we accept the fact of a revelation that counsels perfection and defines charity as entirely other-directed and for the specific reasons that the other is a child of God, loved by God, and, therefore, worthy of love by us.

Justice, like beneficence, is transformed by the Christian experience of Faith in the light of revelation. The pagan notion of justice, like that of the contemporary theories, is ultimately practical and prudential. We owe others their due because we want them to give us our due and because we want to protect ourselves from the unjust claims of others. Justice is a requirement for a peaceable society and the protection of legitimate self interests. If we practice justice, we can thereby assure happiness for all. Justice, in this view, is a claim we have on the community — compliance with which is an obligation of communal living. In its highest expressions, it might be justified as owed to humans because they are worthy of respect and dignity.

In the Christian view, however, justice has its deepest roots in love; it is an extension of the charity we should show to others. Not to do justice would be to relapse into self interest, to turn from love of the other to love of self. Love, charity, *caritas*, *agape* — each notion testifies that the claims of others upon us are the claims of our brothers and sisters in Christ, loved equally by Him and redeemed by Him, and, by that fact, entitled to be loved.

In the Christian view, therefore, love generates and transmutes justice. As St. Augustine held, justice is the concern and love that Christians must show to others. Charity is for him ". . . the root of all good."[32] It truly is the *vis a tergo* moving us to justice. Jesus dedicated his life to justice energized by a love that transcended the legalistic justice of the Pharisees. In the Sermon on the Mount, Jesus calls his followers to follow him and live not only the letter but the spirit of the Law. His own life is the exemplification of the new justice. St. Paul repeats this exhortation when he calls upon us to put on the "new man."

In his own life, Jesus' concern, his practice of justice transmuted by charity, was for the poor, the sick, the troubled, the oppressed, and the outcast. He practiced justice transmuted by charity in the concrete acts of beneficence towards specific persons. He did not argue for charity and justice in conformity with abstract principles. Christian justice does not focus on strict interpretations of what is owed in accordance with some calculus of claims and counter-claims. Instead, it offers the way of love illuminated by an ineffable guide. Christian justice does not obliterate the pagan virtue, but modulates and illuminates it by a principle of a very different sort, the principle of charity.[33] It is not knowledge that generates justice, as in Plato or Aristotle, but the loving concern of charity. Jesus on the cross asked the Father to forgive His crucifiers. He did not ask for the retributive justice of the Old Law.

The ways the classical construals of justice in Plato, Aristotle, and the Roman Stoics intersect with the Christian notion are worthy of continuing examination. The same is true of the intersections with contemporary ethics. Frankena, for example, suggests that the ethics of Christian charity is a theory of its own — "pure agapeism."[34] Justice philosophically derived and justice Christocentrically revealed cannot be fully equated. Their relationships and differences merit closer study in any attempt to answer whether or not, and how, Christian notions of love and justice modify the ethics of health care. Just how the natural and supernatural virtues complement, supplement, or transform each other is a subject of its own, too.[35]

In the Christian view, justice is ultimately grounded in love — a charitable justice, i.e., rendering to others their due, in which "due" is not only what is legalistically owed, but what is called for by love. Charity is the first principle of Christian justice. It could be similarly argued on philosophical grounds that justice is ultimately rooted in benevolence and beneficence. In this way, love can be the first principle of naturalistic as of Christian ethics.

Whether the Christian takes the Augustinian agapeistic, the Thomistic natural law, or the Christian existentialist perspective, one thing is undeniable — each Christian must respond personally to the life, way, and truth of Jesus Christ. The richness of that truth and its call to perfection are the well-springs into which Christians must dip for inspiration and aspiration. This is not to expunge reason, but to require that reason confront the unexpungeable reality of Christ's life and teaching. It is in this teaching that we find the ordering force behind Christian justice and love. It is the illuminating power of

Christ's healing that becomes the obligation that binds Christians to practice a special kind of love and justice.

It is the awareness of God's call to all to live a life of charity and the conscious answer to this call that, for a Christian, transforms a profession into a vocation. This does not mean that high orders of love and justice are not discernible to non Christians, nor that Christians automatically practice these virtues. Rather, the Christian vocation means fidelity to a notion of justice transmuted by charity as a moral obligation. That is a call for every Christian. Health care is one ministry, one way to respond to this call.

B. *Christocentric Health Care Ethics: from Profession to Vocation*

> ". . . the world today needs Christians who remain Christians."
> A. Camus, *Resistance, Rebellion and Death.*[36]

The Christian health professional is bound, like others, by the norms of philosophical medical ethics. From that source he derives principles, guidelines, rules, and codes which specify right and good actions and the criteria by which they may be judged. For the Christian, this is not, however, the whole of ethics. To be sure, the Christian perspective does not add another whole set of specific prescriptions; but, the Christian ethic enjoins one overriding principle: love of God and neighbor.

The distinguishing factor of Christocentric ethics is the fact of revelation — a point which Frankena acknowledged in his classification of Christian ethics as agapeistic.[37] This difference does not yield precise indications, rules, or guidelines to determine what should be done in every given situation. Nor does it, of necessity, preclude the use of deontological or utilitarian principles in this or that decision. It requires only that any principle or ethical theory conform to the spirit of love and justice exemplified in the life, work, and teaching of Jesus Christ.

The Christian perspective, therefore, provides principles of discernment more than a code of rules for action. What it lacks in specificity it gains in insight. It is a beacon and a compass that individual Christians and the Church must use to find the direction which their Faith requires them to follow. This is a task at once more demanding and perilous. The call is to perfection — and the precise recipe for success is not available. Further, as times change and as new technological advances appear, the answer must continuously be re-examined and re-tested.

Christocentric ethics is, therefore, in its deepest sense, "beyond" ethics. Romano Guardini puts it very well, "Once we restrict the word ethics to its modern specific sense of moral principles, it no longer accurately covers the Sermon on the Mount. What Jesus revealed there on the mountainside was no mere ethical code, but a whole new existence. . ."[38] This is not to dispose of ethics or law. Law impels us to limit self interest for fear of punishment and thus assures an orderly society based on rights. Ethics impels us to limit self interest as rational beings who recognize duties to others and thus assures a concerned and responsible social life. Religion impels us to limit self interest because God asks us to do so out of love for Him and his creatures and thus assures a caring society. This is something of what Guardini means when he says, "Only in love is genuine fulfillment of the ethical possible."[39]

Philosophical ethics can define the proper relationship between human beings, but not between God and humans, or between humans as God wants those relationships to be. A Christocentric ethic, therefore, does not repudiate philosophical ethics, but transvalues its highest principles, justice and beneficence, into love and thereby carries them beyond the highest human aspirations.

There are, of course, specific moral principles and rules to guide Catholics. These are found in the promulgations of the Moral Code for Catholic Hospitals, the Pastoral Letters of the Bishops, the writings of the theologians, and the teachings of the Popes and the Official Magisterium. But, these sources are, all in their own way, the products of discernment — of the way the institutional Church "reads" Christ's call to love and justice in health care. There are numerous instances today in which such principles of discernment are needed to guide specific decisions and actions. These touch on some of the most important issues in health care today. Let us turn now to a brief examination of some selected aspects of contemporary health care ethics to see where the vectors of Christian discernment point.

C. *The Physician-Patient Relationship*

In the changed socio-political, economic and scientific climate within which medicine is practiced today, there are conflicting conceptions of the healing relationship. Earlier in this essay, I attempted a phenomenological analysis of the healing relationship. Some of the formulations of this relationship would be more congenial to a Christian perspective than others. Thus, it would not require a high degree of Christian discernment to discern that a biological model of the physician-patient or healing relationship would be insufficient, if not antithetic to a Christian interpretation of healing or helping. The same could be said of the relationship viewed as a legal contract, a commodity relationship, or a strongly paternalistic one. Other models — the covenantal, friendship, or fidelity to promise — would be more congruent.[40]

All the models cited have some versimilitude. Without denying this fact, it is the model perceived as primary received primacy which is of utmost importance, the one which takes precedence over the others. Thus, "strong" paternalism would rarely, if ever, be countenanced while weak paternalism could be.[41] A strictly libertarian relationship would not be consistent since it would forbid intervention in suicide or euthanasia, for example. With these exceptions, respect for the autonomy of the competent patient as a human person would not only be consistent, but required. So, too, would respect for the respective agency of patient and physician with neither imposing on the other except where grave harm was in prospect. There would also be a strong imperative to mutual respect for the personal moral accountability of both the physician and the patient. Neither could ask the other to act contrary to conscience.

Likewise, a strictly contractual model of the healing relationship is insufficient from a Christian perspective. The contractual model requires only a minimalistic ethic—one that obligates the patient and the physician to fulfill the terms of an agreement and nothing more. This model calls for the minimal amount of beneficence. Rather, it is contrived to reduce dependence upon either the physician's benevolence or his fidelity to promises. It is precisely those features of the relationship that a contract cannot cover—the uncertainties inherent in the clinical situation and reliance on the fidelity and good will of the physician and patient that charity most clearly regulates.

The most distinctive characteristic of a healing relationship motivated by the Christian perspective is the higher degree of self effacement it requires as a matter of course. Even on strictly philosophical grounds, the vulnerability of the sick person imposes a special responsibility not to take advantage of the patient. In a more positive sense, the physician commits himself to some degree of suppression of his own self interest, comfort, and preferences in order to serve his patient. This is that "higher degree of self-effacement" which Harvey Cushing called the "common devotion" that should motivate the medical profession.[42]

From the Christian perspective, self effacement is an obligation of charity toward others, motivated by love and without the motive of self interest. Being imperfect, few physicians are expected to practice heroic levels of self sacrifice. But, a Christian physician has a moral obligation to be compassionate, considerate, and courteous even to his "difficult" patients, to be available to them even at some considerable inconvenience to himself, and solicitous for their needs. The Christian perspective precludes some of the excessive expressions of self pity we see today on the part of physicians, the complaints about income, work hours, delayed gratification, or the justification for recreation at the expense of commitment to patient needs. It precludes also the attitude of some physicians who feel that, having worked so hard and paid so much for a medical education, they are entitled to "get it back" financially, or in prestige, privileges, and prerogatives.

Self effacement, it must be said, however binding it may be in naturalistic and Christocentric medical ethics, does not require neglect of one's personal or familial well being. Physicians are entitled to develop and grow as persons, to enjoy recreation, to serve their families, and provide for their own material needs. Moderate and extreme interpretations of the obligation to self effacement can be as morally unsound as its neglect. Indeed, immoderate self sacrifice is too often an excuse for an inability to balance conflicting obligations or even for deliberately neglecting some of them.

The issue is really one of balance—knowing when legitimate self interest should dominate and when self effacement is the product of constant reflection and emotional maturity—something for which no instant formula is at hand. Suffice it to say that prudence, the virtue St. Thomas thought so central to the Christian life, is the virtue to be cultivated here.[43]

The charitable self effacement implicit in a Christian vocation to the health ministry leads the physician away from a series of activities at the moral margin—things neither illegal nor contravened by professional codes, but, nonetheless, fraught with compromises of Christian conceptions of charity and justice. I refer here to most of the practices associated with today's commercialism, competitive and entrepreneural medicine; e.g., investing in the health care "industry," owning shares in hospitals, nursing homes, patenting medical procedures, working in for-profit or corporately-owned hospitals, clinics, and HMOs. The list of investment "opportunities" in health care open to physicians grows daily. The profit motive sooner or later must conflict with the deference owed the sick person by virtue of the inequality of a relationship in which one of the parties is ill and dependent upon the other. Making a profit from the sickness of others in order to produce a return to investors comes too close to exploitation, even in the best circumstances.

The ethics of business, as it is presently understood, cannot be relied upon to guarantee that extra measure of solicitude that Christian ministry to the sick requires. The Christian physician has a positive responsibility to resist, and even to refuse, to participate in actions that endanger a patient out of motives of fiscal necessity. The "economic transfer," for example, of the patient whose insurance is insufficient to pay for care in a private institution is a growing example in point that is causing ethical dilemmas for conscientious physicians.

Equally to be condemned is the practice, becoming too frequent these days, of physicians' asking whether a patient is insured adequately before seeing him. In the same vein, excessive fees, overutilization of diagnostic or therapeutic services, exuberant advertising, maneuvers to "dominate" the market, and a whole host of morally marginal business practices would be eschewed by any physician who claimed Christian authenticity for his ministry to the sick. The physician's "right" to treat whom he pleases would, in a Christian view of medical ethics, be limited.

Another form of behavior antithetical to the Christian notion of love and justice is the refusal to treat certain kinds of patients who represent a threat to the physician. I refer here especially to the AIDS patients. Instances are increasing of physicians, nurses, and other health professionals who avoid caring for these patients. Some even take the view that AIDS patients are victims of their own self abuse and not worthy of care. Similar attitudes are evident with respect to alcoholics, smokers, the very obese, or diabetics who do not follow their dietary regimens.

In short, a Christian vocation of healing imposes a standard of commutative justice weighed heavily in the direction of benevolence and beneficence, even at the expense of inconvenience, cost, and some danger to the physician. Simple non-maleficence would not suffice. Such an interpretation of beneficence is, of course, not closed to the non Christian. It is often exhibited by those without the Christian imperatives to the scandal of Christian physicians. But, for the Christian, such behavior is a matter of moral obligation. The Christian physician or health professional cannot live a life of contradiction in which professional and personal morality are divorced. Such a state is inconsistent with even the most rudimentary interpretations of authentic Christian living, to say nothing of a Christian vocation.

In the realms of distributive and social justice, a Christocentric ethic would, of necessity, favor some interpretations of justice over others. Thus, Nozick's fundamental principle of protecting the inequalities of the natural lottery would be the antithesis of a Christian perspective. The Christian vocation is quite specifically oriented to a charitable redress of the inequities of nature or circumstance. It is, in fact, precisely to the losers in the natural lottery—the sick, the poor, the outcast—to whom Christ addressed his personal ministry and his Sermon on the Mount. This is the basis for the preferential "option" for the poor that inspires the best Christian institutions.

Likewise, distribution of goods and rationing on principles of social worth, merit, productivity, ability to pay, age, or burden on society would be hard to justify. Egalitarian principles of justice, like Rawls', would have much more claim on the Christian, though not for the reason Rawls adduces—that is to say, not because we, ourselves, might be the disadvantaged person. Rather, the Christian should show love and justice to all equally, since all are our brothers and sisters under God, not because we might need help ourselves some day.

Two kinds of justice I did not treat earlier require mention at this point: retributive and compensatory justice. Retributive justice treats of the redress of injury by punishment of the wrong-doer. In health care it is expressed today as an option to control costs by limiting care to those who are responsible for their ill-health—the smoker, the overeater, victim of venereal disease, and the drug addict. An even sterner view of justice would interpret withholding care as just punishment for past indiscretions. This form of justice goes counter to a Christocentric health care ministry as we have defined it here.

Compensatory justice makes amends for injustices in the past. In health care, it would call for extra solicitude for the poor, for minorities, for those who have not had access to health care, and those badly treated by the natural lottery. It is applicable, too, in admission criteria to medical schools and such things as faculty and hospital appointments. In the Christian view, compensatory justice is an obligation implicit in the call to perfection. A preferential option for the poor, the disadvantaged, for all who have been ill-favored by history, environment, heredity, or political or social circumstance, is a necessary extrapolation of the virtue of Christian charity.

In the realm of social justice, the Christian vocation to health care would impose an obligation to participate in designing and operating institutions and policies that would result in a just and equitable distribution of health care as well as other socially important services. Personal involvement is required of the individual health professional, of the health professions as corporate entities, and the entire Christian community. The provision of just and merciful health care to all is thus a shared responsibility in social justice of all Christians. Advocacy for the sick, in all its dimensions, is a responsibility, especially today when our social mores tend to accept inequality and two level medical care as justifiable.

These implications of the Christian concept of social justice are not widely acknowledged by Catholics or other Christians. Too many "delegate" their own responsibility to health professionals, health care institutions, or governmental or voluntary agencies. All Christians share a mutual responsibility to assure that health care institutions, Catholic-Christian or secular, do, in fact, act with justice and love. As members of democratic societies, we are expected to use the means available in those societies to shape our institutions. Those who are bureaucrats have a special Christian vocation to work within their institutional contexts to see that those institutions perform in morally justifiable ways.

Distributive and social justice are also obligations of the institutional Church. Since Christ provided so many examples of his solicitude for the sick, the healing ministry is an essential part of the evangelical ministry of the whole Church. Pope John Paul II has only recently reaffirmed the importance of that ministry. He reaffirms the Good Samaritan parable as a model for Christians who should be impelled by love and justice to help the sufferings of the sick.[44]

The institutional Church must, as it has for centuries, remain involved in sponsoring health care institutions today for several very good reasons. First, hospitals and health care institutions, as we know them

120

today, were born under the aegis of the Church. The reasons for them
are as cogent today as they were then. Then, the Church-sponsored institution is increasingly the last resort of the poor in a community and
the only "safety net" actually available. Third, the Catholic hospital is
the only place in which Christian and Catholic medical moral principles can be exemplified and applied daily in medical decisions. This
option in medical models must be available to Catholics and to non
Catholics. Fourth, hospital and health care agencies provide concrete
examples of what being a Christian means. To be a Christian is to in-
fuse everything we do with the message of love and justice Christ gave
to us, a message which forever changes the way we are expected to live
with each other.

It is important, therefore, to reassert the vocation, call, of the whole
Church to the imitation of Christ. Today, Catholic hospitals everywhere are tempted by fiscal exigencies to retreat from the care of the
poor, to sell out to for-profit corporations, or to compromise with the
commercialization and monetarizing practices adopted by their "com-
petitors." Yet, it is precisely the ubiquity and the non-compassionate
nature of many of today's fiscal exigencies that impose an ever-greater
necessity for continued involvement of the institutional Church. Healing has always been essential to the Church's evangelical mission and is
also witness to the world that Christian belief makes a difference in the
way Christians live.

I have argued elsewhere, and will not repeat here, that Catholic
hospitals and health care institutions can "compete" in today's health
care milieu without compromise of moral integrity, and they must do
so to remain faithful to the call we all share to care for the sick.[45] Survival, so much discussed by Catholic professionals and Boards, cannot
be at the expense of compromise or capitulation. This means a degree
of cooperation, of concrete practice of charity among Catholic and
Christian hospitals not yet fully tried. It means greater personal and
financial support by Catholic laymen and greater volunteer assistance
on a scale not yet practiced.

Catholics and Christians have an additional obligation to all of
society. By uniting in the care of the sick, the poor, and the dependent
members of a society, they demonstrate the need for love in any society. This is a message easy to repudiate when preached in the abstract,
but difficult to ignore when witnessed in action. It is a message vital to
today's world where every force seems to favor divisiveness. Communities cannot survive without something they love in common, some
things that transcend the uninhibited self interest of the competitive
spirit.

All Christians have a vocation—that is, a call from God to follow
Christ, "to proclaim the exploits of God who called us, out of darkness
into this marvelous light."[46] Within that larger call, each person is also
called to follow Christ in some specific activity. Whatever that activity

may be—exalted or humble—it becomes illuminated by the light of faith and love. "Everyone has his own vocation in which he has been called; let him keep to it."[47]

A vocation is a grace, a stirring of the mind and will toward which can be accepted or rejected. When it is accepted consciously, an activity becomes a Christian vocation. In the case of the health worker, the conscious response to God's call transmutes a profession into a vocation.

A vocation differs from a profession. A profession is a self generated declaration of dedication to a certain standard of ethical behavior. A vocation is the same kind of declaration, but one which has its source in a call from God and a desire to do God's will, to be a witness of the Gospel message through a specific life activity.

For the Christian health professional—doctor, nurse, dentist, other health worker—it is not sufficient to remain faithful to the moral imperatives of a philosophical or naturalistic ethic. A Christian vocation includes the obligations assumed by other professionals, but they must be supplemented, enriched, and made congruent with the spirit of a justice transmuted by love that flows from a Christocentric ethic. In a vocation, the seminal principles of beneficence and justice, central to philosophical ethics, are interpreted in the light of the spirit of the scripture: the tradition of the Church and the special teachings of the Official Magisterium.

The objection will be raised that all I have said is unrealistic and far from the behavior of physicians or hospitals. The allegation is often made that not-for-profit hospitals, Christian and non Christian, do make a profit, too, and that the physician's fee is also a form of profit. Why, then, should I be so self righteous about for-profit hospitals or the commercial aspect of medical practices? Have not physicians been the staunchest supporters of the free enterprise system, of untrammeled and unregulated practice, of free choice for patients? Are they not the major opponents of nationalized or socialized centrally-planned systems and fee schedules, et cetera?

Much of this is true. Indeed, I would go further and say that many physicians and their professional organizations are seeing today the logical extrapolations of economic and political philosophies they, themselves, espoused. Now, it turns out that those philosophies are hurtful to them and to their patients. For some, they are simply the fulfillment of their hopes for medicine as a free market enterprise. Like the automotive industry, we are for competition until it hurts us.

While some of this is true, some is not. Not-for-profit hospitals do not make profit the same way that for-profit hospitals do. For one thing, their "excess of revenue over expenditures" does not go into the pockets of the hospital trustees or distant investors. It all goes into capital improvement or expansion for other activities related to the improvement of patient care. This is very different from the primary orientation of a corporate entity to provide a return to investors. That return is a moral obligation, too. It is the way that the obligation to maximize the investor's money and the obligation to the sick conflict that constitutes the major objection to for-profit medicine.

Fees do contain some excess of revenue over expenditure. Presumably, that is the charge for the physician's time and effort — what he receives after he has paid his expenses of practice. The question morally is not whether he should be paid for his time and effort, but how much is legitimate? There is no doubt that many fees are not morally defensible and some investments are morally unconscionable.

Admitting all of this does not vitiate the arguments of this essay. It is in the nature of ethical discourse to define what ought to be done — not justify what is, in fact, done. The present or past activities of physicians or the profession as a whole, of hospitals, Catholic or not, are not self justifying. What this essay tries to do is derive what are morally defensible norms — what *should be,* rather than *what is.*

Pope Paul VI succinctly and eloquently summarized what is essential to a Christian vocation of healing based in love and justice in an allocution he gave to physicians about the profession of medicine:

> Aimez votre profession! Elle est pour vous une grande école. Elle vous sensibilise à la souffrance de vos frères, elle vous aide à les comprendre et à les respecter, elle purifie les plus nobles élans do votre coeur par le dévouement et l'esprit de sacrifice qu'elle exige de vous. Votre activité est encore une grande leçon pour la société tout entière: car c'est encore et toujours l'exemple de la bonté généreuse envers ses frères qui, mieux que toute parole, entraîne les âmes, émeut les coeurs les plus froids et offre à la vie de la communauté un motif de confiance et de stabilité morale.
>
> Combien elle est plus facile, plus belle, plus méritoire lorsqu'elle vient en aide à la souffrance humaine par amour du Christ, le grand Patient mystérieux, qui souffre en chacun de ceux sur lesquels se penche avec bonté et discernement votre profession.[48]

Paul VI's vision of a Christian profession fuses the idea of profession indissolubly with the idea of vocation. His call is one to which each Christian health professional must respond in the measure God's grace and his other capabilities allow. It is a vision that the committed Christian will grasp — without the laborious argumentation I have provided here.

NOTES

[1] *De Trinitate,* XXXV, xviii, 32.

[2] Only a few of the more recent summarizations need be cited: John R. Donahue, "Biblical Perspectives on Justice," in John C. Haughey, ed., *The Faith That Does Justice* (New York: Paulist Press, 1977), pp. 68–112; Monika K. Hellwig, "Scriptural and Theological Bases for the Option for the Poor," in Margaret John Kelly, ed., *Justice and Health Care* (St. Louis: The Catholic Health Association, 1984), pp. 1–12; Peter J. Henriot, "Service to the Poor, a Basis for Spirituality and Mission," in Margaret John Kelly, *op. cit.* Or, we may

EDMUND D. PELLEGRINO, M.D.

recall directly Jeremaiah's exhortation to do justice to the vulnerable
(Jeremaiah 22:3), Sirach's warning not to avert our eyes from the poor (Sirach
4:1-5), Jesus' dedication to his mission to the poor, the blind, the captives
(Luke 4:16-19), or the obligations of Christians to go beyond mere justice
(Luke 6:32-35).
    ³ Here, the foundational documents are so well known as needing only to be
listed: The encyclical of John XXIII, *Mater et Magistra, Christianity and
Social Progress,* Paul VI, *Populorum Progressio,* Apostolic Letter of John Paul
II, *Salvifici Doloris, On the Christian Meaning of Human Suffering,* The en-
cyclical, *Dives in Misericordia, Rich in Mercy.* Also, *Justice in the World,*
Statement of the Second General Assembly, The Synod of Catholic Bishops,
1971; *Gaudium et Spes, Pastoral Constitution of the Church in the Modern
World, Documents of Vatican Council II,* 1965, and *Health and Health Care,
A Pastoral Letter of the American Catholic Bishops,* U.S. Catholic Conference,
1981. See also commentaries on the preceding and Joseph Gremillion, "Papal
and Episcopal Teaching on Justice in Health Care," in Margaret John Kelly,
op. cit., 31-43, and George E. Reed, "Initiatives of the Catholic Bishops in
Seeking Justice in Health Care," Margaret John Kelly, *op. cit.,* 45-59.
    ⁴ See the excellent multi-authored volume edited by Charles E. Curran and
Richard A. McCormick, *The Distinctiveness of Christian Ethics: Readings in
Moral Theology, No. II* (New York: Paulist Press, 1980). Also, Josef Fuchs,
Christian Ethics in a Secular Arena (Washington, D.C.: Georgetown University
Press, 1984); Richard A. McCormick, "Does Religious Faith Add to Ethics'
Perception?," in John C. Haughey, *Personal Values in Public Policy, Conversa-
tions on Government Decision-Making* (New York: Paulist Press, 1979), pp.
155-73. Also, Garth L. Hallett, *Christian Moral Reasoning, An Analytic
Guide* (Notre Dame, Indiana: University of Notre Dame Press, 1983); and
Christian Biblical Ethics, written and edited by Robert J. Daly in cooperation
with others (New York: Paulist Press, 1984); Patricia B. Jung, "A Roman
Catholic Perspective on the Distinctiveness of Christian Ethics," *Journal of
Religious Ethics* 12 (Spring, 1984).
    ⁵ H. Tristram Engelhardt, Jr., "Bioethics in Pluralist Societies," *Perspec-
tives in Biology and Medicine* 26 (1982): 64-78; Alisdair MacIntyre, *After Vir-
tue* (Notre Dame, Indiana: University of Notre Dame Press, 1981).
    ⁶ E. D. Pellegrino, "Religion and the Sources of Medical Morality," *New
York State Medical Journal* (Dec. 1981): 1859-64.
    ⁷ See the anthology, *Concepts of Health and Disease, Interdisciplinary
Perspectives,* edited by Arthur L. Caplan, H. Tristram Engelhardt, Jr., and
James J. McCartney (Addison-Wesley, 1981); and *Journal of Medicine and
Philosophy* 1 (Sept., 1976).
    ⁸ E. D. Pellegrino and David C. Thomasma, *A Philosophical Basis for
Medical Practice* (New York: Oxford Press, 1981).
    ⁹ I have paraphrased Galen's oft-quoted definition of health as that state "in
which we neither suffer pain or are hindered in the functions of daily life" (*De
Sanitate Tuenda,* I, 5). Despite many wordier attempts, this simple definition
has not been improved upon.
    ¹⁰ See Henry Sigerist, *A History of Medicine* (New York: Oxford University
Press, 1961), Vol. II, p. 299. Also Werner Jaeger, *Paideia* (New York: Oxford
University Press, 1944), Vol. II, Ch.I. Plato's notion of health as a balance
centered on his multiform notion of *sophrosyne* — the orderly arrangement of
faculties of the soul. See *Timaeus,* 87E-88A. The idea of balance between body

and soul and the idea of *sophrosyne* run through *Gorgias, Charmides,* and the *Republic* as well.
[11] *Oxford English Dictionary.* For relationship to physicians' obligations, see E. D. Pellegrino, *Humanism and the Physician* (Knoxville: University of Tennessee Press, 1979), p. 225.
[12] Leon R. Kass, *Towards a More Natural Science: Biology and Human Affairs* (New York: The Free Press, 1985), pp. 170-74; and Joseph Owens, "Aristotelian Ethics, Medicine, and the Changing Nature of Man in Philosophical Medical Ethics: Its Nature and Significance," in Vol. 3, *Philosophy and Medicine,* ed. Stuart F. Spicker and H. Tristram Engelhardt, Jr. (Holland: D. Reidel, 1975), pp. 127-42.
[13] E. D. Pellegrino, "Moral Choice, The Good of the Patient and the Patient's Good," in *Ethics and Critical Care Medicine,* ed. Loretta Kopelman and John Moskop (Holland: D. Reidel Publishing, 1985 — in press). Transcript of paper read at Conference on "Moral Choice and Medical Crisis," East Carolina University School of Medicine, Greenville, North Carolina, March 16-18, 1983.
[14] For example, "The Hippocratic Oath and Corpus," Loeb Classical Library, translated by W. H. S. Nones; The Indian Code, "The Charaka Samhita"; the Chinese, "The Thousand Golden Prescriptions"; the Hebrew, "Oath of Asaf"; for an overview, see Donald Konold's article, "Codes of Medical Ethics," in *The Encyclopedia on Bioethics, Vol. 1* (New York: The Free Press, 1978).
[15] For an example of some lofty Stoic sentiments, see Scribonius Largus' introduction to *Compositiones,* cited in Henry Sigerist, *Ancient Medicine, Selected Papers of Henry Sigerist,* edited by Owsei and Lillian C. Temkin (Baltimore: Johns Hopkins, 1967), pp. 336-44. Also cited is Libonius' speech to young physicians, exhorting them to cultivate "love of man," to "share the pain" of the patient (p. 345).
[16] E. D. Pellegrino, "Moral Choice, the Good of the Patient and the Patient's Good," *op. cit.*
[17] James F. Childress, *Who Should Decide? Paternalism in Health Care* (New York: Oxford, 1982).
[18] See the *Journal of Theoretical Medicine* 5 (February, 1984). Also, Tom L. Beauchamp and James F. Childress, *Principles of Medical Ethics,* 2nd ed. (New York: Oxford, 1979), Chapter 3; "Autonomy, Paternalism, Community," *The Hastings Center Report* 14 (October, 1984): 5-49.
[19] Tom L. Beauchamp and Laurence B. McCullough, *Medical Ethics, The Responsibilities of Physicians* (New York: Oxford, 1984), Chapter 2.
[20] *Nichomachean Ethics,* 5,13,1137a,30.
[21] John Rawls, *A Theory of Justice* (Cambridge: Belknap Press of Harvard University Press, 1971); Robert Nozick, *Anarchy, State, and Utopia* (New York: Basic Books, 1974).
[22] I have drawn heavily here on the excellent summarizations of the divisions of justice by David Hollenbach, "Modern Catholic Teachings Concerning Justice," in *The Faith That Does Justice, Examining the Christian Sources of Social Change,* ed. John C. Haughey (New York: Paulist Press, 1977), pp. 219-27. For a different and somewhat opposing view, see J. Brian Benestad, "The Catholic Concept of Social Justice: A Historical Perspective," *Communio,* Winter, 1984, pp. 364-81. Benestad argues that the current concepts of social

justice in the United States are the result of a misunderstanding of Aquinas and Pius XI. Benestad places emphasis on the virtue of prudence and the duty of individuals to the common good rather than on rights and claims of individuals on society.

23 See Joseph Owens, op. cit.

24 For a summarization by Rawls of the essential points in his theory, see pages 302-303 of John Rawls, A Theory of Justice, op. cit.

25 John Rawls, ibid, p. 62.

26 Robert Nozick, op. cit.

27 H. Tristram Engelhardt, Jr., Shattuck Lecture, "Allocating Scarce Medical Resources and the Availability of Organ Transplantation, Some Moral Presuppositions," New England Journal of Medicine 311 (July 5, 1984): 66-71.

28 See the citations under notes 2 and 3 above and the papers in The Faith That Does Justice, ed. John Haughey, op. cit., especially the papers by John Langan, "What Jerusalem says to Athens"; by David Hollenbach, "Modern Catholic Teachings Concerning Justice"; by William J. Walsh and John P. Langan, "Patristic Social Consciousness: The Church and the Poor." This collection is an excellent summarization of the relationships of love and justice; I have drawn heavily on the idea of "charitable justice" in my analysis.

29 See note 15 above and Cicero's De Officiis, the vade mecum of later Stoic morality.

30 For an exposition of Paul's notion of Christian justice and love, see John Haughey, "Jesus as the Justice of God," in The Faith That Does Justice, op. cit., pp. 282-88.

31 William J. Walsh and John P. Langan, "Patristic Social Consciousness: The Church and the Poor," op. cit.

32 St. Augustine, Sermon 72, 4, cited by Walsh and Langan, op. cit.

33 The question about the continuity or discontinuity of the supernatural and the natural virtues is still an intriguing one. Robert Sokowloski has examined this relationship in a brilliant monograph, illuminating both kinds of virtue, The God of Faith and Reason (Notre Dame, Indiana: University of Notre Dame Press, 1982).

34 William Frankena, Ethics, 2nd ed. (Englewood Cliffs, New Jersey: Prentice Hall, 1973).

35 Robert Sokowloski, op. cit.

36 Albert Camus, Resistance, Rebellion, and Death (New York: Alfred Knopf, 1961). p. 70.

37 William K. Frankena, op. cit.

38 Romano Guardini, The Lord (Chicago: Henry Regnery, 1954), p. 79.

39 Ibid., p. 84.

40 See William F. May, The Physician's Covenant (Philadelphia: Westminster Press, 1983); Pedro Lain Entalgo, La relación médico-enfermo, historía y teoría (Madrid: Revista de Occidente, 1964), pp. 235-88; and E. D. Pellegrino, "Toward a Reconstruction of Medical Morality: The Primacy of the Act of Profession and the Fact of Illness," The Journal of Medicine and Philosophy 4 (1979).

41 See James Childress' discussion of strong and weak paternalism in Who Should Decide?, op. cit., pp. 102-12.

42 Harvey Cushing, "The Common Devotion," in Consecratio Medici and Their Papers (Boston: Little Brown and Co., 1929), pp. 3-13.

[43] Josef Pieper, *The Four Cardinal Virtues* (Notre Dame, Indiana: University of Notre Dame Press, 1966); also *Summa Theologiae*, IIa,II,ae,47:4-5.

[44] John Paul II, Apostolic Letter, *Salvifici Doloris, On the Christian Meaning of Human Suffering* (Washington, D.C.: U.S. Catholic Conference, 1984).

[45] E. D. Pellegrino, "Catholic Hospitals: Survival Without Moral Compromise," in *Health Progress* (New York: Catholic Health Association of the United States, 1985), pp. 42-49.

[46] 1 Peter ii, 9. See article, "Vocation," in *A Catholic Dictionary*, ed. Donald Attwater, 3rd edition (New York: Macmillan, 1958).

[47] 1 Cor vii, 20. Also, *A Catholic Dictionary, art. cit.*

[48] Paul VI, "Allocution àdes médecins," 18 October 1969, *Documents Pontificaux de Paul VI* (Suisse: Editions Saint Augustin-St. Maurice), 701.

Business: A Vocation to Justice and Love

William J. Byron, S.J.

In the first draft of their famous pastoral letter on "Catholic Social Teaching and the U.S. Economy," the Catholic bishops of the United States make the following interesting and quite challenging assertion: "The work of business people, managers, investors, and financiers is a genuine Christian vocation when carried out as a form of stewardship."[1] In making this statement, and indeed in undertaking the project of drafting a pastoral on the economy, the bishops acknowledge that they want "to encourage and support a needed renewal of this sense of vocation in the business community."[2]

This essay will attempt to facilitate that "needed renewal" by discussing the notions of vocation and stewardship in the context of the United States business system. Business is a true vocation "when carried out as a form of stewardship." And stewardship, as I will argue below, is a work of justice and love. It should be acknowledged here at the beginning and remembered as this argument develops that an ethical reflection deals with what ought to be; it is not a simple description of what is. If ethics ruled the world of business, the world of business would be a better place. A vocation to business implies an opportunity to better the human condition through business. One need not be ill in order to get better. Hence, the notion of a vocation to business is not an implied condemnation of business. It is a positive idea with potential for releasing ethical energies capable of bringing the "is" of business a good deal closer to the "ought."

In the United States, it is commonplace for persons to express their interest in what others "do." "How do you do?," is a conventional greeting. "What do you do?," is a question of far greater interest; so much so, that it amounts to a problem which is not new in America. It was brought to our attention in 1968 by the report of the Kerner Commission which made the point by quoting Daniel Patrick Moynihan:

> In America what you do is what you are: to do nothing is to be nothing; to do little is to be little. The equations are implacable and blunt, and ruthlessly public.[3]

Moynihan was writing about the importance of employment and the devastating effects of unemployment for blacks. The problem of doing over being is a very real one for poor blacks. It has serious implications for members of any socio-economic group. It has special relevance in a reflection on the idea of vocation in a business context.

A vocation is, of course, a call. Ordinarily, it is a call to do something, but it is more than that. In every instance, it is a call to be something. More precisely, it is a call to be someone. The being is more important than the doing.

As Thomas Merton used to explain to young Trappist monks who consulted him as they struggled with the decision to remain in or leave religious life, it is more correct theologically to say, "I am a vocation," than, "I have a vocation."[4] In this view, a vocation is not something that comes and goes; it is not something that can be "lost" like luggage during air travel. The person is the call. The call may take the person, in fidelity to the will of the Caller, in or out of religious life. The call may lead into business or any other occupation. The vocation is the called person with all of his or her changeabilities. The person called depends on the Caller for life itself and for the occupational definition of that life. The Caller is, by nature, faithful to the person called. The person called is, by nature, fickle and frail. If the person called is to be faithful to the call, he or she must become intent on maintaining fidelity to the Caller. Such maintenance is the work of prayer, but it is more than that. Theologically speaking, it is the gift of grace. It takes grace to remain faithful to the God who calls. No matter what the occupational circumstances of the called person, the call received (involving, as it does, both prayer and grace) is a call to holiness. Holiness is a precondition to fidelity in the person called. "The call to holiness is addressed to every Christian, in every walk of life."[5] As the bishops put it in their pastoral on the economy, "Sanctity is the vocation not only of bishops, priests and religious, but it is equally the call of parents, workers, business people and politicians."[6]

The task, therefore, of the called person is to cooperate with grace and grow in holiness as a way of maintaining one's availability, responsibility, and fidelity to the God who never stops calling. Where God's call will lead the called person is, for the person called, the challenge of discernment. One may never assume, as one relates to a God of both mystery and majesty, that a call to a particular set of occupational circumstances is an over-and-done, once-and-for-all thing. The called person may be called to something else. Or, more likely, the called person may be called to do something new within the broad occupational context of an earlier call. In every case, however, and at all moments in the journey of faith, the person is called to be faithful to the Caller. In this sense, the person is the vocation regardless of what the person does.

The focus of these reflections will, therefore, be on the person in business—the person whose vocation is business, the called person whose discernment, decisions, and daily responsiveness to the Caller is in the context of business.

As I noted by citing the bishops in the opening sentence of this essay, the qualifier that differentiates business as a "genuine Christian vocation" from business as a happenstance situation is the condition that business be "carried out as a form of stewardship."

I have written a small book on stewardship;[7] I will take just a paragraph or two here to outline the notion of stewardship and some of its implications. The idea of stewardship is essentially this: wealth possessed is held in trust for others. The possession of wealth involves social responsibilities. "The earth is the Lord's, and the fulness thereof" (Psalm 24:1). God is the owner. Humans, who may hold legal title, do not really own; they manage and care for that which God intends to be at the service of all. Human interaction with the land and natural resources produces wealth. Entrepreneur, industrialist, innovator, organizer, worker—all are called to interact with the land and natural resources, but always as stewards, as managers and developers, not as owners in any absolute sense that would leave them unaccountable to God and their fellow humans. They are to be rewarded for their risk, worry and work, but not to a point where the wealth produced is withheld from meeting the essential needs of others who are within their reach or reasonable range of influence.

Some of my friends in business are not comfortable with the idea of stewardship. They say the notion smacks of communism, socialism at the very least. It is a concept, they say, that is hostile to capitalism. This problem, I think, has to be handled with prayer. Can a creature, conscious of his or her real and eternal relationship to the Creator, remain convinced for long that private ownership is, in the true sense of the word, absolute?

The immaterial realities of God's creation also come as gifts to humans. Imagination, spirit, creativity, and intellectual capacities are all to be held in trust, managed well, and put to the service of others. This is a requirement of stewardship. Invariably, a rise to positions of influence and leadership in business is a function of one's possession of material and immaterial gifts which are really not one's own. The person in a position of power is a steward. Failure to recognize this inevitably produces a spiritual problem for the individual in question and a societal problem of badly used, inadequately shared, and insufficiently conserved resources.

The vocation to business requires stewardship. Stewardship, in turn, requires a spirituality that keeps these realities in proper perspective.

Spirituality, as Doris Donnelly has said so well, is "prayer elevated to a lifestyle." The called person in business must be a praying person; otherwise, contact with the Caller will be lost, and both discernment and decisions can go astray. Prayerful reflection on the gifts of creation and on the graciousness of the Creator, whose essence is love and whose promise is fidelity, will shape in the person of prayer attitudes which, in turn, will shape a lifestyle, a lifestyle characterized by gratitude. The prayerful sense of wonder has a way of producing a practical sense of gratitude. Gratitude, rooted in a prayerful relationship to the Creator, is a safeguard against insensitivity, pride, avarice, and greed — qualities that contradict the idea of stewardship. The called person, whose stewardship is practical in business, will, if faithful to the call, exhibit traits of character that reflect compassion, humility, and trustworthiness. Character, of course, is the internal source of external behavior. Success in the business vocation, as vocation, is not a matter of luck; it is a question of character. In this connection, it is interesting to note that the Greek word *ethos,* the root form of *ethica* (ethics), referred to a person's fundamental orientation toward life. Originally, the word meant a dwelling place. With Aristotle, it came to mean an inner dwelling place or what we have come to call character.[8] The ethical person in business is the person of sound character.

In an essay on "The Ethics of Stewardship,"[9] I mentioned that stewardship says that no human person owns anything absolutely and that everything we possess we hold in trust. I then added:

> The conditions of that trust are set by the Creator who "entrusts" to our care varying proportions of material creation. An ethic of stewardship concerns itself with fidelity to, and violations of, that trust.
> The unethical steward is the person who violates that trust (1) by neglecting to care for that which has been entrusted; (2) by destroying without adequate reason the substance of that which has been entrusted; or (3) by appropriating or assigning to oneself the exclusive use of that which has been entrusted, and doing so in a way which denies the legitimate claims of others.

For examples of settings in which these ethical considerations might be raised, think of land ownership in rural America, plant ownership in smokestack industries of the United States, or those escalating and inflated financial activities far removed from the production of goods and services, but closely linked to disproportionately high personal rewards.

It is my view that the character required of the good steward, the ethical person in business, is one marked by virtues available to us only through divine grace. It is also my view that the contradictory vices (selfishness, avarice, greed) are sins or sinful tendencies which await the healing power of divine grace.

Again, the bishops of the United States in their pastoral on the economy were theological realists when they remarked that people in business are called to holiness, and sanctity is the vocation of "workers, business people and politicians" just as much as it is the vocation of "bishops, priests and religious." They would acknowledge, of course,

that the "what is" among bishops, priests and religious, no less than
among workers, business people and politicians, falls considerably
short of "what ought to be."

Later in this essay, mention will be made of the unavoidable influence of structures on behavior, of organizations on individuals. But,
there is no escaping the question of individual integrity and the
development of one's own character in this discussion of the vocation
to business. Organizations are collections of individuals; structures are
relationships between and among individuals. There is a pressing need
today for active business leaders to think about the integration of
human values with economic institutions, as they think about their
own integrity and character.

Only persons active in the business system of the United States know
to what extent they are influenced by that system and the way they
themselves can influence others in that system. They can also influence
the system itself. This reciprocal influence goes on—for better or
worse—every day. Is the result of this reciprocal influence of human
persons and corporate structures depersonalizing and dehumanizing,
or is it life-enhancing and affirmative of human values? Those who feel
this tension may be experiencing a call (within their call to business) to
contribute what they can to a further humanization of the business
system. I am raising questions here, not rendering judgments. I think
those who are now in the system and have with them a properly
cultivated sense of vocation will have the clarity of moral vision to see
the system's goodness, despite its failings, and the moral courage to
recognize the failings as they note the system's virtues.

Those now in the system, if they take a moment to reflect (I have
suggested that they should be persons of prayer), and if they are free
enough to respond non-defensively (prayer yields that kind of
freedom), could address the questions of depersonalization and de-
humanization for their own benefit and for the benefit of those who
will follow them into the system. Is is true, for instance, that in comparison with the welfare of the corporation, the welfare of the individual person in that corporation does not really matter? Is the price
of employment in the corporation the surrender of individuality? Is
corporate life in the United States diminishing of human potential?
Again, these are questions, not assertions. It should satisfy no one of
integrity to say, "Yes, but our corporately produced goods or services
do a lot for others." The fundamental question is not whether the
product serves a useful purpose but rather, "What happens to the pro-
ducers in the production?" Those in the system know. Whatever it is,
for good or ill, has been happening to them. They can determine to do
what they can to make the system more friendly to human potential. Is
a humanistic capitalism possible? The question deserves examination
inside out, beginning with the personal experience of those now inside
the corporations.

Max Lerner observes in contemporary America "the continuing ero-
sion of the ideal of work and the satisfaction of a task well done; mean-
ingful work has been replaced by the job, in which the goal is to give as
little of yourself as possible, to get as much for it as possible and to
retire as soon as possible."[10] Would those now inside the corporations
agree or disagree?

To bring some of these questions and concepts closer to the everyday
experience of business, I have decided to "mine" the June 24, 1985,
issue of *Fortune*. This decision limits, of course, the universe of individuals in business whose example could tell us something about the
human side of enterprise and the reciprocal influence of persons and
organizations in business. It just so happens that the *Fortune* cover
story for that issue deals with "The Executive Addict." Since addiction
to drugs and alcohol is found among physicians, lawyers, clergy and
others, there is no particular significance to an examination of addiction in the corporate context, except insofar as the context might encourage the addiction. There is no evidence that the business environment is more likely to induce addiction than the medical, legal,
parochial, or political. The opposite could indeed be argued. But, the
Fortune cover story does provide a glimpse of "A Boss Who Stepped
In" and an instance of corporate compassion for the troubled individual. David J. Mahoney, former chairman of Norton Simon, Inc.,
was recommended for the *Fortune* interview by a New Jersey drug-
treatment specialist experienced in the care of corporate executives.
Mahoney is legendary as a tough-minded chief executive officer. Less
well known was the firm but almost fraternal approach he took to the
problem of addiction among subordinates when he was running a
company. His words are instructive:

> "You've got to tell him in a no-nonsense but nonthreatening way that
> you and his colleagues know about his drug use."
> "Make him aware that you are concerned that he is harming not only
> his career, but also his marriage and family."
> "If you make them feel secure, they're much more willing to help
> themselves. I tell them that we'll send them on a trip or check them into
> a hospital on a hernia diagnosis." Mahoney would thus provide "cover"
> as well as reemployment assurance for the person with the problem.
> Explaining the importance of visits by the boss to the employee in the
> treatment center, Mahoney said: "This relieves the pressure at home.
> You know, his wife is scared, and during treatment a lot of her aggres-
> sions come out. If you show how much you care this way, they'll both
> relax. At least the executive (i.e., the patient) will not have to be fighting
> on three fronts."

Mahoney would take the executive back, even after relapses. "The
key question is, is there improvement, is he really trying?" There are,
however, cases where—for the sake of the company—the boss must
fire the executive. "Yes, you are allowed to give up. But the tom-toms

in an organization will know that you tried your best to help a guy. Even if you lost him, the next one will be more willing to come forward. And when help works, the company is infinitely better off. You develop a loyalty that transcends business."[11]

An unrelated story in the same issue of *Fortune* describes the efforts of Anthony J. F. (Tony) O'Reilly, chief executive officer of the H. J. Heinz Co., the food-processing giant, to cut costs. Production efficiencies, not cheaper raw materials, will reduce costs, according to O'Reilly's strategy; some of the wider operating margin will regard shareholders, but significant portions will be spent on new products and additional advertising. An interesting dimension of the story is related by *Fortune* as follows:

> If Heinz's operating managers need any further incentive to save, O'Reilly's determination to eliminate one layer of management should spur action. The idea is to force decision-making further down the hierarchy, under what the company calls the principle of subsidiarity. Compensation is structured accordingly. "We pay very little money for coming to work," says O'Reilly. About two-thirds of the pay of each of the top 300 managers takes the form of performance incentives based on everything from brand profitability to corporate return on shareholders' equity. To further power the drive to cut costs, some of the Super Fund money [O'Reilly's term for the savings accumulated through cost reduction] will be distributed as bonuses to those who survive the pruning of the managerial ranks.[12]

This could represent a classic managerial tension between corporate efficiency and executive fulfillment. With the targeted responsibilities resulting from the application of the "principle of subsidiarity," some managers will not only experience the fuller "stretch" of managerial responsibility, but they will also win greater financial rewards. They will be paid relatively little just "for coming to work"; they will derive the deeper satisfaction of earning as opposed to simply receiving their higher rewards. But, what about the managers who fail to produce the right numbers? There will be no place for them at Heinz. Similarly, there will be job losses for production workers displaced by additional automation and other cost-cutting production innovations. "Under the whip of Chief Executive Tony O'Reilly," says *Fortune*, "Heinz managers are squeezing the last penny of excess cost out of all 57 varieties, and then squeezing some more. Profits are flowing."[13]

So is the ketchup. One can only speculate about possible managerial bloodletting and loss of production jobs at Heinz. And, one can only hope the system will be capable of absorbing those for whom there is no longer room in that corner of the economy controlled by Heinz.

In still another article in the issue of *Fortune* I have at hand, the question of loyalty arises in the context of "The Soft Drink Wars: The Next Battle."[14] Coca Cola and PepsiCo are now battling one another in the non-cola soft drink market. Pepsi has a new soft drink called

Slice; Coke now has Minute Maid Orange Soda. Coca Cola's extension into orange soda pits the cola giant against Sunkist and Crush, holders respectively of 1.5 percent and one percent of the soft drink market in an industry where one percent of the market is worth three hundred million dollars in retail sales. As *Fortune* explains, Coca Cola and Pepsico will have to persuade bottlers across the nation to take their new products:

> Bottlers have a symbiotic but occasionally fractious relationship with the syrup makers. Although Coke and Pepsi own some of their own bottling companies, most bottlers are still independent. They do the bulk of their business selling colas, counting on Dr Pepper, Sunkist and other non-colas to fill out their line. But because exclusive contracts with the syrup makers prevent bottlers from distributing competing brands, the cola giants must persuade them to drop established products to take on Slice or Minute Maid Orange Soda.[15]

Fortune asked Charles Millard, chairman of the $600-million-a-year Coca Cola Bottling Company of New York, the second largest Coke bottler, whether he intends to drop Sunkist for Minute Maid. Even though Coca Cola owns thirty-one percent of Millard's company, he has decided to stick with Sunkist. "They have made a big investment in this company and in our business. The smart bottlers will leave the dance with the girl they came with."[16] Loyalties run in many directions; their pull can add tension to human relations within and around a business enterprise.

One last selection from the June 24, 1985, issue of *Fortune* provides a profile on Edward L. Hennessy, Jr., "Allied-Signal's Tough Skipper."[17] In summarizing the article, *Fortune* notes: "The proposed merger of Allied Corp. and Signal Cos. will combine two huge companies and three strong executives. The job of holding it all together will go to Edward Hennessy, a onetime candidate for the priesthood who's 'as tough and as mean as they come.' " The assessment of toughness is the quoted opinion of an unnamed investment banker. *Fortune* acknowledges that "others find Hennessy remarkably warm, open-minded and fair," and then goes on to make its own non-committal comment: "Hennessy's abhorrence of scandal and gossip either is evidence of a strong moral code or proof of prissiness."[18]

The article makes a lot of Hennessy's three years in the seminary and reports his uncomplicated reason for dropping out: "I just didn't have the calling." But, he did and does still have a calling to business. Business is the vocation of all the people *Fortune* profiles. I suspect very few of them think of it that way. But, the point of the argument I have been making and am about to resume is that business is just as much a vocation as priesthood, medicine, teaching, or the law. It just is not regarded as such. Moreover, as regard for business as vocation rises, so will the humanistic quality of the business and corporate environment.

The vocation under consideration in this essay is a call to justice and love. That might be said of any Christian called, of any Christian calling. Justice, we would acknowledge even without the prompting of Pope Paul VI, "is love's absolute minimum." The "new" Christian commandment (John 15:12) is a call beyond the Old Testament norm to which the gospel of St. Matthew refers (7:12) in relating Jesus' teaching to "Treat others the way you would have them treat you: this sums up the law and the prophets." He was speaking of the Old Law. St. John records a new law of love given by Jesus to his followers: "Love one another as I have loved you." Not as you would have the other love you, but as Jesus loved you—to the point, therefore, of laying down your life for the other. That represents a significant leap beyond an Old Law justice that does not tax individual self interest quite so heavily.

We live under a new law of love—to love one another, not simply as we love ourselves, but as Christ loved us. He laid down his life for us. We are expected to be prepared to lay down our lives for one another. We have a new law of love to live up to. I see this law as applicable to us on a day-to-day basis; we lay down our lives for one another day by day—in considerate behavior, courtesy, service, sacrifice—in business or wherever else our vocations place us.

Our prophet, Jesus Christ, is also priest; and not only priest, but victim as well. To imitate this prophet means to enter into His paschal mystery. The Jesus who, as rabbi, taught His disciples to treat others as they would have others treat them; the Jesus who, as rabbi, required His disciples to live according to the law and the prophets, actually changed the lesson He taught by His own subsequent teaching on the night before He died, the night He established His priesthood. He then, as priest, translated His farewell discourse—particularly His "new commandment" of love—into action, the action which we remember now in the breaking of the bread. This action is the death by which we live. It is the action which was His as priest and victim; it is ours as sacrament and sacrifice. The baptized person who is called to business must not, when answering that call, leave these theological and religious realities behind.

Before leaving this quite positive, and what cynics would dismiss as an other-worldly view of love, inapplicable to the world of business, I want to borrow from the this-worldly wisdom of Harold Geneen whose management credentials are well known. He saw the way self love, the reversal of the Christian ideal, can hurt a business enterprise. "No one has yet devised a reasonable basis for measuring what a company should have accomplished as opposed to what it did accomplish and how much of that lost potential was caused by the blinded, closed minds of men wrapped in self-love." [19]

No need to apologize for regarding business as a vocation to love when you have the retired chairman of I.T.T. reflecting on this ex-

136

perience and finding that self love, the contradiction of the Christian
ideal, is, in fact, bad for business. That love is really good for business
requires daily demonstration in the deeds of those whose lives are
rooted in the "good news" of Jesus Christ.

As a call to love, therefore, the business vocation simply provides a
particular context for one's living out the so-called "new commandment." Business deals with material reality, with scarcity and limitation, with goods and services that are not so easily shared as immaterial
reality, like knowledge, might be. In dealing with material reality,
people tend to gather in and hold (if not hoard), rather than open up
and give.

Economics is an intellectual discipline, a way of knowing what people are likely to do if they behave rationally in relationship to their external, material environment, and to one another, as they share that
environment which is the very basis for their material existence. And,
a given business system is a way of imposing some order on those personal interrelationships in the struggle to meet material needs. The
system develops its own way of doing things. It fashions its own institutional arrangements for production and distribution of goods and services intended to meet material needs of people.

The potential for materialism, a preoccupation with the material
side of existence to the exclusion of the immaterial and spiritual, is
great in any business system. The person called to business must
beware of materialism. This warning is not just for the rich and powerful; it applies to everyone. We all need material things. We all know
the way "need" can expand to "want," and we never seem to be quite
ready to fix the boundary of "enough." We know the way "things" can
crowd "ideas" out of our range of interest. We also recognize our
capability of valuing and protecting property in our possession over
persons not closely related to us. (And even when the relationship is
close, we sometimes act as if the dented fender is of greater value than
the offending driver, the money lost of greater value than the child
who lost it, the damaged machine of greater worth than the distracted
machinist.) All of us have a great potential for materialism! But, we
have a greater potential for love, the immaterial reality that is the
"stuff" of the "new commandment" which calls all of us to love one
another and some of us to do so in the business system.

I promised earlier to bring structures and systems into this discussion. They are human constructs which take on a life of their own.
Like it or not, they do condition behavior. The words "system" and
"structure" are often used interchangeably. A third word, "institution," is often part of the same mix. I think of a social structure as an
institutionalized set of interdependent relationships.[20] Structures influence social behavior. They regulate the life chances, the potential
for human development available to persons at given times and places.
I favor the use of "system" as a more comprehensive term than "struc-

ture." Within a given system, a variety of structures (institutionalized sets of interdependent relationships) will be found. For instance, prison life and appeals courts are structures within a criminal justice system. Wage structures and market structures are part of the business or economic system. And yet, we often speak of market systems, wage systems, prison systems, and court systems. So, the distinction is not crucial. It is crucial, however, to have a correct understanding of institution. It should be regarded as "a way of doing things," not as something designed by an architect and fixed in stone, concrete, or other building materials. Institutions are constructs of the human mind, reflective of human values and set in human behavior patterns. Slavery was an institution in America. It serves as a reminder, among other things, that institutions can be changed. Marriage is an institution, so is dating. Think of the institutionalized sets of arrangements that constitute an economy, and recognize their potential for change under the impulse of love and toward the goal of justice—love's absolute minimum.

One hears of oppressive and depersonalizing structures and systems. My preference for structure over system is tactical and, perhaps, ideological. I think it is wiser from a tactical point of view to aim analysis and corrective action at structures (the critical parts) rather than at systems (the whole). From an ideological perspective, I see no need to replace the United States' business system with something altogether different. I see a need to work for structural reform within the system in order to enhance the participation of all those the system should be serving. I have in mind particularly the poor and the unemployed. This, it seems to me, is an important part of the vocation of the person called to business.

Emily Stipes Watts has written an interesting book on *The Businessman in American Literature*.[21] In it, she describes Ralph Ellison's Invisible Man as one who has had "to escape from corrupt corporate capitalism, from suffocating communism, from selfish unionism, from social and racist paternalism, from racial prejudice and militancy, from insanity, and from many other evils in order to proclaim and affirm the meaning of the Tinker"[22] (a term expressing an embodiment of the innovator-inventor-entrepreneur like Ford and Edison, and running back through American technological-business history to Benjamin Franklin). Although not finally an inventor of gadgets, Ellison's Invisible Man draws this insight from his reflection on experience:

> Now I know men are different and that all life is divided and that only in division is there true health. Hence again I have stayed in my hole, because up above there's an increasing passion to make all men conform to a pattern. . . .
>
> Whence all this passion toward conformity anyway?—diversity is the word. Let man keep his many parts and you'll have no tyrant states.[23]

138

BUSINESS:

Ellison's book was published in 1952. Have we progressed to a point of
rendering this kind of rhetoric quaint, or is the "passion toward conformity" still presumed to be a precondition of successful upward
mobility in the typical business organization and the larger business
society? For at least a decade after World War II, the uniform of
business was the "gray flannel suit." It yielded, of course, to IBM blue,
but fashions aside, to what extent does the stereotypical expectation
persist — conformity in dress, behavior, and lifestyle? Is the formula for
"How to Succeed in Business" simply doing it "the company way," or is
there more room today for self determination and personal fulfillment
in business?

In his essay, "The Major Novelists View the American Businessman," excerpted from the *Wharton Quarterly* and published in *The
New York Times* on June 29, 1975, Dr. Robert F. Lucid, chairman of
the graduate group in the University of Pennsylvania's Department of
English, suggests that it is possible to envision a society in a micro-
cosmic way, and the microcosm used by many novelists — Hemingway,
for example — to symbolize all of our social institutions is the military.
"For him (Hemingway) the military is a perfect symbol, revealing the
essence of institutionality, for it acknowledges candidly what most institutions — including industry, of course — often cover up. It acknowledges that, by comparison with the welfare of the institution, the welfare of the individual doesn't matter." Is the vocation to business a call
to resign oneself to this kind of personal oblivion, or is it a challenge to
commit oneself to do whatever one can to humanize the system, to protect the person from the depersonalizing potential of those pressures
for conformity within any complex organization? To the extent that
the business vocation is a call to justice and love, there can be no doubt
about the answer to that question. It cannot be answered easily. And,
in every case it must first be answered from within:

> Our very life depends on everything's
> Recurring till we answer from within.
> The thousandth time may prove the charm.
>
> Robert Frost, "Snow."

The integrity of the person in business and the "very life," humanis-
tically speaking, of the system itself depend on attempts, well beyond
"the thousandth time," to permit that which is most human in each
participant; namely, the impulse for justice and love, to flower and
flourish. It requires of each participant in the system an "answer from
within."

Justice, as I have already indicated, is love's absolute minimum. It is
something of an anomaly, however, that the higher virtue love is more
readily understood and accepted in its demands than justice. There is
something of a cultural contradiction in a Christian society which
acknowledges love as a central value and tolerates injustice in its
economic arrangements. The vocation to business places a daily "lay-

down-your-life" demand (the new commandment of love) on the
Christian whose call it is to work for justice in and through the business
system. Without justice, love is absent. Without love, a Christian
presence in the business system, or anywhere else, is illusory.

In turning now more directly to the notion of justice, I want to make
two transitional comments. First, if the argument thus far sounds
idealistic, naïve, or otherwise unrelated to the real world of business,
that should be taken as a measure of the distance the Christian called
to business must travel if the business vocation is to have any meaning
whatsoever. If love and justice are not part of it, the Christian in
business is demonstrably deaf to a God who calls. Second, if the drift of
this argument seems excessively individualistic and insufficiently
systematic, it is not intended to be. Such an impression does, however,
correctly reflect my understanding of the implications of Mark
1:14-15: "After John had been arrested, Jesus went into Galilee. There
he proclaimed the Good News from God. 'The time has come,' he
said, 'and the kingdom of God is close at hand. Repent, and believe
the Good News.' " The call to "repent" means, of course, a personal
metanoia. It requires a value reversal, a change of heart, a new
outlook, a personal conversion. The point of this personal turnaround
is a grasp of the kingdom values of justice and love. The values are "at
hand," but not yet grasped. With the grasping comes a fresh perspective, a new mindset. It is my view that this is a matter of personal conversion dependent on grace. As more and more persons grasp the "at
hand" kingdom values, the community constituted by those persons
and the organizations they populate will themselves embody the kingdom values. It will not happen unless we, individually and collectively,
"answer from within."

To live is to adjust. The question in the case of a Christian called to
business is: who is adjusting to whom (or what)? Does the system impose a conformity that impedes a full and free response to a God who
never stops calling? Or, does the called Christian impose upon the
system adjustments conducive to love and justice? For the Christian,
the answer to that question is a measure of vocational integrity. With
these transitional comments, I turn to the question of justice.

The relationship of the business vocation to the idea of justice will be
better understood to the extent that an image of justice is also grasped.
The plumb-line image in the Book of Amos is useful: "I am going to
measure my people Israel by a plumb-line; no longer will I overlook
their offenses" (Amos 7:8). The nation is to be measured for its
uprightness, its integrity. Sidewalk superintendents and others fascin-
ated by building construction activity know that the plumb-bob points
to the exact center of the earth. The string between the surveyor's
fingers, holding the bob, and the bob itself is plumb or "upright." It is
an image of justice. Construction-related phrases like "on the level,"
"up and up," "fair and square" become the vocabulary of
justice—human relationships measured for plumb-line integrity.

Another image of justice is the familiar scales of justice—trays in balance on a scale. The figure holding equally balanced trays or scales has, since antiquity, been a symbol of justice.

Relationships in the world of business which are uneven are not necessarily unjust. If you want to inspect the justice quality of the relationship, you must first establish relatedness. In the symbol, it would be relatedness between the trays; in business, it would be relatedness between persons—one to one, one to group or organization, organization to individual, organization to organization, system to society. Not every imbalance is also an injustice. An imbalance is an injustice when one side's advantage (the down tray) has been taken unfairly at the expense of the other side (the up tray). Related to the downside gain is an upside injury (in-*jure*), a violation of the other's right. If the beneficiary of the downside gain is the perpetrator of the upside injury, then the relatedness is obvious and direct, i.e., I cheated the other party and thus gained the advantage. If the advantage is really a passive benefit derived from an injury inflicted on the other party from another source (even by impersonal social forces), the relatedness is not so clear. The closer my relatedness to the source of injury, the deeper my implication in the injustice and the greater my obligation to bring the trays into balance.

The person called to work for justice in the world of business will grow more sensitive to justice issues by adopting the scales of justice as a framework through which he or she can simply look at business reality. One begins by locating oneself (owner, manager, producer, consumer) or one's group (firm, industry, union, association, profession) on one of the two trays. In any business relationship, one's tray will be balanced over against the other, or in a disadvantaged upward position, or weighted with a downside gain. What problems in the world of business and the larger society are in no way related to you and your firm? What problems are related, and to what extent does that relationship involve obligations in justice? Few, if any, problems in a business society will survive scrutiny through the framework of the scales of justice without revealing some trace, however slight, of relatedness to any participant in the system. To deny the possibility of relatedness is to pretend to avoid moral participation in the system; it would also negate the notion of vocation in business.

There are those today who simply deny the existence of economic rights. In their pastoral letter on the economy, the bishops of the United States make a point of stressing the existence of economic rights that are going unprotected today. Society is far more protective of civil and political rights—like the rights to vote, to assemble, and to speak freely—than it is of economic rights to food, employment, housing, and health care. The bishops explain our failure in this regard as stemming from (1) our tendency to give primacy to civil and political rights, (2) our inability to agree on the means to assure economic rights

WILLIAM J. BYRON, S.J.   141

once we grant their existence, and (3) individual and corporate
selfishness that runs deep in our society.[24]

In an exchange with Milton Friedman, upon whose paper I was in-
vited to comment in a symposium on the pastoral letter, April 23-24,
1985, at the University of California, Berkeley, I discovered still
another reason for resistance to the notion of economic rights. In com-
menting on John Kenneth Galbraith's paper, delivered earlier in the
symposium, I outlined the bishops' discussion of economic rights. Dr.
Friedman took the occasion of his presentation the next night to
separate himself from the position that economic rights exist. "For instance," he said, "if a person has a right to food, then someone else has
an obligation to produce that food." That was unacceptable to him. I
pointed out that the bishops were not saying quite that. They were
calling for full participation in the economic system so that all people
would have the means to produce or purchase food, shelter, and other
economic necessities. Those who could not participate still had a right
to the necessities, and the system, therefore, should, by some form of
sharing, acknowledge that right. It became clearer to me then that Dr.
Friedman's moral vision which, in his words, "differed profoundly"
from that of the bishops, was influenced by a species of materialism
that touches many others today. I am not referring to a callous, selfish
consumerism or a greedy grasp on wealth. I do see, however, a
readiness to grant rights in the area of immaterial reality (speech, vote,
belief, knowledge), where sharing does not require one with more to
yield from his or her possession in favor of one with less, and a
resistance to the recognition of rights in the realm of material things,
where one must have less if another is to have more. The "pain" of
sharing is eased, of course, to the extent that the pie produced grows
ever larger. But as limits set it, rights to food, shelter, employment,
and health care carry a higher price. Willingness to pay the price is not
unrelated to recognition of the existence of economic rights.

The justice issue involves an unavoidable return to the notion of
stewardship. And stewardship, it will be recalled, is the condition that
qualifies business activity for the status of "a genuine Christian vocation." The person called to business is, therefore, a steward whose
fidelity to the call will bring, in every instance, some measure of love
and justice to the business system. Infidelity to the call and insensitivity
to the demands of love and justice are always possible. We see abun-
dant evidence of that. Also possible is the grace of fidelity. We have
the promise of that in abundance. Cooperation with that grace is
everybody's business every day. That is just another way of understanding the meaning of vocation. Everybody has one. Everybody is
one. Business is one environment wherein much of that cooperation is
intended to take place. If that cooperation is of true vocational quality, the level of both justice and love in business will surely rise.

Realism requires the acknowledgment that the world of business is a

place where hard heads are expected to rule over soft hearts, where
hard drivers take hard lines on the way to hard bargains. Some would
say that to survive in business one must have a "killer instinct." The
Sunday-School picnic belongs to a world far distant from the three-
martini lunch. Or does it?

It is a competitive world, the world of business. It is often called a
"jungle" and rarely regarded as a safe harbor for the meek and humble
of heart. Attention must, therefore, be paid, in any reflection on the
vocation to business, to the hard edge of business reality.

Business does not own the word reality. Love and justice, poetry and
philosophy are just as real as buying and selling, hiring and firing,
profit and loss. So are kindness, caring, forgiveness, and love real. But,
reality's hard edge is more evident in business, probably because our
ways of doing business not only tolerate but encourage and reward
hardness in those multiple human relationships that weave the basket
we call business. No one should be scandalized by this. Life has its
hard edges. Conflict is to be expected. The only conflict-free zone in
human society is the cemetery. So, it is really a question of the way we
deal with conflict, not a matter of pretending that conflicts do not or
should not exist.

Life is always uneven, often unfair. The person called to business as
a vocation aimed at promoting justice and love (and what other
business vocation is there?) has to carry some protective principles into
the business arena. This is nothing new. Throughout the ages, wisdom
has had its warnings for those facing hard practical realities. One example from Confucius will suffice:

> Fan Ch'ih inquired about what was essential in a moral life. Confucius
> answered, "At home be serious; in business be earnest; in relations with
> other men be conscientious. Although you may be living among bar-
> barians, these principles cannot be neglected.[25]

Principles cannot be neglected. This simple statement is something
of a first principle for those called to business. But, what are the principles? Where can they be found?

The ancient scriptures are replete with moral principles. So are the
oral and written traditions of virtually every nation and culture.
Modern codes of business ethics are often general, occasionally
platitudinous, but helpful nonetheless. Moral maxims still decorate
schoolroom walls and are sometimes proffered in poster art. In a society of slogans like our own, T-shirts dialogue with bumper stickers in
moral discourse that is no threat to Plato but simply indicative of our
penchant for reducing principles of action to crisp phrases or short
sentences.

The person called to business should, through proper self interest
and regard for the system, look within and around for well articulated
principles capable of guiding personal commitment and preserving
personal integrity. Even the most unreflective person could recall some

appropriate principles: "Honesty is the best policy." "Do unto others as you would have them do unto yourself," "Early to bed, early to rise. . . ." Serious study and deeper reflection will produce a longer list, but the point of the exercise should be the quality of the principles, not the quantity of the moral maxims. Since most people tend to confuse thinking with rearrangement of their prejudices, thought directed to construction of a principles list must be disciplined, disinterested and, above all, honest.

It is possible for a person of complete good will to be both quite honest and dead wrong. Honesty refers to a moral condition. A dishonest person deceives others knowingly and willfully, and this, of course, is morally wrong. But, an honest person can also be wrong. Without intending to deceive, an honest person can mislead himself or herself and others as well. Latin is precise in defining a lie: *locutio contra mentem*. The "locution"—external word, sign, or gesture—is contrary to what the mind knows to be true. What if the mind is mis-or ill-informed? The external "locution" can accurately convey the internal knowledge (no deceit intended), but the message communicated is simply wrong. Hence, the person in business should guard against self deception in framing principles that will guide business choices and practical policies. The reflective business person will want to ask: "What do I really stand for?" "Where do I draw the line?" "What is most important to me?" "What do I want to do with my life?" "What does it mean to be human?" "What is the basis of human dignity?" "To whom and for what am I ultimately responsible?" "Where are my moral boundaries?" "What are the measures of success?"

Reflection on these and similar questions will yield not just answers, but declarative statements of principle which define values and direct action.

It is not enough to look for a code of ethics written by someone else. Nor is it sufficient to take the Ten Commandments or the Golden Rule and adopt these as a guide to business behavior. What is needed is for persons in the system to write their own specifications of principled behavior for the world in which they work, principles of behavior to which they can commit themselves. Aware of their capacity for self deception, such persons should be willing to disclose their principles to certain trusted others whom they respect for their experience, their integrity and, let us say it, their holiness. If such persons are hard to find, their scarcity only serves to emphasize the need for the kind of reflection I am recommending; it underscores the need for a reduction of principles to paper so that they can be recalled and translated into practice.

Cynics will say this cannot be done. Many business people will regard it as not worth trying. Some would fear certain defeat when they tested their principles in the marketplace. As one writer, drawing on both his experience in business and his creative imagination, put it, "the only mintage that paid the piper was hard cash, so that our talents and principles ceased to be strengths and became shackles; so that we found ourselves not exalted but enfeebled by our best and noblest qualities, left by the roadside to scavenge among our memories while the rest of life rushed by, noisy and heedless and hoggish."[26]

I am personally convinced that it is not and need not be that way in business. This is not to say that business is as it ought to be. Far from it. I would argue that God is calling people to business to bring the "is" closer to the "ought" and, in the process, find greater fulfillment through a gift of self for justice and love.

NOTES

[1] See *Origins* (the Documentary Service of the National Catholic News Service, 1312 Massachusetts Avenue, N.W., Washington, D.C. 20005) 14 (November 15, 1984), p. 354, No. 122.

[2] *Ibid.*

[3] *Report of the National Advisory Commission on Civil Disorders* (New York: Bantam Books, 1968), p. 252.

[4] See Colman McCarthy, *Disturbers of the Peace* (Boston: Houghton Mifflin Company, 1973), pp. 67-68.

[5] "Catholic Social Teaching and the U.S. Economy," *op. cit.*, No. 326.

[6] *Ibid.*

[7] *Toward Stewardship: An Interim Ethic of Poverty, Power and Pollution* (New York: Paulist Press, 1975).

[8] See James Drane, *Religion and Ethics* (New York: Paulist Press, 1976), p. 6.

[9] See Mary Evelyn Jegen and Bruno V. Manno, *The Earth is the Lord's* (New York: Paulist Press, 1978), pp. 44-50.

[10] "The Interplay of the Generations," *Notre Dame Magazine* 14 (Spring, 1985), p. 29.

[11] *Fortune* 111 (June 24, 1985), p. 28.

[12] Bill Saporito, "Heinz Pushes to be the Low-Cost Producer," *ibid.*, p. 54.

[13] *Ibid.*, p. 44.

[14] Monci Jo Williams, *ibid.*, pp. 70-72.

[15] *Ibid.*, p. 72.

[16] *Ibid.*

[17] Colin Leinster, pp. 90-96.

[18] *Ibid.*, p. 91.

[19] *Managing* (Garden City, New York: Doubleday & Company, Inc., 1984), p. 176.

[20] See William J. Byron, *Toward Stewardship, op. cit.*, pp. 45-46.

[21] (Athens, Georgia: The University of Georgia Press, 1952.)

[22] *Ibid.*, p. 123.

[23] *Ibid.*, pp. 123-124. Quoted from Ralph Ellison, *Invisible Man* (New York: Vintage Books, 1972), p. 563.

[24] *Origins, op. cit.*, Nos. 83-85.

[25] *The Analects*, trans. Ku Hung-ming (Taipei: The Shin Sheng Daily News, 1984), p. 72.

[26] Michael W. Thomas, *Hard Money* (New York: Viking Penguin Inc., 1985), p. 449.

Science and Technology: Vocations to Justice and Love

Kenneth Vaux

My theme for this volume is: "Science and Technology: Vocations to Justice and Love." Justice and love or mercy are the basic normative forces by which all societies order their common life. Sometimes complements, sometimes antagonists, they are integral forces fundamental to any civilization; no culture can survive without them. America is now struggling with its conception of the mutuality of justice and love.

Case in point: an advertisement of First Jersey Securities Corporation — Children singing in the background "My Country 'Tis of Thee" . . . A banker in dark pin stripe suit with yellow tie — suggesting seriousness and power — the pitch: "What is the promise of America?" The answer: "Opportunities, *not* guarantees." Justice/Mercy.

Case in point: Gary Dotson is released, reincarcerated, then released again. The woman whose accusation of rape six years ago put him in jail, experiences a spiritual "change of heart" and retracts her story. The judge holds firm and will not let him go. Governor Thompson commutes his sentence, though without clemency. Justice/Mercy.

Case in point: As lawyers and industry representatives talked with Bhopal residents about compensation, the following insightful comments were heard:

"If only I could get 10,000 rupees ($850), I'd be very happy," said one woman who had lost family members. "India is a spiritual world. We don't understand millions. Americans started all this talk of compensation," said another. Mr. Patel, whose wife and 17-year-old son died, said, "I am a man, not an animal. Money cannot give satisfaction. Suppose I would have died, this body would be thrown away." He looks up, eyes tearing. "Reality is God! Do Americans believe in God — tell me?"[1] Justice/Mercy.

In this essay I would like first to develop an understanding of the

145

basic qualities of justice and mercy. Secondly, I will show the way these qualities shape the cultural ethos, especially the ethos of science, technology, and medicine. Finally, we will explore the opportunities afforded by these specific professions to animate or violate, to activate or vitiate the power of justice and mercy.

I. Justice and Mercy: The Fundamental Requirements of Worldliness and Transcendence

Justice and mercy are the two fundamental moral forces in the universe. Justice is the power of equilibrium, maintenance, and homeostasis. Love is the power of risk, enhancement, and outreach. Justice and mercy are at once human constructs to order and redeem society and divine energies to uphold and endear the creation. We live in space and time. Space (*physis,* nature) is the natural environment of our life. We exist in a web of nature ordered by certain predictabilities and powers. Justice is one way to speak of nature's fundamental, inherent order. We also exist in time. Time is characterized by *chronos* and *kairos,* duration and meaning. We live in long arching *chronos,* the endless time of the cosmos. We live at the end of the age, the end of the entropic drooping age of the earth and cosmos. We also live in the fullness of time. We act not only as if the world will go on forever, but as if the world could be made new or destroyed by our thought and deed. We live, therefore, in the history of nature: subject to order and finitude, yet animated by spirit and creativity. We live in the worldly context and divine milieu of justice and mercy. Conditioned and free, our lives are shaped by equality and liberty. The sun shines on the just and the unjust. We are both finite and infinite, moribund and immortal.

Justice and mercy are the finest impulses ever to have animated the human spirit. They bear on almost every human transaction. They have especially profound bearing on the human activities of science and technology. Justice and mercy are the most forceful, analytic concepts and action precepts in human ethics.

They are natural and primitive values and virtues. Having biological and sociocultural basis, they are found in all societies. Perhaps you have read the book or seen the film, "Never Cry Wolf." This remarkable diary of an ethologist studying a wolf community in the north tundra shows the exquisite sense of justice, order, and even altruism that prevails in this family of beasts once thought to be vicious and predatory. At one level, justice and mercy are found in our precursor animal societies and the primitive forerunners of civilized societies. Justice and mercy are also cultural artifacts, orders we create. Imputing rights with implied obligations is an example of what we might call contrived justice. They are responses within particular and provincial groups to universal and transcendent signals. Ordering life in justice and mercy is a sympathetic response back to the mysterious and sympathetic overtures we receive from beyond.

Justice and mercy are also spiritual insights and thus appear in all religions. Religion, indeed, can be defined as the enactment of justice and mercy. Religion is the human endeavor of believing and acting within the confines and corruptions of the actual world in the light of a sense of what the world is meant to be. Justice is a prophetic statement of what reality is. Love is a proleptic statement of what the world could be. Religion is the human endeavor to remember and hope, to discern a sense of one's intrinsic nature and destiny and thereby bring active life to coincide with that perceived moral purpose.

Justice and mercy are commingled virtues. They are the turgor of the twin pillars of ethics: philosophy and theology. They are the twin impulses of mutuality and human care. They are the crucial expressions of God's care for his creation. They inform interhuman concern wherein we take others and their well being seriously. The powers are commingled at their ultimate source. God's justice is mercy; his mercy is justice.

In the Judaeo-Christian tradition, justice and mercy reflect of the inner nature of God. Building on the Psalms, a Jewish Midrash pictures God as reigning from two thrones. From the throne of justice, cosmos is maintained against the threat of chaos. Justice holds things together. The throne of mercy is that condescension without which the world could not go on. If justice alone prevailed, divine wrath at human evil and rebellion would overwhelm the cosmos. Mercy is, in Chesterton's phrase, God saying to the sun each morning, "Rise!"

As we reflect on the conceptual foundations of justice and love, we can base our reflection on this Midrash which attempts to characterize the moral quality of reality. Justice and mercy, like all human words, are attempts to describe the inner moral architecture and disposition of the universe. Like Psalms 89 and 97, Psalm 98 depicts this vision:

> Sing a new song to the LORD,
>   for he has done marvellous deeds;
> his right hand and holy arm have won him victory.
>   The LORD has made his victory known;
>   he has displayed his righteousness to all the nations.
>   He has remembered his constancy,
>   his love for the house of Israel.
> All the ends of the earth have seen
>   the victory of our GOD.
>
> Acclaim the LORD, all men on earth,
> break into songs of joy, sings psalms.
> Sing psalms in the LORD's honour with the harp,
> with the harp and with the music of the psaltery.

With trumpet and echoing horn
acclaim the presence of the LORD our king.
Let the sea roar and all its creatures,
    the world and those who dwell in it.
Let the rivers clap their hands,
let the hills sing aloud together
before the LORD; for he comes
    to judge the earth.
He will judge the world with righteousness
    and the peoples in justice.[2]

Justice and mercy are space/time membranes. They are synapses
where spirit penetrates matter, where eternity penetrates time. Not
only are justice and mercy symbolized by two thrones, but also by two
mountains: Sinai and Golgotha. Sinai draws together those moral
insights of Ancient Near Eastern culture where the passion for truth,
monotheism, and conscience first dawn. Egypt, Sumer, Babylonia,
Assyria all contribute their wisdom to the Hebraic law of life. When
the time (*kairos*) was ripe, when the Greek *lingua franca* and the *Pax
Romana* had united the world and created universal history, Golgotha
gave the world the law of love as Jesus of Nazareth died to rescue the
world (John 3:16). To this day, the world lifts its eyes to these two hills
from whence strength comes.

Justice is human response to God's cosmic regulation, the *Tao* in
Oriental philosophy. Mercy is human response to divine ingratiation.
Grace in Hebrew is the raw onomatopoetic sound of the cry of a
mother camel searching the desert for a lost son. In Christian thought,
it is the shepherd searching for the lost sheep. Now that the long span
of geologic time has been punctuated by the events of Sinai and
Golgotha, now that moral law has been ascertained at the heart of
nature itself, we can argue that time and space are now different. We
now live in the stream of Holy history (*Heilsgeschichte*) which
interpenetrates secular history.

We also live in the age when nature is being made new under the
power of Christ, the redeemer of the cosmos. In this new aeon, reality
is being reconstituted. The world is now presented to us in a new way.
It yields itself knowable to our rational quest and pliable to our
technical act in an eschatological or proleptic sense. Our knowledge
and technology can fathom and participate in the new reality that the
world is becoming. The world is not just there as brute matter. It is
going somewhere. An inner dynamic animates the history of nature
which, in theological belief, is nothing less than the consummating
purpose of God. I can truly say that I am quite convinced that our
unfolding science, especially astrophysics, molecular biology, and
neuroscience, will one day give us words to describe this notion of the
inner character and outer *telos* of nature.

For the time being, suffice it to say, I am giving a theocentric description to the world view of modern science which Koyre has described as the picture of an infinite universe. I am also sketching an understanding of nature and history which is imbedded in Judaeo-Christian philosophy. As Whitehead has shown, this is the world picture that cradles the birth and nurtures the growth of modern science. I understand justice and love as ontologic and teleologic features of the body of this world. Justice and mercy are mysteries of nature and history. Rather than overt and explicit manifestations of time and space, they are secret inner meanings imbedded in the character of God, the creator and consummate will of the cosmos. It is his handiwork. The inner direction of the world itself is an expression of the divine will.

One additional moral image may further illumine the nature of these powers. Justice and mercy are expressions of the shalom of God for creation. The intended peace, wholeness, perfection, splendor of the created world is there, although it is not yet complete. Justice and mercy are premonitions of the implicit promise of the cosmos. Injustice and violence, though ubiquitous and endemic in the human situation, are already doomed. Therefore, we resist and even outlaw these antitheses, and civilization is a name reserved for communities that embody the virtues. At a simple level, justice is decency, the human decision to right wrongs and to help where help is needed. *Zedka* and *mishpat* are the bottom line of a life that seeks to be right, whole, and useful. "What does the Lord require of you, but to do justice, love mercy and walk humbly with your God?" Abraham's life is rescued from oblivion and is given direction and meaning as he chooses in faith to be in this way, to be on this move. Choosing to live in response to the justice and mercy of God, he pioneers a new humanity and becomes the progenitor of a new race, chosen out of the human race. Justice becomes the substance of the universal covenant, mercy the exceptional dispensation. If you will allow that Marxism is a variant of Abrahamic faith, then today in the world ninety percent of the population seeks to order its life by moral standards anchored in that Abrahamic concept of justice and mercy. These powers become the transcending standard of their lives and the substance of their consciences.

As Whitehead, Weizsacker, and Lynn White have shown, Abrahamic monotheism, which yields the full-orbed physics and metaphysics of cosmic justice, becomes the precondition and impetus of modern science and technology. The conviction also grounds all law and philosophy. It is, if you will, the basis of the true, the good, and the beautiful, as well as the impetus to that eros in the human spirit.

At one level, the laws of nature, especially of physics and causality, are expressions of cosmic justice. "What you sow, you will reap," is not only a moral equation, but a predictability that farmers have relied on since the dawn of human civilization. In the Broadway musical, "The

Fantasticks," the same necessity is expressed in the song, "Plant a radish, get a radish."

In sum, justice is the human idea given to describe the cosmic sense of order and predictability and the moral sense of reliability that appear to the human mind as soon as reality is conceived monistically and monotheistically, a universe and not a pluriverse. Mercy, on the other hand, arises out of Hebrew *Hesed*: that undeserved, unmerited concern, that faithful continence expressed by the God-Lover in the prophet Hosea. Mercy becomes a full-blown power in human life as the Christian Gospel joins primitive natural law, Hebrew monotheism, and Graeco-Roman humanism.

People, empowered by spirit and heart, seem to be made to give and receive love and care. When we seek to describe the foundations of justice and mercy, it is important that we realize that we speak of givens and artifacts, inherent realities and human constructs. They are qualities both discovered and invented. The incisive delineations of justice given by Plato, Immanuel Kant, and John Rawls, or the portrayals of love given by the Apostle Paul, Augustine, or Shakespeare, are rational constructs, the speech of man to be sure. But, at a deeper level they are merely appropriate responses to the moral morphology and momentum of the universe. These are not, as Freudians or Nietzschians might say, "Fignewtons" of our wishful imaginations. Now, on the basis of this somewhat lyrically described conceptual analysis, let us move to something more concrete.

II. The Antinomies of Justice and Love

In the second part of this essay, I wish to show the ways in which justice and mercy can inform the basic cultural ethos of modern society and shape all of our endeavors, including those of science, technology, and medicine. As they become manifest historically and politically, justice and mercy are dialectical and contrapuntal virtues. One calls forth the other and then echoes back to the former. The dangers of exaggerating the rules of justice are corrected by the impulses of mercy. The sympathetic excesses of mercy are counterbalanced by the requirements of justice. Justice upholds. Mercy reaches out. The fiduciary imperatives of justice can be juxtaposed against the altruistic opportunities of mercy. The following chart illustrates the complementarity and interdependence of some of the features of justice and mercy:

Requirements of Justice	Possibilities of Mercy
Survival	Sacrifice
Stability	Hospitality
Equality	Favoritism
Distribution	Compensation
Retribution	Forgiveness

A. Survival/Sacrifice

Two quotes highlight the tension between survival and sacrifice as functions of the justice/mercy dialectic: "Are you better off than you were four years ago?" (Ronald Reagan, candidate for re-election) and, "He who saves his life will lose it" (The New Testament Gospels).

"Can mercy survive in politics?," asks historian John Patrick Diggins in a new book entitled *The Lost Soul of American Politics*. "The quality of mercy," says Diggins, "struggles to stay alive in the political soul of Washington today." "The principle of sacrifice is completely missing in our politics."[3]

In certain periods of history, we have oriented our public life around the principles of benevolence and help. At other times, the principles of power and self sufficiency predominate. The direction is set in part, of course, by the sense of external threat or internal need felt among the people. The scientific project and the specific technological priorities of a society are directed by this underlying value. In our own society at this time, for example, priorities in research and development focus on defense, space, information technology, and exotic medical devices. The concerns for agricultural development, socioeconomic improvement, food production, biologicals and health needs for the poor have receded in importance.

An interesting irony should be noted at this point. It is often out of a sense of security that individuals and groups rise to the nobility of sacrifice and sharing. Similarly, living for the benefit of others often enhances the security of individuals and nations. The observation that aggrandizement leads to destruction is true for both individuals and societies.

Only survival in order to serve others fully edifies. Abraham Maslow has shown that the natural biological, psychic, and territorial demands of our being require that we first survive. All other values are built on this prerequisite. To repel threats, to defend ourselves, to secure our fragile life is an extraordinarily powerful impulse. To breathe and not suffocate or drown, to see and not be plunged into darkness, to move freely and not be confined, indeed, to eat and not starve, to drink and not dehydrate, all are fundamental human impulses of security.

Sacrifice is an equally compelling instinct. Edwin Wilson has shown the genetic ethological basis of self sacrificing altruism in fire ants, bees who sting at mortal cost to protect the hive, wolves, and primates. While fathers are creatures of apathetic justice, mothers are creatures of empathic mercy. I am quite sure my dear wife would sacrifice herself for her children—watching her, through one sleepy eye, walk the floor all night with four babies has convinced me that she would gladly sacrifice herself, or me, for them.

Let me take a more serious illustration: seventy-five-year-old

Roswell Gilbert was recently sentenced to life imprisonment with a mandatory twenty-five years. Justice tempered with mercy probably will insure a suspended sentence or at least early release. Even our sense of justice is offended by the sight of a one hundred-year-old gentleman in jail. Gilbert shot his wife of fifty-one years, Emily, to end the terror of her Alzheimer's disease after she begged to die.[4] Was this an act of survival or sacrifice? The prosecutor claimed, "The old man solved his problem, not his wife's."

Hans Jonas has gone so far as to suggest that human experimentation, perhaps even our compulsions to artificial life prolongation, may be enactments of primitive rituals of human sacrifice to appease divine justice, that is, to survive. That we sacrifice others to ensure our survival is beyond doubt. We even use the phrases, "human guinea pig," "cannon-fodder," "faggots," beings to be sacrificed. Bhopal, India, or Botswana, South Africa, or Buchenwald and Bitburg — and that is just the Bs. Or, if you will excuse the compulsive alliteration, think of the sacrifice of Barney Clark and Baby Fae. The ritual of sacrificing others for our safety, security, and satisfaction, perhaps even survival, is ubiquitous. Vicarious sacrifice is believed to save and edify. The words of Hosea the prophet come to mind: "I desire mercy, not sacrifice" (Hosea 6:6).

Beyond the justice or injustice of sacrifice there is also merciful sacrifice that ennobles human history and society. Consider the ragged train of Viet Nam Vets at last honored in a New York ticker tape parade. They remind us of the tattered heroes of that great painting of 1776, the drummer, piper and flag bearer. As Lincoln said, "These honored dead shall not have died in vain."

Science and technology grow out of a society's search for security and out of its ability to share sacrificially. Star Wars technology is an interesting though controversial attempt to secure a nation with a non-aggressive mechanism. As Jacques Ellul has shown, humans build the city in pride and the impulse to secure, to enclose, and exclude. The city is a hiding place; even God cannot come near, that is, until we learned that the Lord was in New York City. But, the city must sacrifice for its survival. Leningrad endured massive starvation and death when encircled by Hitler's army. Unless commerce and communication, indeed, unless conviviality, i.e., sacrifice for others, is maintained, the city shrivels and dies. This truth is illustrated not only in the technologies of urban construction and food production, but in the techniques of health maintenance and contagion control. These also involve mutuality as much as self protection. Science and technology are the broad enterprises of *techne*, our transformation of the non-human world. Now, with the human sciences and technology, we are extending technical dominion over the human being as well.

The artificial heart is an expression of technology serving the survival urge; the calculator, the sacrificial urge. The one technology

KENNETH VAUX

153

isolates and elevates a selected few certainly (not including the fifty thousand Brazilian peasants with chargas induced cardiomyopathy who might benefit from this exotic technology). The calculator and communication technology in general *can*, if implemented justly, diffuse and disseminate power. Here, the market mechanism as a guide for technological development is a salutary force. Assessing popular needs and interests and making artifacts to fulfill those ambitions are noble actions. Sacrificing the wider world community's well being for the sake of presumed security, as we now do with defense expenditures, is morally intolerable. Sacrificing future generations and the habitable planet for small scale instant gratification now, despoiling the creation by our action, is equally unconscionable.

B. Stability/Hospitality

When the world is perceived paranoically, when demonic forces are projected onto one's adversaries, when a siege mentality is concocted, individuals, groups, and nation-states construe the Justice/Mercy imperatives so as to require gestures of stability rather than hospitality. Among Ancient Near Eastern tribal peoples, notably the Habiru, impulses of justice were seasoned with stipulates of sanctuary. Even if an enemy wandered into your territory, you were obliged to be hospitable and not harm him.

I turn to Philadelphia, the great city of Brotherly Love, for illustration. The West Side row-house neighborhood provided hospice, we understand even sympathy, to MOVE. Then, as hospitality was abused, garbage and rats proliferated, stability was felt to be threatened. When letters predicted violence, when gasoline and weapons were being stored up, rightly or wrongly Mayor Goode sensed profound threat to stability and, reminiscent of Viet Nam, bombed and destroyed the village in order to save it. Was this act justified? Was it just? Would an act of mercy, at least waiting for the children to leave for the playground, have been more appropriate? Hospitality renders one vulnerable, opens one to danger. It may be that we entertain angels unawares. We also can invite destroyers into our homes. Right now, I know several persons, poor, homeless, mentally ill—in mercy, I wish I could bring them into my home. I am quite sure that a few months of intensive TLC (tender loving care) would significantly improve the lives of these persons. Yet, I will not do it. The stability of our family, our busy schedules, our privacy, our pleasures preclude it. The dialectics of stability and hospitality express the underlying antinomies of justice and mercy. Throughout society, these passive and protective or active and redeeming virtues are lived out daily.

In one sense, science and technology are human endeavors to obviate the need for personal help, attempts to care with effect. Transportation technologies, such as the underground in London, Paris or Moscow, certainly the most decent trains in the world, seek to rescue persons from helplessness and immobility. Schools are evasions of *our* personal and familial responsibilities to civilize the rising generation. Hospitals are not only measures to bring sophisticated knowledge and technique to ameliorate disease but also vehicles to displace the burden of care from our hands and hearts. There is a moral equivocation deep within our personal and collective soul having to do with the basic Justice/Mercy and derivative Stability/Hospitality dialectic, now manifest in our science and technology. This equivocation makes all the more crucial the central theme of this volume, the vocation to justice and love.

C. Equality/Favoritism

Another source of the Justice/Mercy imperative is found in moral rationality. We have argued that these virtues are forces of nature, biological energies, and theocentric impulses. They are also the fruits of human philosophical reflection.

In John Rawls' monumental study, *A Theory of Justice*, he reflects on the ideal and practical qualities of justice. Principal among these are equity, fairness, and a concern for the least advantaged. In the philosophical statements on justice, at least in the modern egalitarian history of the doctrine found in Hume, Mill, Sidgwick, and Rawls, we have the central notion that the fundamental quality of justice is non-discrimination, fair reaction and response to insult and equity. Crudely stated, this doctrine implies that persons should get their due, receive what is coming to them, and obtain their fair share. "Equal work deserves equal pay," a doctrine we seem to affirm on the domestic front but abhor internationally, is an example of this commitment. The doctrine contends that all citizens have an equal claim on the resources of the commonwealth and that all the world's citizens have an equal right to the earth's commons: lands, minerals, seas, and skies. The labor movement, Marxism as an egalitarian ideology of the industrial era, women's liberation, the pedagogy of the Third World oppressed, all are recitations of this fundamental human right. This noble sense of justice has increased its hold on individuals and societies in the modern era and, although it has yet to create a state where "Earth shall be fair and all her folk be one. . . . ," it has at least heightened sensitivity to the requirements of justice and disturbed our complacency in the face of injustice. The world is outraged at the plight of blacks in South Africa or Browns in Bhopal.

Despite its power, the notion of justice as reciprocal equilibration is outweighed by another virtue. The pole of mercy draws forth in human affairs a virtue that stands in some tension with equity. For lack of a better term, let us call it favoritism, preferential treatment, or affirmative action. In the deep recesses of our moral traditions, we find a commitment to overcompensate the oppressed, to side in solidarity with victims. The impetus to this virtue is more rooted in the nature of God than in the nature of nature. The world, as Darwin rightly described it, favors the strong and the fittest. God, however, is the champion of the weak, the sick, and the helpless. Mercy, as a response to that pole of the divine nature and thereby to that side of our moral nature, seeks to reach out and lift up those who have been cast down or walked all over.

The theme of God's bias toward the poor permeates the history of Israel and the emergence of primitive Christianity. Wandering nomadic Semites, not the elegant Egyptians, are chosen as the messianic people. Slaves are delivered from Egypt in the constitutive event of Judaism. The prophets extol God's siding as Avenger with the oppressed. Jesus the Nazarene identifies with the outcasts. The early church ingathers those impotent in the eyes of the world:

> Divine folly is wiser than the wisdom of man, and divine weakness stronger than man's strength. My brothers, think what sort of people you are, whom God has called. Few of you are men of wisdom, by any human standard; few are powerful or highly born. Yet, to shame the wise, God has chosen what the world counts folly, and to shame what is strong, God has chosen what the world counts weakness. He has chosen things low and contemptible, mere nothings, to overthrow the existing order (I Corinthians 1:25-28).[5]

Though Christian history often baptizes the exploitation of the powerful over the weak, just as often it stimulates an uprising of the downtrodden. One need think only of the Reformation, with its attendant social and political revolutions, or the emergence today of Africa and Hispanic America as the centers of World Christianity. No longer are the centers of global privilege and power the centers of vital Christianity.

The implications of this value of compensatory concern, though evident for school busing, desegregation and affirmative action for hiring in city police departments, are more subtle but equally important for science and technology. In many ways, technology serves the favoritism value as much as the equity value. Technology, at least in its consumer aspect, seeks to make haves of have-nots. Though the yield of science is weighted to the intellectual élite because of the ability of that group to understand and appropriate its impact, it is also ultimately democratic, even merciful. Any new breakthrough quite quickly becomes universally known, eventually ameliorating some harsh condition of life. Such conditions are disproportionately experienced by the powerless in a society. Therefore, the very activity of science and technology has revolutionary effect if only because it generates discontent with one's lot and a desire to improve it. In real terms, technology allows advantage, even though it may not close the chasm between the empowered and the impoverished.

D. Distribution/Compensation

Again, the diad of distribution and compensation further illumines our understanding of justice and love. The imperative flowing from equity and fundamental justice proscribes exploitation while endorsing distribution of benefit and proportionate participation. Compensation, an imperative of mercy, goes beyond by requiring going the second mile and coming to another's aid. Distributive justice is a rich theme in ethics. Most moral systems call for sharing the resources and opportunities of a society among its members. Acknowledging the unequal distribution of genetic endowments, fortune and misfortune, the commitment seeks, via the mechanism of distributive justice, to provide basic sustenance, housing, health, and education for all. The Western democracies, the Soviet Union and satellite nations, China, and Japan are animated by the conviction that social justice requires distributive provision given in terms of a welfare state, social security, guaranteed minimum incomes, socialized medicine, and a variety of other measures.

Compensation holds back a pool in reserve from the common resource to help those in acute need or provide recompense for those injured in the public service. Programs of this type include insurance plans, workman's compensation, catastrophic health insurance, and disaster relief. Compensation is a hesitation of distribution. It is a response of pity and mercy, as opposed to a meting out to one his due. There is a nobility but also a certain flaw in this compensatory feature of human justice.

For example, we will spend tens of thousands of dollars to rescue a trapped coal miner, but would never spend the same amount to preventively safeguard his life. An even more poignant illustration: In merciful, heart rending impulses of care we have created a network of neo-natal intensive care units. These centers bring the awesome powers of hi-tech medical care to distressed newborns, a great number of whom are premature babies born to poor mothers. Our own NICU at the State University Hospital now has about twenty babies, mostly premature, mostly black, mostly born to young unwed mothers. We could prevent the problem in great measure by programs such as New Orleans had before federal funds were cut. In this program, wise older black women were paid modest salaries to visit all the pregnant women in a given slum or shanty village. They made regular visits, imparting basic preventive and maternal care lessons that these "barefoot doctors" had learned in a training course. For these moms with child the incidence of premature births was reduced by seventy-five percent. That is, until the funds were cut.[6] By reason of some irrational quirk in the structure of our conscience, heroics turn us on; prevention is less gratifying. We will risk our lives to save persons in a burning building, but pleas to aid in fire proofing the structure *before* a blaze fall on deaf ears.

Nevertheless, compensation is a central ingredient in human moral response. It is merciful response to those harmed by cruel circumstance. It is a counterbalancing impulse to distribution, a radius off of the pole of mercy that sweeps around an imaginary sphere; it transmutes into distribution as it approaches the pole of justice.

E. Retribution/Forgiveness

As we consider the ultimate grounding of Justice and Mercy in the transcendent reality of God, another fundamental issue emerges. Most people in most cultures down through the ages saw in the background or beyond of life some ultimate structure of Judgment yielding benefit or punishment. In the Old Orient cultures of Egypt and Mesopotamia, for example, one's life was assessed day by day in the moral balance. Then, at death the virtue and vice of one's living was tallied up and weighed and judgment meted out. The daily dynamics of retribution and reward were seen to be based on a crude stimulus-response mechanism driven by a natural moral law. The primitive mind, as it has been disclosed to us by Levi-Strauss, Levi-Bruhl and others, saw in the world retaliative and remunerative forces that reacted with inevitable necessity to personal or collective righteousness or evil. Tangible effects would be felt from one's own actions, either prosperity and fortune or degradation and misfortune. "Be sure your sin will find you out," is a biblical version of this ancient awareness. King David can commission Uriah the Hittite to lethal combat in order to seduce his wife, but his deed will eventually be revealed, and he will be punished. "Those who sow to the flesh will of the flesh reap corruption." This mentality still found expression in the nineteenth century by those who found insanity as the just punishment for the masturbation inversion. It finds expression today in those who see in the AIDS epidemic the natural consequential punishment for the homosexual perversion. Very often this naturalistically conceived vindication/indication, "you'll get yours," "I told you so," approach was thought of in terms of a purity/contamination quotient. This mindset was confounded when the pill, auto-back seat, and antibiotics eliminated the ancient natural fears of conception, detection, and infection as enforcers of human sexual responsibility.

Of even greater importance than causal retribution to our topic was the end of the life line vision of judgment in the belief in everlasting punishment or forgiveness in heaven or hell. Upon death, the young King of Egypt must sail into the underworld, endure a cardiectomy, have his heart weighed on the scale of good and evil. (Think of the recitation of Book of the Dead texts on Tut's funeral bier: "I was considerate to my wives, paid my bills, did not defraud, etc.") If good deeds outweigh misdeeds, he sails up into the sunrise of eternal reward. At the root of the metaphysical and supernatural imagination that undergirds Western culture, including the culture of science and technology, is the vision of heaven and hell born in Jewish apocalyptic, medieval Christendom, and the Puritan theology of Judgment and grace. Indeed, as Lynn White and others have shown, this imagery supplies much of the subconscious positive and negative motivation for both the ameliorative and destructive impulses of science and technology.

Now, the vividness and grasp of this ultimate backdrop of heaven and hell, of punishment and forgiveness, have lost their hold on human consciousness and conscientiousness. The architecture of judgment and grace expressed in a natural and temporal mode, though still viable and, as Niebuhr has said, empirically called for, is, nevertheless, for our time, unbelievable. The ultimate ratio of good and evil now focusses on the constructs of human natural reason, on the ethics of consequence, and on the stipulates of duty and decency that we have retained from Kant's deontology: a faint smile long after the metaphysical Cheshire cat is gone. We now live in the moral terror of *saeculum*: in the grip of this present age and reality, in the here and now.

Yet, despite the demise of the classical world picture of grace and judgment, heaven and hell, the impulses of justice and mercy still order human affairs. Retribution is the harshest form of justice, verging on injustice. Forgiveness is the most radical form of mercy.

Two pictures: Violating even the primitive talion justice of Hammurabi, "an eye for an eye, a life for a life," Arabs and Jews retaliate against each other: hijacking, taking hostages, killing ten lives for one; justification: to set a precedent, to instill a terror. These days, as I write, the assassin trials in Rome search for the facts in the attempt on Pope John Paul's life. Our mind goes to that poignant scene in the jail cell of the assassin: the Pope kneeling at the side of Ali Agca, his attacker, offering forgiveness and mercy.

Retribution seeks to uncover wrong, assess damage, and demand repayment or appropriate punishment; only when the punishment fits the crime has justice been done.

Forgiveness seeks, not to cover up, but to cover over wrong, to invoke confession and restitution, to set the guilty free, so that life might began anew. Retributive justice assumes and demands moral perfection; merciful forgiveness acknowledges human frailty and fallibility. Retribution and forgiveness are the most intensive expressions of divine justice and mercy. For that reason, both qualities are unfathomable and offensive to human sensibility. Abraham Lincoln recognized this after the carnage of the Civil War when he spoke the Second Inaugural Address:

> If we shall suppose American slavery one of those offenses which, in the providence of God, must needs come, but which, having continued through his appointed time, He now wills to remove, and that He gives to both the North and South this terrible war, as the woe due to those by

whom the offense came, shall we discern therein any departure from those divine attributes which believers in the living God always ascribe to Him? Fondly do we hope, fervently do we pray, that this mighty scourge of war may speedily pass away. Yet, if God wills that it continue until the wealth piled by bondsmen's two hundred and fifty years' unrequited toil shall be sunk, and until every drop of blood drawn with the lash shall be paid by another drawn with the sword, as was said three thousand years ago, so still it must be said the judgments of the Lord are true and righteous altogether.[7]

As in that Great Domestic War, science and technology can today be the ideology and instrumentation of retribution or forgiveness. Weaponry is the instrumentation of attack, defense, and retaliation. Science, even medicine, can be the ideological vehicle to incarcerate, even banish. In some parts of the world, physicists or psychiatrists can be accused of either unscientific thought or mental illness. Torture is the supremely evil technological act. The computer can enter a bit of information that will never be erased. In international trade wars, in balances of terror maintained by technological supremacy, the worst impulses of hostility and fear are expressed. We can also exchange scientific and technological information and skill. They can lift up and reconcile. The Second World War was a technological feat. So was the Marshall Plan.

"Vengeance is mine, saith the Lord," remarked G.B. Shaw. "This means it is not the Lord Chief Justice's." At our best, we humans are capable of only a facsimile of justice and mercy. Indeed, we should be content with the imperfect approximations of which we are capable. Ultimate reward or revenge is not our responsibility. Why? We simply cannot see all that is involved. We are too quick to condemn, and, yes, to forgive. We do not have perspective *sub specie aeternitatis*. In sum, retribution and forgiveness, the extreme extrapolates of justice and mercy, show us that we humans cannot and should not seek to fully master and arbitrate these divine powers. To take justice into our own hands is as harmful as seeing ourselves as ultimate vehicles of mercy. In the final say, we are only instruments to those transcendental powers which always lie over against our poor efforts, chastising and inspiring. Justice and mercy are simply spiritual forces that we may allow to live through us. If we can only temper our own revenge and sentimentality, we will benefit both agent and recipient. Objectively grounded, justice and mercy are subjectively mediated. Portia captures the spirit in her famous speech:

> The quality of mercy is not strain'd,
> It droppeth as the gentle rain from heaven
> Upon the place beneath: it is twice bless'd;
> It blesseth him that gives and him that takes:
> 'Tis mightiest in the mightiest; it becomes
> The throned monarch better than his crown;

His sceptre shows the force of temporal power,
The attribute to awe and majesty,
Wherein doth sit the dread and fear of kings;
But mercy is above this sceptred sway,
It is enthroned in the hearts of kings,
It is an attribute to God himself,
And earthly power doth then show likest God's
When mercy seasons justice. Therefore, Jew,
Though justice be thy plea, consider this,
That in the course of justice none of us
Should see salvation: we do pray for mercy,
And that same prayer doth teach us all to render
The deeds of mercy.[8]

In this second section, we have searched some of the lineaments of justice and mercy. We have hinted at the character of their personal and societal manifestation. It now remains for us to relate these powers, as they are affirmed and negated, to the activities of science and technology.

III. Science and Technology: Vocations to Justice and Love

It is interesting to observe at the outset that many of these particular professions are indeed in some sense works (vocations) of justice and mercy. They are also synchronized to the levels of those virtues we have described. Let us select five spheres of scientific technology and show in each the potential to either enlarge or diminish justice and mercy. We will now consider the science and technology of:

Space
Agriculture
Energy
Information
Biomedicine

A. Space Science and Technology

One of the major questions of political priority today is whether space science will be primarily expressed as peaceful or military technology. What originally was proclaimed as a venture "peace for mankind" is now the vehicle for spy satellites and missile launching. Orbiting installations in the heavens can track weather patterns, perhaps saving entire populations, or they can serve as launch platforms for defensive and offensive missiles. Ironically, while the research and development of Strategic Defense initiatives are seen as necessary to survival, survival in truth requires that these same instruments never be used. Indeed, some say that security is possible only when such weapons no longer exist.

The sacrificial potential in space technology is also impressive. The space club of nations could share with the world acquired information (e.g., drought patterns) and technical innovations (e.g., close quarters habitation, high efficiency foods, et cetera). Whether the SDI, with its ground-based lasers, its space-based guided munitions, lasers and particle beams, will serve the purposes of justice, such as survival and stability, let alone the purposes of sacrifices, is highly questionable.

The imperatives of justice appropriate for astrophysical science and technology come from a naturalistic and a theological source. Tersely put, by nature the skies are our global heritage, not the domain of national interests. Theologically understood, the heavens are God's domain. They should not become the environment for human malevolence.

A fascinating moral question regarding space science and technology is the claim of the SDI program that only research, not development and testing, will take place. But, can knowledge acquisition be separated from technological utilization? Is justice at stake when pure knowledge and no actual tangible impact is involved? The question devolves on two systems of ethics. Principle and deontological ethics give primacy to ideas and intentions, while consequentialist ethics accent calculable effects. The ethical concerns of space science and technology show us that responsibility in general and justice and love in particular have to do with both rules and deeds, with will and action.

This domain of human enterprise not only shows the inextricable unity of ideas and object, but it also points to the cosmic dimension of these virtues. Human ethics has often focused on personal and interpersonal transactions. The space age makes it clear that our power and influence, our ability to create, maintain and destroy, now extend to the outer reaches of the cosmos. Our responsibility now is not local and provincial, but global, universal, cosmic. As Teilhard showed us, we must now speak of global and cosmic justice, global and cosmic love.

At this point in our discussion of the economy of justice and love in the creation, we must mention the activities of war and peace. In this day we must indeed speak of the science and technology of war and peace. We speak of the "Just War": the justification of our excursion into Viet Nam. We remember the *Pax Romana*, the peace of Versailles, the pacification of the Cambodian countryside. At the root of this concern is the question of whether war or peace is the basic nature of man. If the state of struggle, animosity, and violence is fundamental to human nature and peace the ideal or eschatological condition, then the achievement of stalemate and the present ideology of cold war balance of power is the best we can hope for. In that case, we should use all the resources of the Hoover and other defense institutions to forge the scientific structure and the Pentagon to fashion the technological armamentariums to activate this idea and will.

Alternatively, if peace and reciprocity are the more fundamental character of human life, if the optimists of human progress toward a better world, those great nineteenth century visionaries who dreamed

of world order and a global community of nations living in peace, if
their reading of fundamental human nature really is correct, then the
Max Plancik Institute of Friedensforschung, the other peace studies
centers, and the technologies of disarmament should claim our
loyalties. The fundamental issue is the way our reading of the justice/
mercy dialectic causes us to read the Peaceable Kingdom vision of the
Hebrew exile: "They shall beat their swords into plowshares." Is this an
image fulfilled, only history bound, or is it a present moral mandate?
My hunch and the belief I will build my life on is that it is both.

B. Agriculture

Agriculture is a human science and technology that functions in two
ways: it is, in part, a transformation and management of nature's own
growth (e.g., foresting, sea food farming) and, in part, new creation
(e.g., hybrid corn, recombinant DNA, nitrogen-fixing bacteria to
displace chemical fertilizer). In the first sense, taking what is there and
using it well, we manage natural resources, exploiting the minerals,
plant, and animal life of this provident earth so that all benefit from
its generosity. This stewardship is active justice, serving the stability of
earth's family.

In certain times and places, from the power of human creativity a
largesse is fashioned. Some nations enjoy a concentration of natural
wealth and resource; others are victims of blight and drought. The
great wheat belts are the blessings of North America and Central Asia.
Oil beds lie under the Middle East and the Southern shelf of America.
Platinum, uranium, and copper are found in other local concentra-
tions. In mercy, or better, kindness and sympathy, we share mal-
distributed resources, and we are hospitable in the finest sense of that
word.

Moral anguish is now felt for two communities of farmers. Ponder-
ing the nature of that anguish helps us understand further justice and
mercy and their derivatives: stability and hospitality. These two crises
illumine the ethics of the agricultural profession. The plight of small
farmers in Europe and North America is surpassed in gravity by the
devastation caused by typhoons and tidal waves to the present farmers,
scratching out a meager existence along the Bangladesh delta. In both
cases, economic policies and questions of human domicile mingle with
circumstances of nature and fate to create human turmoil. Placed in a
position of impotence by unjust economic policies which through sub-
sidies favor large technological farms, the small farmer is losing the
ability to support his family, keep some beauty in rural America, and
provide modest grain, vegetable, and dairy contributions for the community. It can be argued that the farmer, especially the small family
farmer, is vital to the nation's stability. Here is also found the seedbed
of the virtue of hospitality which strengthens any society. Stabilizing

justice in this case means simply to live and let live, not to jeopardize by preferential subvention.

In Bangladesh, a land plagued by drought and over population, desperate, homeless families have sought, in their displaced wandering, a small parcel of wet delta soil on which to eke out a subsistence. Then came the tidal waves. Not only mercy, resources, and a kind of global hospitality can save and stabilize that wretched populace. Only massive subsidy, education, and family planning, relocation and restabilization of homes, and some provision for sharing in the global economy can heal this disgraceful wound on our provident planet. Indeed, we can in justice refocus more resources on this planet away from destruction toward human need, and in mercy hold up those who have been beaten low. We may find that proleptic harmony where swords are beaten into plowshares.

C. Energy

The science and technologies of energy and the persons who will make their professions in these fields will have a vital impact on the future of the human race. For the race to survive (and for its vast membership to achieve quality life), imaginative and innovative energy insight and technique will be required to fashion a usable future. The frugality and equality requirements of justice will be absolutely necessary, as will the outreaches and dispensations of mercy. Whether we speak of the minerals of the earth; oil, gas, coal, uranium, geo-thermal and hydro-powers; the surface substance; wood and refuse, for example, or solar and wind power, we must exploit, conserve and distribute, guided by the wisdom of justice and mercy.

Without energy, homes are without heat or light. Production of foods and consumer products is halted. Transportation grinds to a stop. Indeed, our entire high-tech based civilization depends on the flow of energy.

Even so, the Luddite and Romantic wax nostalgic when New York City has a blackout. I remember the night my Dad walked home (twenty miles) on the Long Island expressway, after all power gave out. The tales of delight, of revelry, of at long last talking to other people, of being drawn into great adventure, were thrilling to me as a young boy. Not so exciting is the recent power failure at our County Hospital, when several deaths occurred. We are an energy dependent civilization. We need to find ways to produce it economically, utilize it ecologically, and distribute it equitably. Foolhardiness on both the time and space axis of justice is illustrated in the work by my colleague, Dr. Chakrabarty, featured a few years ago in the historic *Time* magazine issue on "Patenting Life." Dr. Chakrabarty works by contract with General Electric. One of his projects is to produce, via recombinant DNA technologies and gene splicing, new organisms, in this case, bugs which devour oil spills when such mishaps occur. When a deep sea rig blows or when a great oil tanker fractures in the ocean, the bugs will go to the rescue. These micro organisms will be released to absorb the spill. The organisms are especially designed to self destruct by means of some programmed factor, such as temperature. But, just in case the bugs proliferate out of hand like some alien Andromeda strain or HTLV III virus, Chakrabarty is also charged with fashioning the technical fix-the-oil-spill-bug-eater. When we rush in to create or distribute energy without careful eco-planning, i.e., giving attention to the household effect which is what economics and ecology are all about, we are violating the nature of justice in its spatial and temporal sense. We must proceed slowly and carefully to satisfy the spatial and temporal demands of justice; yet, we must move with deliberation.

Though all of the couplets of the justice/mercy polarity that we have described are applicable to the sciences and technologies of energy, we must note the particular bearing of Equality and Favoritism. Since energy emerges up out of the resources of earth and drops down in providence from sun, wind, and rain, we are bound through the instrumentality of gathering, storing, and utilizing to equitable distribution.

The mechanisms of wealth, profit, and payment are causing havoc with this imperative of natural justice. The day may come, as it already has in great urban slums or along the beaches of the United States east coast, that only the wealthy can see the sun or walk along the seashore.

For this and other reasons, mercy commends herself to us in the name of favoritism. Last winter, an ambulance rushed into our University Hospital carrying an older woman who had frozen to death. The heat in her apartment had been turned off because she had failed to pay her heat bill. Even the most laissez-faire capitalist and most avid cost conscious actuary found this unconscionable.

In the parishes of Medieval Europe, firewood was stored away in the Church to fuel the fires of destitute neighbors. Since today we cannot see our neighbors, feel their moans and shudders, tucked away as they are in anonymity, we must have social policy that makes this provision.

Here again, the disposition of concern for the least advantaged, the positing then shoring up of the one most vulnerable, the one most likely victimized by the policy under question, is the mercy-animated imperative of justice. That special concern for those shut out in the cold should pervade the values of those who find vocation in these scientific and technological professions.

D. Information

The sciences and technologies that we have reviewed thus far (space, agriculture, and energy) have to do with the domains of human life, the spheres of our dominion in and above the earth. I have suggested that Justice and Love, as we have described them, are brought into force through human vocation in those spheres. The science and technology of information is also a human act which both reads out of and reads into fundamental nature. Logos or speech is written through the nature of God into the constitution of the universe:

> The heavens tell out the glory of God,
> the vault of heaven reveals his handiwork.
> One day speaks to another,
> night with night shares its knowledge. . . . (Psalms 19, 1-2).[9]

Because knowledge and expression are encoded in nature itself, language has a universal structure, as is being shown by psycholinguistic research. But, speech is also a human vocation. Through concepts and articulation we are projecting a new word into the world. Marshall McLuhan's Global village, that shimmery envelope of information energy that flashes around the globe, and Teilhard's noosphere, that dimension of nature that emerges in human evolution within the biosphere, are symbolic attempts to name this phenomenon.

Justice, with reference to information science and technology, is, therefore, conformation and contrivance. Freedom of speech, freedom of information, open channels of communication, are all responses to the natural imperatives of justice. Conversely, to control the media, to propagandize, to restrict access to information, to condone and enforce illiteracy, all are attempts to stifle and impede the natural and salutary flow of knowledge throughout the world.

The requirements of justice in the world of information and knowledge are that we not exclude any from access — therefore, we make public all but the most classified information, and we sustain public and university libraries open to all. Justice mandates distribution or accessibility. Mercy mandates compensation. This requires that we reach out and take information to people regarding critical influences on their lives. The injury of smoking must be more vigorously conveyed to persons. People must know the risk involved in living in certain areas. Universities must develop knowledge that affects the vital interests of people and transmit it to the populace. In sum, the realm of telecommunications, the media, education, and computers constitutes a science and technology that exert a profound effect on human beings. Only the minimalist imperatives of justice and the maximalist imperatives of mercy can wisely guide this enterprise.

E. Biomedicine

The most radical moral qualities of justice and mercy are retribution and forgiveness. The final science and technology professions we consider are those of biomedicine. Here, human dominion and, therefore, moral accountability extend over human nature itself. The final illustration before our minds these days is Josef Mengele. Some words from a splendid essay by Otto Friedrich in *Time* magazine, entitled "Mengele: Non Requiescat in Pace," follow:

> Mengele, the most hated man in the world, was . . . the perverted emblem of his origins. He came from a wealthy commercial family in Bavaria. He studied Kant, earned a Ph.D. at the University of Munich and his medical degree at the University of Frankfurt. . . . On the railroad ramp at Auschwitz, where Mengele presided over the selection process, deciding which of terrified prisoners were fit for slave labor and which for only the gas chambers, he wore white gloves and highly polished boots, and occasionally whistled fragments of Wagner. In doing so, he defiled music, just as his cruel "medical experiments" defiled science and his whole life defiled philosophy. . . . If ever anyone deserved to be hanged — or worse — it was Josef Mengele.
>
> The New Testament condemns such a view as sinful. "Judge not that ye be not judged," Jesus said. "Love your enemies, bless them that curse you, do good to them that hate you." St. Paul decried the hunger for revenge as a blasphemy. "Vengeance is mine; I will repay," saith the Lord. "Therefore, if thine enemy hunger, feed him." One can admire these teachings, and yet sometimes find them impossible to accept, or act upon. Must one not make an exception in the case of someone as vile as Mengele? Would mercy toward him not mock his victims?
>
> In these secular times, it is the state that claims, "Vengeance is mine," and insists on the sole right to decide what is just and to impose punishment. Any personal attempt at retribution is dismissed as vengeance and vengeance is dismissed as psychotic, almost taboo. Yet as Susan Jacoby points out in her interesting book, *Wild Justice*, vengeance comes to appear necessary when the state (or the gods) fails to provide justice.[10]

Mengele knew the science; he possessed the technique; he lost the soul. Unless the moral fabric is there, in personal character and in societal structure, the science and technology become demonic.

Biomedicine is a professional art, based on a body of knowledge and technique. It is also a societal manifestation of care for its citizen. The society licenses, defines, and rewards the practice of biomedicine. It, therefore, must add a social dimension of justice and love to the required dimension of knowledge and technique. It is, therefore, the task of the profession and the professional schools to inculcate these dimensions.

The AIDS victim suffered with Karposi's malignancy when he entered our oncology unit. A surgical resident was called to see him. He appeared in a triple sterile jumpsuit, tripled masked, tripled gloved. "Man! you have destroyed your immune system, contaminated yourself, and now subjected your body to lethal infection and malignancy (This was the thought conveyed). Justice has caught up with you. I'm not going to expose myself." It was hard in the conference that followed to introduce the theme of vulnerability. I used

Camus' *The Plague*, where, you recall, the doctor continued to expose himself to risk out of care for the sick. It was even more difficult to introduce the opposition impulses of forgiveness, when the prevalent posture was justice, security, protection, rightful deserts, retribution.

"That young man does not deserve a heart transplant," said the resident, as we discussed in morning report whether to refer John to Dr. Shumway's program at Stanford. "Yes, he is 34 years old; the transplant is the only hope to cure his end-stage cardiomyopathy. But, he got himself into this fix. His heart has turned to stone because of his abusive life style. Alcohol and drugs. Besides, Stanford would never take such an unpromising patient!"

The primary moral antinomy that is found in medical care is the tension between blame and acceptance, complicity in cause or innocence. The dialectic is as old as we have historical records. "Why did this happen to me?" "Who caused this?" "Why am I being punished?" "What did I do wrong?"

In a new study done here at the University of Pennsylvania, the Cousins-Symington thesis of attitudinal influence on the causation and progress of disease is questioned by Dr. Barrie Cassileth and colleagues. Do the voluntary powers of our own being (our minds, emotions, habits, and will) exert a causal influence on whether we get sick or not? Do they interplay in the way we transact disease, and the way it runs its course?

In the here and now in which we live, we are to live primarily in mercy and against the propensity of our nature, which is to live in vengeance.

In this essay, we have sought to understand the meaning of justice and love. We have delineated the characteristics of these virtues as these influence specific realms of human efficacy and help — what we are calling professions. Finally, we have related these themes to representative vocation in science and technology. We have surveyed these moral forces in their natural and supernatural power. We have surveyed human responsive action in very concrete endeavors.

NOTES

[1] *Wall Street Journal*, 19 December 1984, p. 16.

[2] *The New English Bible* (New York: Oxford University Press, 1970).

[3] Benjamin R. Barber, review of *The Lost Soul of American Politics*, by John Patrick Diggins, in *The New York Times Book Review*, 13 January 1985, p. 9.

[4] See *USA Today*, 10 May 1985, p.3A

[5] *New English Bible*.

[6] "McNeil-Lehrer Report," 2 April 1985.

[7] Abraham Lincoln, *The Second Inaugural Address,* quoted in Carl Sandburg, *The War Years, 1864–1865* (New York: Dell Publishers, 1954), pp. 772-773.

[8] *The Merchant of Venice,* Act IV, Scene I, *The Complete Works of William Shakespeare,* ed. David Betington (Glenview, Ill.: Scott, Foresman and Co., 1980), p. 284.

[9] *New English Bible.*

[10] Otto Friedrich, "Mengele: Non Requiescat in Pace," *Time,* June 24, 1985, p. 90.

Index of Persons